THE BETRAYAL OF SUBSTANCE

# The Betrayal of Substance

DEATH, LITERATURE, AND SEXUAL DIFFERENCE
IN HEGEL'S *PHENOMENOLOGY OF SPIRIT*

Mary C. Rawlinson

Columbia University Press
*New York*

Columbia University Press
*Publishers Since 1893*
New York   Chichester, West Sussex
cup.columbia.edu
Copyright © 2021 Columbia University Press
All rights reserved

Library of Congress Cataloging-in-Publication Data
Names: Rawlinson, Mary C., author.
Title: The betrayal of substance : death, literature, and sexual difference in Hegel's "Phenomenology of spirit" / Mary C. Rawlinson.
Description: [New York : Columbia University Press], 2020. | Includes bibliographical references and index.
Identifiers: LCCN 2020013864 (print) | LCCN 2020013865 (ebook) | ISBN 9780231199049 (hardback) | ISBN 9780231199056 (paperback) | ISBN 9780231552929 (ebook)
Subjects: LCSH: Hegel, Georg Wilhelm Friedrich, 1770–1831. Phänomenologie des Geistes.
Classification: LCC B2929 .R39 2020 (print) | LCC B2929 (ebook) | DDC 193—dc23
LC record available at https://lccn.loc.gov/2020013864
LC ebook record available at https://lccn.loc.gov/2020013865

Cover image: Widayat, *while fishing, he has to pee,* woodcut print on cloth, 80 x 40 cm. Copyright © OHD Museum. Courtesy of Dr. Oei Hong Djien.

Cover design: Lisa Hamm

At a time when the universality of spirit has gathered such strength, and singularity, as is fitting, has become correspondingly less important . . . the share of the total work of spirit which falls to the individual can only be very small. . . . less must be expected of him, just as he must expect less of himself, and may demand less for himself.

—G. W. F. HEGEL, *PHENOMENOLOGY OF SPIRIT*, PREFACE, ¶72

Appearance is the arising and passing away that does not itself arise and pass away, but is 'in itself,' and constitutes the actuality and the movement of the life of truth. The true is thus the Bacchanalian revel in which no member is not drunk; yet because each member, as he detaches, is immediately dissolved, the revel is just as much transparent and simple repose. Judged in the court of this movement, the singular shapes of spirit do not persist any more than determinate thoughts do, but they are as much positive and necessary moments, as they are negative and evanescent. In the *whole* of the movement, seen as a state of calm, what distinguishes itself therein, and gives itself a differentiated and specific existence, is preserved as something that *remembers* itself, whose existence is self-knowledge and whose self-knowledge is as well immediate existence.

—G. W. F. HEGEL, *PHENOMENOLOGY OF SPIRIT*, PREFACE, ¶47

The ethical substance having withdrawn from its outer existence back into its pure self-consciousness is the aspect of the concept or of the *activity* with which spirit brings itself forth as object. This activity is pure form, because the individual, in ethical obedience and service, has worked off every unconscious existence and fixed determination in the same way that substance has become fluid essence. This form is *the night in which substance was betrayed* and made itself into subject. It is out of this night of pure certainty of self that the ethical spirit is resurrected as a shape freed from nature and its own immediate existence.

—G. W. F. HEGEL, *PHENOMENOLOGY OF SPIRIT*, ¶703 (MY EMPHASIS)

[Philosophers] are like children who imagine that when they come to the end of a plain, they shall be able to touch the sky with their hand.

—ÉTIENNE BONNOT DE CONDILLAC, *AN ESSAY ON THE ORIGIN OF HUMAN KNOWLEDGE*

# CONTENTS

*Acknowledgments* ix
*On Reading Hegel's* Phenomenology of Spirit *xi*
*Beginning: Philosophy and the Problem of the Preface* xxiii
*Our Time Is the Birth-Time of Spirit: Kant and the Bird on a Lime-Twig* xxxv

## PART I: EPOCHĒ

1. Critique of Immediacy: The Unreality of the Sensuous 3

    a. Determinate Negation: Interrogation Between Certainty and Truth 3
    b. Contradiction: The Sophistry of Perception 11
    c. Inversion: Appearance, or Hegel's Concept of Experience 23

2. Self-Consciousness: The Fate of the Singleton 34

    a. Struggle Unto Death: The Myth of Originary Violence 34
    b. Slave Narratives: Freedom in Detachment from Life 45
    c. Mastering Life: Unhappy Consciousness and the Beyond 51

3. Happiness: Reason at Work 70

    a. Inner/Outer: Human Exceptionalism and the Mastery of Nature 73
    b. I/Others: The Struggle Between Virtue and the Man of the World 82
    c. *Die Sache Selbst*: Action, Law, and Antigone on the Moral "Insolence" of Reason 95

CONTENTS

## PART II: THE PHENOMENOLOGY OF SPIRIT

4. Spirit, or Transubstantiated Life: Infrastructures of Community   113

    a. Ethics of Family and Nation: Sexual Difference in Action, or Leaving the Sister Behind   117
    b. Culture or Alienation: Realizing the We in the I   131
        I. The World of Culture: Transforming the Mortal Singleton Into Language, or Leaving the Singleton Behind   131
        II. Enlightenment: The Struggle of Reason with Faith Over Truth   142
        III. Absolute Freedom and Terror   150
    c. From Dissemblance to Forgiveness in Hegel's Critique of Morality: Freedom Beyond Terror and the Law   158

## PART III: ABSOLUTE KNOWING: THE BETRAYAL OF SUBSTANCE

5. Leaving Literature Behind: The Return to Immediacy in the Life of the Concept   183

*Bibliography*   201
*Index*   205

# ACKNOWLEDGMENTS

Many thanks to Wendy Lochner, my editor at Columbia University Press. Wendy combines generous support with real discipline to great effect. I am grateful to her and to her team for shepherding the work into print with such care.

Many thanks to the Institute of Advanced Studies at University College London for the Senior Visiting Research Fellowship in 2018–19, during which I completed the manuscript. Under the leadership of its director, Professor Tamar Garb, the IAS provides a vibrant, challenging, and supportive intellectual environment where it is easy to thrive.

Many thanks to Elizabeth Morcom and the excellent staff of Senate House Library, University of London, where I completed the manuscript, for offering the best working conditions I have ever enjoyed.

Many thanks to Dr. Oei Hong Djien, the founder and owner of the OHD Museum in Magelang, Java, Indonesia, for allowing me to use as the cover of the book the woodcut "while fishing, he has to pee," by the great Javanese artist Widayat. Dr. Oei's collection includes over two thousand works of classical and contemporary Indonesian art, and he is actively engaged not only in supporting contemporary artists, but also in various art education programs aimed at developing an appreciation for the art in younger generations.

## ACKNOWLEDGMENTS

Many thanks to Caleb Ward for the extraordinary care he took in reading and editing the manuscript. Touching everything from punctuation and syntax to style and meaning, Caleb's firm hand has made this a more accessible and a much better book in every way.

Many thanks to James Sares for his astute comments on an earlier version of the manuscript. Reading Hegel with James over the past few years has been a source of immense pleasure and illumination.

For nearly four decades I have been teaching a seminar on Hegel's *Phenomenology of Spirit* to students in the PhD program in philosophy at Stony Brook University in New York. I arrived at Stony Brook a Husserl scholar, but it quickly became clear to me, as the very junior (and only female) member of the department's "continental wing," that if I waited to teach a course on Husserl in the PhD program, my turn might be a long time coming. It seems odd now in retrospect that no one was teaching Hegel. Having come from Northwestern and the tutelage of its great Hegelians William Earle and Errol Harris, who even in their twilight burned bright, I had read my Hegel. Most importantly, I had spent two quarters meeting every Friday morning with Bill Earle to read the *Phenomenology*. I wasn't so sure about the rest of Hegel's encyclopedic project, but this book, I knew, had to be read.

And, so we did.

Many thanks to all the students in the seminars for many hours spent together in the *Phenomenology of Spirit*. I hoped not only to facilitate your access to the text, but also to engender a passion for reading it.

I hope this book will engage not only those who are already reading Hegel, but also those who are coming to the *Phenomenology* for the first time.

## ON READING HEGEL'S
## *PHENOMENOLOGY OF SPIRIT*

What does it mean to *read* Hegel's *Phenomenology of Spirit*? How is it to be read and to what end? What is at stake in this reading? What could be *said* about a text that, from the very beginning, puts the reader to the test at every point, challenging him to say what he means? The reader will be the site of the research. It is in his thought and experience that the concept will be demonstrated. The *Phenomenology* puts at stake for the reader nothing less than the truth of his own life. As *phenomenology*, the text tests itself against the reader's experience or rather initiates in him a performance in which he tests himself. Can he say what he means? Can he give voice to his experience? Does his claim to know the truth actually stand up when tested against his own experience?

In Hegel's philosophy the concept is produced neither by abstract argument nor by reason alone, but only through a phenomenology of experience that takes into account all the registers of life. The *Phenomenology of Spirit*[1] provides a "ladder" to philosophical science insofar as the concept of logic must emerge first from the material conditions of life. Philosophy has

---

1. G. W. F. Hegel, *Phenomenology of Spirit*, trans. A. V. Miller (1807; New York: Oxford University Press, 1977). I have frequently altered Miller's translation to restore the clarity and consistency of Hegel's argument. I have also often used he/himself for it/itself in referring to a shape of self-consciousness. In-text references cite paragraph numbers in the Miller translation.

a duty to demonstrate to "natural consciousness" how the position of philosophical science already lies implicit in his experience (¶¶26, 29).[2] The concept proves its truth through its power to organize and sustain forms of life. As the very infrastructure of experience, the concept can be discovered only through phenomenological analysis.

In the magisterial narrative of the *Phenomenology of Spirit*, the reader discovers a language adequate to unfold the transparency of the concept through all the regions and registers of life, from sensuous immediacy and the family, to science and politics, to art and religion. As the phenomenological interrogation unfolds, every identity proves to be an identity in difference, always already having given way to the two that is implicit within it (¶18).[3] Any identity immediately sunders itself, so as to reveal that its truth lies in what first appeared to be its opposite. Through the phenomenological project of giving voice to experience or attempting to "say what we mean," the apparent opposite of each identity proves instead to be its essential other. The man of virtue, for example, might seem to be the opposite of the man of the world, who acts only in his own self-interest, but the former is not as good as he seems, nor the latter as bad. The man of virtue selfishly prizes his own moral purity above all else, while imposing his particular truth on everyone else. The man of the world, though he might seem to act for himself alone, actually benefits the whole: he creates a business and gives others employment or creates something transformational—the transcontinental railroad, the airplane, the iPhone, the Nike running shoe—that changes the way the community lives. Even the identity of the singleton[4]

---

2. I refer to the subject of Hegel's phenomenology with masculine pronouns out of philosophical necessity. Doing otherwise would constitute an egregious error in reading: as I will demonstrate, Hegel's philosophical subject is *necessarily* masculine. Writing as if one could simply insert sexual difference into Hegel's subject would obscure Hegel's insistence on the necessity to philosophy of the gender division of labor. Hegel takes women's experience and labor seriously as a distinct domain of human agency, but he means to efface that difference in an absolute 'I,' in a philosophical subject that is always already marked masculine. So, while it might be politically correct to employ 'he/she' or 'they' in referring to the subject of the phenomenological analysis, it would be philosophically incorrect, and, moreover, an erasure of Hegel's very attempt to erase sexual difference, letting Hegel off the hook on this issue.

3. *Entzweiten*, or "two-ing," occurs throughout the text. In ordinary German, *entzweigehen* means "to come apart" or "to break in two." *Etwas entzwei schneiden* is to cut something in half. The opposition comprising identity is a belonging together, as one half belongs to the other.

4. "Singleton" translates *der Einzelne*. Miller's translation, "individual," obscures the crucial distinction of this term from *das Individuum*, the "individualized" singleton who has learned that he is only a member of a whole. "Singleton" avoids the paleonymic effects of the terms *subject* or *human being*, while emphasizing the "self-standing" (*Selbstständigkeit*) of self-consciousness. Philosophy must appropriate this "immediate self-certainty" in which the self-conscious singleton

himself proves to be an "incommensurable" difference between a changing determinate self and an 'I' that persists as the same through the flux of becoming.[5]

The truth of phenomenology, then, would seem to be the irreducibility of difference and the inability of the concept to master the proliferation of differences in life. The method of interrogation that yields the transparency of the concept seems to describe an infinite movement of becoming that could never terminate in an absolute identity to which nothing is other, that could never be fully anticipated in any concept, as physical events are known in advance in the laws of physics. As a phenomenologist, Hegel seems to subscribe to the novelist's epistemology: only the impression is a guarantor of truth. The truths of the abstract intellect may be logically coherent, but there is no guarantee that they are about anything real. They are "less profound, less necessary" than the truths that "life communicates to us against our will in an impression which is material because it enters us through the senses but yet has spirit which is possible for us to extract."[6] As a phenomenologist, Hegel not only insists on the singular singleton as the site of the realization of the self-conscious concept, he also insists that the concept cannot be thought apart from its materialization. The truth is not only the "result" but also "the process by which it came about" (¶3). The concept will always be marked by its emergence from life and can only be realized in the singleton's thought. While the concept must be thought as distinct from the self-conscious singleton, as surpassing the singularity of his experience, this proves to be a "distinction which is no distinction," as there is no other "medium" for the concept but that experience.[7] Thus, just as phenomenology discovers the living singleton to be

---

knows himself as existing on his own. In so doing, phenomenology demonstrates that the singleton is in truth only a member of multiple communities, only a "moment" in the tides of generations across which the whole of spirit is realized. The movement of identity, sundering itself and discovering itself in relation to its other, unfolds the whole of human history and culture. The movement, not the moment, proves to be the truth of spirit.

5. See ¶705: "Incommensurability" is the "essential nature" of the "organic." The metaphor of the organism controls the text. The development of the concept is "organic," as the "bud disappears in the bursting-forth of the blossom" (¶2). The individual comes forth from the singleton, as the man from the boy. Spirit emerges out of material life, as the oak from the acorn (¶13).

6. Marcel Proust, *In Search of Lost Time*, vol. 6, trans. C. K. Scott Moncrieff and Terence Kilmartin (1927; New York: Modern Library, 1983), 273.

7. This phrase "distinction which is no distinction" occurs throughout Hegel's text. See ¶166, where the difference between knowing and being is in question—a difference that, as phenomenology reveals, "falls within consciousness."

an "incommensurable difference," so too the interrogation reveals an incommensurable difference between language and experience, between philosophical narrative and life, between the abstract concept and its material realization. Philosophy, as phenomenology, reveals a concept that is always marked by this difference and, thus, always wears a singular face.

At the same time, Hegel's phenomenological analysis aims at "that point at which knowledge need no longer go beyond itself because nothing is other to it" (¶80). Phenomenology will prove to be only a propaedeutic to logic and to an encyclopedic project meant to exhaust the field of knowledge. The *Phenomenology* sets as its goal an absolute knowing in which all difference has been surpassed and comprehended, so that nothing is "*left behind.*"[8] Nothing is "other" to absolute knowing: it is the exceptional identity in which all difference is at once articulated and reduced. All the possible shapes or forms of human experience will have been taken up in it and accorded, each one, its proper place as a moment in a completed system of shapes. Absolute knowing may be manifest only in the self-conscious singleton, but in its master narrative, his very singularity has been reduced to a mere passing moment, surpassed in a thought that belongs to each and all.[9] With the arrival of absolute knowing, the singleton "must expect less for himself and less must be expected of him" (¶72).

Absolute knowing only comes on the scene at the "time that is ripe to receive it," at that moment in human history when all the possible shapes and forms of life have already been articulated in experience and stand ready to be reflected in thought (¶71). The appearance of absolute knowing marks the "end of history" and the "end of art" insofar as it reflects the completed system of shapes that comprise human experience. There will be more history and more art; but these domains are no longer philosophically interesting, as they can offer no novelty. They can yield only a repetition of the essential forms already reflected in the completed whole of absolute knowing. In absolute knowing, the concept is "grasped," so as to "annul" (*tilgen*) time itself (¶801). Absolute knowing inaugurates the project of logic, where

---

8. As I will discuss in chapter 4, in the installation of the gender division of labor as necessary to the life of spirit, the sister is "left behind" (¶458).

9. As Hobbes remarks, "all men by nature reason alike." Thomas Hobbes, *Leviathan* (1651; Cambridge: Cambridge University Press, 1991), chapter 5, ¶16.

the concept is to be thought *as such*, apart from its materialization and in its "pure" conceptuality.

Hegel, then, writes with both hands. On the one hand, he insists on the materiality of the concept as an infrastructure of life, on the singleton as the site of its realization, and on the ineluctable sundering of any identity into the two that constitutes it. On the other hand, he aims at the purified concept of a science of logic beyond phenomenology, the science of experience. He aims at a thinking in which singularity has been erased, and he means to install an identity in which difference has been comprehended "so that nothing is other to it." The phenomenological interrogation will master any difference that appears by incorporating it into a system of differences thought as one. The one returns to itself in the many, mastering difference, and leaving nothing unsaid or unthought.

This double writing requires a double reading.

Reading with Hegel, the reader will discover in the phenomenological interrogation how identity and difference, the movement of self-sundering and return from otherness, operate across the registers of life, how this movement is reflected in nature, the body, the family, and Earth, at the same time that it produces natural science, politics, and philosophy itself. In this capacious narrative, the singularity and novelty of materiality mark the emerging concept. Identity belongs to a movement of differentiation that creates knowledges, solidarities, and cultures. And the truth of experience lies in this becoming. On this reading, philosophy must be phenomenology, for only the interrogative method can capture the specificity of the concept as it emerges from the movement of becoming.

Reading against Hegel, the reader will discover that Hegel's attempt to complete the phenomenological project, *leaving it behind* for logic and a "purified" concept, comes undone at three points. Three dangling threads refuse to be woven into the completed fabric of absolute knowing. Sexual difference, the mortality of the singleton (which differentiates him as *this one and not the others*), and the differences of style in art and literature each resist Hegel's attempt to knit them up. Perhaps, these differences entangle the writing hands so that the seams of absolute knowing cannot be sewn closed and remain indefinitely unfinished. Perhaps, the attempt to "purify" the concept and "pulverize" singularity remains tangled in the threads of these recalcitrant differences.

## SEXUAL DIFFERENCE

Hegel's account of sexual difference unfolds in his interpretation of the figure of Antigone and his analysis of the relation between family and state. The gender division of labor is necessary, Hegel argues, for two reasons. First, it is *practically* required, because only if women tend the body will men be free for the discursive pursuits of science, politics, and philosophy. Without this assignment of the care of the body to women, the community will have no way to feed itself, to raise its children, and to care for the sick and aged.[10]

Second, it is *philosophically* required. Unlike other philosophers of the tradition who render woman a man without reason[11] or an emotional supplement to man's rationality,[12] Hegel accords to women's experience an essential place in the phenomenology of spirit, as the embodiment of the ethical and the guardian of the body. Her distinctive experience cannot be reduced to man's, and it is just as essential as his to the life of the community.

Only her assignment to the care of the body and her exclusion from the discursive pursuit of philosophy prevent this irreducible difference from undermining the aim of absolute knowing. She is to be "*left behind*" in the family, so that her difference may not mark the master narrative (¶458). On the one hand, her difference is absolutely essential to the self-realization of spirit; on the other, this difference must be effaced if self-consciousness is to reach "absolute knowing," in which "knowledge need no longer go beyond itself because nothing is other to it." Existing as this

---

10. Hegel has a point here. When women leave the home for public life, there is no one left in the domain of the family to care for the needs of the body. The community is undermined by social problems: latch-key children, elders in nursing "homes" because there is no longer a daughter available to take care of them, or an obesity epidemic because processed or fast foods have replaced home-cooking. I certainly would not argue for maintaining the gender division of labor, but Hegel's point that *some* infrastructure is necessary to negotiate the claims of family and public life cannot be denied. The challenge for feminism and the political community is to create new infrastructures, other than the gender division of labor, that are capable of sustaining the claims of both family and public life, both the body and thought.

11. Hobbes frequently groups women, children, and "savages" as a single class, identified by their incapacity for rational thought.

12. For Rousseau, woman's purpose, to which her education should be directed, is to soften man's temper and supplement his rational judgments with compassion. See Jean-Jacques Rousseau, *Emile: Or, On Education*, trans. Allan Bloom (1762; New York: Basic, 1979).

aporia, she remains the "eternal irony of the community," an irony that remains unresolved in absolute knowing (¶475).

## THE MORTALITY OF THE SINGLETON

Hegel insists that the singleton "comes into existence as such" only through the "force [*Kraft*] of speech" (¶508). Self-consciousness exists only in language, as a *transcended* self. Thus, substance is "humiliated" (*erniedrigt*) and the immediacy of experience rendered a "vanishing moment" (¶532). Only language can embody the identity of the pure universal 'I' with the particularity of the singleton in the flux of becoming.[13] Just as in the interrogation of sensuous immediacy the 'now' preserves itself as the form of experience through the negation of determinate 'nows,' so, too, the pure 'I' of language and the concept maintains itself through the negation of the determinate contents that distinguish the singleton as *this one*.

The logic of appearance—the "arising and passing away that never arises or passes away"—turns out to be the truth of self-consciousness, who exists only as this "vanishing" (¶47). Hegel means to *leave behind* the substance of the singleton by transforming him into a linguistic being, who exists only as something *conceptual* or as thought. Hegel's terrestrial faith, his belief in the immortality of Earth, the "eternal individual," sustains his belief in the immortality of appearance and the genus life (¶452). The mortality of the singleton does not trouble this faith, for if "the universal is only actual in the singleton," the eternal tide of generations will always assure its realization despite the death of the singleton. The truth of the singleton is to be the site of this complex process of mediation through language; thus, the universal is actualized in such a way as to transcend the specificity and mortality of each and all. What persists is the logic of mediation, and the death of the singleton leaves no trace.

Perhaps the singleton and his mortality can no more be *left behind* than the sister can. Hegel's own method stipulates that nothing can be left

---

13. As Derrida remarks, "my-death" is structurally necessary to pronouncing "I am." For the speaker's utterance to make sense, he must be subject to a phenomenon of displacement, whereby another speaker could come to take his place and make the utterance his own. Jacques Derrida, *Speech and Phenomena*, trans. David B. Allison (1967; Evanston, IL: Northwestern University Press, 1973), 96.

behind, unarticulated in the 'I' that produces the conceptual narrative, but, perhaps, the irreducible specificity of mortal life—for the reality of death is always *my* death and never an abstraction—resists and always exceeds the grasp of the concept.[14]

Hegel can claim the closure of the phenomenological project in "that point at which knowledge need no longer go beyond itself because nothing is other to it" only through violent acts of erasure. Woman and the mortal singleton have each already been erased. Hegel completes this effacement of specificity through the erasure of the irreducibility of the signature in art. These erasures not only violate the phenomenological method; they leave a trace and give to the universal a singular face.

## ART/LITERATURE

> Plato's theory of art *is* his philosophy, and since philosophy down the ages has consisted in placing codicils to the platonic testament, philosophy itself may just be the disenfranchisement of art.
> —ARTHUR DANTO, "THE PHILOSOPHICAL DISENFRANCHISEMENT OF ART"

At least since Plato, who calls this "old quarrel" an "ancient enmity," philosophers have found it necessary to subjugate art in order to establish the sovereignty of philosophy as the discipline of truth.[15] What is at stake here is nothing less than philosophy's aim of an absolute knowing freed from the finite perspective. The irreducible differences of style in literature and art undermine the pretensions of philosophy to offer a master narrative beyond finite difference. Art portrays the shattering of the one world into the aspects of the finite perspective, its multiplicities and differences. Art promises no absolute vision of the truth beyond the world of appearances, in which these differences would be comprehended and effaced. Thus, the

---

14. "The syllogism 'Caius is a man, men are mortal, therefore Caius is mortal' had always seemed to him correct as applied to Caius, but certainly not as applied to himself. That Caius—man in the abstract—was mortal, was perfectly correct, but he was not Caius, not an abstract man, but a creature quite, quite separate from all others.... 'Caius really was mortal, and it was right for him to die; but for me, little Vanya, Ivan Ilych, with all my thoughts and emotions, it's altogether a different matter. It cannot be that I ought to die. That would be too terrible.'" Leo Tolstoy, *The Death of Ivan Ilych*, trans. Rosemary Edmonds (1886; New York: Signet Classics, 1960), 131–32. Death may be universal, but it always wears a singular face.

15. *Republic*, lines 598–99. See also *Phaedrus*, lines 275–76.

pretension of art to express truth undermines the aim of a knowing "that need no longer go beyond itself because nothing is other to it." While religion and philosophy aim to think the whole of reality at one go in a master narrative, the artist strives to embody in his work only a distinctive style or way of seeing. Thus, the history of philosophy is, as Danto remarks, "a cosmic labyrinth designed to keep art, like a minotaur [a monstrous being], in logical quarantine."[16] Philosophy, to maintain its concept of truth, must be protected from the problem of style.

Hegel takes an approach to art that reduces the work to a symptom of culture, or the "embodiment" of the spirit of a "free people" (¶700). A work of art is a conscious production "made by human hands." However, in creating his work, the artist has "depersonalized" himself: "to himself as a particular singleton he gave in his work no actual existence" (¶708). The work, Hegel claims, represents a worldview or form of life, rather than the differentiating style of the artist.[17]

Here, and in his *Aesthetics* too, Hegel reduces the work to an instance of a general form. Works are subsumed under the general categories of the symbolic, the classical, and the romantic. A hierarchy of arts is established, in which the self-conscious linguistic art of literature surpasses the unconscious, inarticulate spirit of the plastic arts of sculpture and painting. Beyond a few references to the genius of Homer, Sophocles, Shakespeare, and Raphael, Hegel offers no sustained analyses of specific works of art on their own terms.[18]

In claiming for philosophy an absolute knowing, Hegel attempts to erase or leave behind the specificity of its conditions of emergence and the specificity of its narrative, thereby violating his own admonition that the truth is not the result alone but the result and *the process by which it came*

---

16. Arthur Danto, "Philosophizing Literature," in *The Philosophical Disenfranchisement of Art* (New York: Columbia University Press, 1986), 165–66.

17. Many contemporary philosophers follow Hegel's approach. In *Les Mots et les choses* (Paris: Gallimard, 1966), Foucault analyzes Velázquez's *Las Meninas* as a depiction of the logic of classicism without saying anything about its sensuous qualities. Similarly, Starobinski comments on David's *Oath of the Horatii* as an emblem of revolutionary fervor rather than a visual experience. Jean Starobinski, *1789: The Emblems of Reason*, trans. Barbara Bray (1973; Charlottesville: University of Virginia Press, 1982).

18. Despite the importance of the figure of Antigone to his argument, Hegel gives no sustained analysis of the trilogy of Sophocles's Theban plays. He ignores *Oedipus at Colonus* altogether, as so many feminist commentators do, and, like them, he misses the role of Ismene in advancing the very virtues that in his own analysis prove essential to community: Ismene's generosity, solidarity, and forgiveness against the hardheadedness and hardheartedness of Oedipus, Antigone, and Creon.

*about* (¶3). Hegel attempts to write as if he were style-less or the zero degree of style, as if he could erase his own authorship and leave behind a book that was nothing but the anonymous self-articulation of spirit.

A genuine phenomenology of aesthetic experience, however, discovers joy and truth precisely in the differences between Vermeer and Rembrandt, Mozart and Beethoven, differences that cannot be subsumed in or predicted by any general form, which the signatures always exceed. Each name presents not only an easily recognizable style, but also a *specific universal*. Each name unfolds the whole of a world in a distinct way that proves its universality by creating for itself a community of adherents. Style exhibits the unity and wholeness that Hegel accorded to absolute knowing, but in a universe of differentiated styles of experience. Hegel thought he would articulate *the* truth; the artist, less grandiose and bound to the specificity of sensuous life, only claims a place in a universe of styles, each one an access to truth. As Proust argues,

> Thanks to art, instead of seeing one world only, our own, we see that world multiply itself and we have at our disposal as many worlds as there are original artists, worlds more different one from the other than those which revolve in infinite space, worlds which, centuries after the extinction of the fire from which their light first emanated, whether it is called Rembrandt or Vermeer, send us still each one its special radiance.[19]

The differences of style in art make accessible individual difference as something universal, as a specific difference or perspective from which the whole of the world unfolds. Art teaches us that, contrary to philosophy's pretensions to an absolute knowing, to a master narrative, all is not to be thought at one go. It gives access to the novel difference of the other, who cannot be reduced to the same. Far from betraying substance, as Hegel claims, literature betrays instead the empty pretension of the philosopher to have found the narrative of the one, as if he could touch the horizon of the sky with his hand. Hegel's own phenomenological analysis, his own insistence on the concreteness of the concept as a material infrastructure of

---

19. Proust, *In Search of Lost Time*, 6:299.

life, will undermine the legitimacy of the project of logic, where the concept would be thought not in its specificity but in general or *as such*.

---

Hegel demonstrates that the essence of being is "two-ing" (*Entzweiten*). Any unity immediately sunders itself into its constituent moments. Hegel's own attempt to install absolute knowing, the one truth or master narrative, will always be undone by the sister and the irreducible two of sexual difference. It will always be forestalled by the reality of the mortal singleton, by the ineradicable difference between his determinate being and the pure 'I' of language. And it will always be deferred indefinitely by the incommensurable differences of style in art and literature, which cannot be subsumed by a cultural form or erased in a general concept.

Hegel's move to logic founders on his fidelity to the phenomenological evidence: while aiming at the installation of a purified 'I' that exists only conceptually in language, he continues to insist on the material difference of the singleton as a necessary and ineffaceable moment. His own logic requires that he maintain this incommensurate difference as irreducible, rather than resolve it in a purified 'I.' Against his own phenomenological analysis and his demonstration of the concept as a material infrastructure of life, Hegel works the themes of "purifying" the concept and "pulverizing" singularity, as he works toward the claim of an absolute voice. He employs the most violent language in his attempt to "pulverize" the singleton (¶364) and to "humiliate" and "betray" substance (¶¶532, 732). He attempts to tear the concept away from its adherence to the sensuous, but this would produce only the sort of empty abstraction that he himself decries. Perhaps, adherence to the phenomenological method and the materiality of the concept will undermine forever the philosopher's attempt to touch the sky with his hand.

Reading the *Phenomenology of Spirit*, pay attention to *what is left behind* in a narrative that claims to articulate the whole of experience. Pay attention to the erasures of difference that eviscerate the "two-ing," which is synonymous with life for Hegel. Pay attention to the price to be paid if phenomenology itself is to be left behind.

# BEGINNING

## Philosophy and the Problem of the Preface

> The well-known [*das Bekannte*], just because it is well-known [*bekannt*], remains unknown [*nicht erkannt*].
>
> —G. W. F. HEGEL, *PHENOMENOLOGY OF SPIRIT*, PREFACE, ¶31 (1807)

> The affirmation of passing away *and destroying*, which is the decisive feature of a Dionysian philosophy; saying Yes to opposition and war; *becoming*, along with a radical repudiation of the very concept of *being*—all this is clearly more closely related to me than anything else thought to date.
>
> —FRIEDRICH NIETZSCHE, *ECCE HOMO* (1887)

> When we wish to see an oak with its massive trunk and spreading crown of branches and leaves, we are not content to be shown an acorn instead.
>
> —G. W. F. HEGEL, *PHENOMENOLOGY OF SPIRIT*, PREFACE, ¶12 (1807)

Hegel's *Phenomenology of Spirit* puts off... indefinitely... any actual beginning. Indeed, the text begins and begins again six times, and only in chapter 6 does the *phenomenology of spirit* actually commence.

This will not be an accident, but necessary to the future perfect in which life and the analysis take place. Immediacy will always be the site of the loss of what we thought we knew, and the truth always *will have been the case*, known only *after the fact*. There is no presence that is not always already a return (¶¶18, 47).

Life and history will have been the preface to philosophy, and the *Phenomenology* arrives only at a time that is "ripe to receive it" (¶71). The history of philosophy will have been the preface to Hegel's text, and his own life and education, the preface for actually writing it. The preface announces a "new era" and a radical break with history and the history of philosophy, but this breach will take the form of an incorporation and fulfillment. The *Phenomenology* will incorporate the totality of thought positions in the history of philosophy by showing how each contributes to the truth of the whole, just as it will show how each historical epoch or form of life belongs to a totality of moments and forms. Like the preface, the *Phenomenology* presents itself as the part that encompasses the whole.

In "our time," life and history stand "ready for conversion" (*bereit umzukehren*).[1] This metamorphosis will not only complete history but also create a universal 'we' and a narrative that sustains the infrastructures of life. There will be exclusions, but they will have been necessary. There will be war and violence, but it will be rational and regulated and will serve to loosen those tribal associations that might undermine the unity of the 'we' (¶475). At a time when the universal has permeated every domain of life, the individual can expect less for himself and less must be expected of him (¶72).

Yet, Hegel's preface proclaims almost as soon as it begins that actually *writing* a preface should be prohibited, at least in philosophy. It would be wrong and illicit from the beginning (¶1). A summary of results will not do. In philosophy the result is not the truth; only the result *and the movement by which it was produced* constitute truth. A mere statement of aims will not suffice either, because not the abstract but the materially realized concept is the truth. It would seem that there could be nothing for a philosopher *to do* in a preface.

If "ours is a birth-time and a period of transition to a new era," still "this new world is no more a complete actuality than a newborn child" (¶¶11–12). The beginning, precisely because it is the beginning, will necessarily not be the truth. That does not mean it will have been false, because the truth is not merely the opposite of what is false (¶¶2, 38–39). The cat may or may not be on the mat, but that has very little to do with truth. The oak is the truth of the acorn, just as the man is the truth of the boy. "Though the embryo is indeed *in itself* a human being, it is not so *for* itself; that is only

---

1. The *Phenomenology* relies on a metaphorics of *kehre*, or "turning": *umkehren* (to return or reverse), *verkehrte* (perverted, turned in the wrong direction or inverted, turned inside out), *die Rückkehr aus dem Anderssein* (the return from otherness.) All these terms reinforce the critique of immediacy and the way in which being or presence results from the movement of appearance, so that it does not take place in the present tense, but always *will have been*. I had the honor of working with Michael Naas on the dissertation that became the book *Turning: From Persuasion to Philosophy: A Reading of Homer's Iliad* (Atlantic Highlands, NJ: Humanities Press, 1995). It was Michael's work on persuasion as turning that made me pay attention to all the turnings in Hegel's thought. Self-consciousness is a "return from otherness." The understanding turns the world inside out, inverting or perverting it. The boy turns into the man. Life turns out to be spirit.

acculturated reason, which has *made* itself into what it is *in itself*" (¶21). The truth takes time. The beginning must unfold its moments to the end. To think that truth can be expressed in a proposition is to make a category mistake. The truth, philosophical truth, requires the temporal dehiscence of the narrative. The embryo will become itself only by acting (or being acted upon), only through a history of unfolding that culminates in its own self-narration.

Hegel repeatedly emphasizes that the reader of the *Phenomenology* must retrace the long road of history and the "laborious emergence" of culture from the immediacy of life (¶4). The reader—natural consciousness—cannot rush his formative education.² "Impatience demands the impossible: the attainment of the end without the means" (¶29). The reader—natural consciousness—must "linger" with each figure or moment, each form of life, in order to "devour" it in all its wealth (¶28).³ He cannot skip ahead to the end result, any more than the boy can become the man without passing through adolescence. The "*length* of this path must be endured," because each moment is a "complete individual shape" in which truth or the whole is thought and experienced from the point of view of that determination. Only after running through all the essential perspectives or moments will the reader/natural consciousness arrive at his fulfillment in philosophical thought or absolute knowing. Only then will he arrive at his end, where "knowledge need no longer go beyond itself" because nothing is other to it (¶80).

Deferrals and delays will be required to open the place for the unfolding (*aufheben*) of self-consciousness.⁴ The slave liberates himself through work. By holding desire in check and exteriorizing himself in his products,

---

2. In performing the phenomenological analysis, the reader will step into the place of the natural consciousness to be interrogated. The phenomenologist is analyst and analysand at once. Natural consciousness is no abstraction but lives in the reader who performs and reconfirms the analysis.

3. Metaphors of experience as a matter of ingestion and digestion abound in the *Phenomenology*, and Hegel, unlike many philosophers, pays attention to eating and other "animal functions," giving their analysis an important place in his argument. The phenomenologist ingests or takes in experience in order to reproduce it as a concept. Perhaps the philosopher has not pursued the metaphor to its logical conclusion.

4. I translate *aufheben* as "unfold" or "unfolding," in keeping with Hegel's reliance on organic metaphors. The concept unfolds in experience, as the bud unfolds in the flower or the boy in the man, preserving and superseding at the same time. *Die Aufhebung* names the principle of both life and thought—of what is created, of what is born, grows, and dies. Contrary to Hegel's confidence in his abstract logic—a forgetting of his own phenomenology—Proust will turn out to be right: "immortality is promised no more to men's works than to men." Marcel Proust, *In Search of Lost*

he creates the distances and differences within himself that unfold the landscape of thought, expanding its horizons across richer possibilities. Knowing consciousness makes distinctions that turn out to be at once not only necessary differences for thought, but also in immediacy completely resolved and no distinctions at all. Still, these "distinctions which are no distinctions" will have been made . . .

The truth is the whole, and, though thought takes time, it must be thought all at once. The truth of any moment will be its relation to all the others. The beginning on its own cannot possibly be the truth. Neither can the end.

Yet, for this very reason, the preface must be written. Precisely in order to begin the long process of education, the reader's expectations must be contradicted.[5] This dismissal of the preface's conventions initiates the reader/natural consciousness into the experience of loss that he will endure over and over again, as he discovers repeatedly that he was neither right in what he knew to be the truth, nor right in who he understood himself to be. The education of consciousness does not consist in the acquisition of information or the accumulation of data, but in the constant loss of commitments and identities that turn out to be untrue on their own or apart from the claim of all the other moments.

The preface introduces the idea that the reader/natural consciousness does not know what he is saying or even what the object of study is. The theme of *die Sache selbst*, or "the real issue," provides the central nervure of the narrative.[6] In the phenomenological education of consciousness, neither the subject matter nor the method can be assumed. The reader/natural consciousness will be interrogated, and every identity tested, until all have been demonstrated to be moments of an organic whole, like the bud and the flower or the boy and the man. The reader/natural consciousness will learn repeatedly that he did not know what the real issue was and, hence, had been approaching it in the wrong way.

---

*Time*, trans. C. K. Scott Moncrieff, Andreas Mayor, and Terence Kilmartin, 6 vols. (1913–27; New York: Modern Library, 1982–83), 6:524.

    5. The reader is "natural consciousness." Every reader must be the site of the "little research" (*das kleine Versuch*) and produce the truth for himself, or it will not be truth.

    6. The text begins and begins again six times because natural consciousness repeatedly discovers that he did not know what the real issue was or that he had been focused on the wrong object.

BEGINNING

> The bud disappears in the bursting forth of the blossom, and one might say that the former is refuted by the latter; similarly, when the fruit appears, the blossom is shown up in its turn as a false manifestation of the plant, and the fruit now emerges as the truth of it instead. These forms are not just distinguished from one another, they also supplant one another as mutually incompatible. Yet at the same time their fluid nature makes the moments of an organic unity in which they not only do not conflict, but in which each is as necessary as the other; and this necessity alone constitutes the life of the whole. (¶2)

Hegel applies the metaphor specifically to the history of philosophy and the task of educating consciousness. Whereas many readers see simple disagreement and believe that the point of reading philosophy is to accept or reject a given "system," in fact, the history of philosophy embodies the "progressive unfolding of truth" (¶2). An organic logic of birth, growth, and development sustains the history of philosophy, no less than history itself and no less than the singleton (*der Einzelne*).[7]

This organic metaphor controls the logic of the preface and of the entire text. Human history embodies growth and development analogous to that of the acorn and the oak or the boy and the man. The acorn is not the oak, nor is the boy the man: each must give way to the other in a necessary logic of genetic development, each shape or identity prefigured in what has come before. The reader/natural consciousness will travel a "highway of despair" due to the many deaths of many selves through which he must pass on the way to philosophy and to the 'we' of the universal. "The life of spirit is not the life that shrinks from death and keeps itself untouched by devastation, but rather the life that endures it and maintains itself in it. It wins its truth only when in utter dismemberment, it finds itself" (¶32). Embracing death and "tarrying with the negative" provide the "magical power" (*die Zauberkraft*) required to "convert" (*umkehren*) the "substance" of man's history and culture, his "inorganic nature," into self-conscious thought (¶¶28, 32). Man's

---

7. Miller indiscriminately translates both *der Einzelne* and *das Individuum* as "individual," but the terms are crucially distinct in Hegel's usage. The singleton (*der Einzelne*) exists as a separate and particular being. Human history unfolds his transformation into an individual who exists as and knows himself to be a member (*das Glied* or *das Mitglied*) of a community. I translate *der Einzelne* as "the singleton" in order to mark its distinction from the individual and to emphasize its sense of standing on its own.

"inorganic nature" exhibits an organic logic. Courage and acceptance of loss will be required if the boy is to disappear in the man of spirit, the historical subject into the philosopher, and the reader or natural consciousness into the 'we' of philosophical consciousness, as the bud becomes the flower.

Under Hegel's metaphorics of the organism, the ancient world provides the seed from which the great canopy of European civilization grows. Historical epochs displace one another as the oak, the acorn or the man, the boy. For the Greeks, only the heavens exhibited the regularity of form and law, while the stars at the same time sustained myth and the narratives of identity:

> The eye of spirit had to be forcibly turned and held fast to the things of this world; and it has taken a long time before the lucidity which only heavenly things used to have could penetrate the dullness and confusion in which the sense of worldly things was enveloped, and to make attention to the here and now as such, attention to what has been called 'experience' [*Erfahrung*], an interesting and valid enterprise. (¶8)

Hegel refers to the long and arduous efforts of the natural sciences to order and classify the lavish profusions of plants and animals on Earth, as well as to the success of the physical sciences in reducing ordinary events to forms and laws. There is nothing mysterious about the "lucidity" to which Hegel refers. It is the result of the practical activity of the natural sciences in regularizing the world through tables and laws, activity that also creates the community of practicing scientists who confirm and reconfirm one another's results.

In "modern time," conversely, the universalizing power of thought, which transforms the particular into an instance and the singleton into a member, has so permeated all the domains of life that "the individual finds the abstract form ready-made" (¶33). While the ancients engaged in a practice of abstraction and universalization in order to produce the concept or form from the "concrete variety of existence," in our time every dimension of the singleton's life has been permeated by the universal. The singleton's distinction as an independent existence seems to be dissolved in the "ready-made" general figures of husband, citizen, worker. Life itself—and above all human life—submits itself regularly to observation, discipline, and law. Life is disposed of on the basis of calculations of utility, statistical generalizations, and an economics of probabilities that reduces the singleton to an abstract unit (¶33). In "our time" the singleton finds himself already generalized through the infrastructures of family, science, and state at the same time that history, knowledge, and the law tie him ever more tightly to sensuous immediacy and actual life. If for the Greeks man was an animal capable of politics, in "our time" man has become an animal whose politics and philosophy interrogate nothing less than "life itself."[8] This will prove to have been the "real issue" (*die Sache selbst*).

Phenomenology, as the "science of the experience of consciousness," attending to the "here and now," attending to "what has been called 'experience' [*Erfahrung*]" as "an interesting and valid enterprise," defines philosophy in "our time." Phenomenology will require the reader to make his "living consciousness" the site of the investigation. He will supply his own sensuous immediacy and all that will turn out to have been implicated in it to the unfolding of natural consciousness into philosophical consciousness. It is his experience, his "saying and meaning," that will be interrogated, through all the registers of life.

At the same time, the "zealous" treat the reader/natural consciousness as if, because of his "preoccupation with the sensuous" and his "ordinary, private affairs," he had forgotten all about spirit and the divine (¶8). Hegel insists, however, that men are not "ready like worms to content themselves with dirt and water" (¶8). Spirit or the divine in Hegel's account is not the opposite of the profusion of life and the sensuous but permeates it. For that reason, the thick richness of life must be worked through until the lucidity of spirit shines through, just as the botanical table illuminates the extravagance of plant life. The truth cannot be reached by a thought that has not engaged with every aspect of concrete life. Insight, faith, intuition, edification, and speculation zealously proclaim that thought may reach the true or the absolute *immediately*, so that the reader/natural consciousness is only offered an abstraction or a mere representation of spirit. He remains thirsty, like "a wanderer in the desert craving for a mere mouthful of water, [who] seems to crave for refreshment only the bare feeling of the divine in general" (¶8). In the end, neither revelation and faith nor "healthy common sense" will be adequate to the life of spirit (¶678).

---

8. Cf. Michel Foucault, *The History of Sexuality*, vol. 1, *An Introduction*, trans. R. Hurley (1976; New York: Pantheon, 1978), 143.

The problem for philosophy in our time is to dislodge the ready-made abstractions and fixed thoughts, so as to set them in motion in relation to one another. This task of "bringing fixed thoughts into a fluid state" in order to "give actuality to the universal and impart to it spiritual life"—the task commenced by the preface—proves much more difficult than the labor of abstracting the concept or the universal from sensuous life (¶33). The phenomenologist tests every attachment, every claim to truth, setting it in motion in relation to other claims like a star in a constellation. Yet, these claims are living and animate and have the force of desire in them. Dislodging these fixed thoughts will prove a more difficult philosophical performance than the abstraction of the concept from the sensuous as form and law. Only phenomenological interrogation will turn out to have been adequate to complete the transformation of the "precarious fullness of life" into the "depth of the concept" (*der Ernst des Begriffs in ihre Tiefe*) (¶4). This conversion of "substance" into "subject" constitutes phenomenology's guiding aim. Converting his experience into language, through the effort to say what he means, the phenomenologist/reader/natural consciousness produces a history of figures or characters, each one a perspective on the whole. Each one must be set in motion in relation to the others, but this will not happen without violence.

Like any organism, including Earth, the species, and the living singleton, thought undergoes metamorphoses. The fixed determination of a thought or identity will give way inevitably to the movement in which it is produced, but not without "despair" and violence. The preface introduces the "Bacchanalian revel" as a controlling image for this belonging-together of rest and motion, the fixed and the fluid. Hegel may not be a *tragic philosopher* in the end, but eighty years before Nietzsche he invokes the Bacchanalian revel as an image for the logic of becoming.[9] The image invokes not only the multiple births and rebirths of Dionysus and his legendary metamorphic abilities, but also the reduction of the singleton in the frenzy of the group that survives his collapse. Dionysus figures the transformative

---

9. In the passage from *Ecce Homo* quoted as the epigraph of this preface, Nietzsche claims the "right to understand myself as the first *tragic philosopher*." He insists, "before me this transposition of the Dionysian into a philosophical pathos did not exist." "The affirmation of passing away and *destroying*" and embracing becoming over being, however, define Hegel's philosophy, as does the motif of the Bacchanalian revel. See Friedrich Nietzsche, *Ecce Homo*, trans. Walter Kaufmann (1908; New York: Vintage, 1996), §3.

power of life and thought, truth unfolding from life, like the man from the boy, but the revelry, on the other hand, also signals something darker. "The true is thus the Bacchanalian revel in which no member is not drunk; yet because each member [*Glied*], as he detaches [*sich absondert*], is immediately dissolved [*sich auflöst*], the revel is just as much transparent and simple repose" (¶47). In the unfolding truth of history and life, the loss of the singleton proves insignificant. If life only exists in the living being, it is the unfolding of the species that provides the vehicle of truth.[10] "Appearance is the arising and passing away that does not itself arise and pass away ... the movement of the life of truth" (¶47). The differentiated thought positions of philosophy, the historical epochs, and the phases of a life are all necessary, but they belong to a fluidity that surpasses them. Identities exist and persist only as unfolded moments in the movement of life, thought, and history. Thus, the great task of the text, commenced by the preface, will have been to detach the reader/natural consciousness from his adherence to any moment. Philosophy addresses the hardheadedness and hardheartedness of fixed thought and feeling as an "abnormal inhibition of thought" or as blockages that threaten the fluid life of spirit (¶¶47, 63).

The organic metaphor, particularly as refigured in the Bacchanalian revel, not only imposes a certain temporality of negation and deferral, a landscape of horizons and fluid motion; it also installs a logic of *membership* and the idea of the *body politic*. Just as the integrity of an organic body depends on the function of each *member* (*das Glied*), so too the reader/natural consciousness will turn out to be, not so much an instance of a form, but a *member* (*das Mitglied*) of a body politic. Rather than imposing the botanical logic of classes and kinds, the universal determines the reader/natural consciousness according to the biology of the organism and the model of sovereign power. Just as the organism differentiates its members according to their function, so too the body politic will dispose itself in a logic of membership that puts some under the command of others. The body politic, too, will have its hands and feet that serve the ruling head. The narrator, philosophical consciousness, commands the unfolding of the characters or thought positions and the articulation of the 'we' of

---

10. Hegel's analysis of the life of spirit assumes Earth to be the "eternal individual." The horizon of Earth's identity provides the figure of closure that ensures the regenerative power of the organic logic. One generation gives way to the next without loss only against the horizon of an infinite Earth. See section 3.a., on human exceptionalism and the mastery of nature.

philosophical and political community. Some will speak, and others will be spoken about, disposed of in an abstract concept or law, like the gender division of labor or the law of property.

The organic metaphor forestalls any possibility of being otherwise. Transgression of the logic of genetic development could never serve life, as it will have been determined in advance to be a genetic defect, a monstrous miscarriage, not a birth. The reader/natural consciousness proceeds according to the logic of the embryo. Once the interrogation of ordinary certainty begins, the end result and the entire movement toward it already will have been determined. Each shape must of necessity come out of the one before, without the interference of any of our "bright ideas." Nothing can be added to the beginning from outside, as it will have been the case that there is no outside. The analysis will return to immediacy as the seed from which the lush growth of the text began. Transgression will always have produced a deformity, a deviation from the logically necessary path of the life of spirit.

The preface promises a ladder from the certainty of immediacy in everyday life to philosophy or the thought of the whole, where the living being will know himself to be only a passing member in the fluid truth of the whole (¶26). Death will have been the reader's constant companion in the course of his education. Spirit takes the form of the living individual, but the singleton unfolds into an "achieved community of minds," and that community will flow in waves of generation that pass the singleton by. Each singleton "only really exists" in this community that unfolds beyond him (¶69).

Philosophy, Hegel concludes, belongs to the book that can be revivified and set in motion by generations of readers. The book transforms "what is as yet a matter for [the author] alone" into something "universally held" (¶71). The book circulates and creates for itself a community of readers that confirm and sustain the author's narrative as belonging to each and all, just as a community of scientists will confirm the results of a member. And, just as truth takes time, so too does the book and reading. The difficulty of reading philosophy lies in the necessity that "so much has to be read over and over before it can be understood" (¶63). This necessity arises not merely from the complexity of its prose or the subtlety of its arguments. Because philosophy takes place in the future perfect, the beginning and the path can be understood only at the end, when the philosopher must go back and read the book again. The book must be read and reread because of the temporal logic of the future perfect that defines not only philosophy but life itself.

While the public is generally "good natured" and inclined to blame itself when philosophy fails to "speak to" it, those who fancy themselves its "representatives" and "spokesmen," "certain of their own competence, put all the blame on the author" (¶72). These "dead men" deal only in conventions and ready-made abstract ideas or in faith and immediate insight. Their deadly fixity of thought and feeling impedes the fluid life of spirit. Fixed in their positions, they do not participate in the living movement of thought. Their books do not circulate and create a community of readers but are instead dead on arrival. Despite the fact that the feet of these dead men are "already at the door" and ready to carry Hegel out, he confidently cites "the more gradual effect which corrects the attention exhorted by imposing assurances and corrects, too, contemptuous censure, and gives some writers an audience only after a time, while others after a time have no audience left" (¶71). The truth will prove its truth by sustaining life and an "achieved community of minds" (¶69). For the singleton "less must be expected" (¶72). On the one hand, Hegel insists that the concept can only be realized in the self-conscious singleton, as a material infrastructure of life. On the other, he maintains that the death of the singleton leaves no trace on the concept, as the tides of generations and forms of community supersede the singleton's actual life. Perhaps, however, the phenomenological analysis itself will prove resistant to this effort to erase the singular face of the reader.

Hegel writes the preface after the book has already been written, installing, as Derrida remarks, an "intention-to-say after the fact."[11] If it is true that "the dispersion of the seed" at the same time "excludes all loss and all haphazard productivity," it still does not seem fair to say that "Hegel never investigates in terms of writing the living circulation of discourse."[12] The "exteriority" of writing and its "repetitive autonomy" prove essential to the production of the "achieved community of minds" and the "we" of the universal. Perhaps, "literature is also the *exception to everything*: at once the exception to the whole, the want-of-wholeness in the whole, and the

---

11. Jacques Derrida, *Dissemination*, trans. Barbara Johnson (1972; Chicago: University of Chicago Press, 1981), 7.
12. Derrida, 48.

exception to everything, that which exists by itself, alone, with nothing else, in exception to all. A part that, within *and* without the whole, marks the wholly other, the other incommensurate with the whole."[13] But, if literature can escape the organic logic, it will not be because Hegel failed to interrogate writing as an element of life. He interrogates the preface for seeming to stand in for the unfolding of history, the actual life of the concept and the living being. He interrogates the book as the infrastructure of community. And his interrogation of the discrepancy between writing and the certainty of ordinary life, the very incommensurability to which Derrida avers, launches the education of the reader/natural consciousness. It remains to be seen whether this discrepancy can be overcome, so that thought discovers that "nothing is other to it." It remains to be seen whether this organic logic preempts diversion and transgression, so that the end returns to the beginning as its seed with no remainder or excess. The preface's interrogation of itself stages the problem of writing life.

---

13. Derrida, 56.

# OUR TIME IS THE BIRTH-TIME OF SPIRIT
## Kant and the Bird on a Lime-Twig

> If, then, on the supposition that our empirical knowledge conforms to objects as things in themselves, we find that the unconditioned *cannot be thought without contradiction*, and that, when, on the other hand, we suppose that our representation of things, as they are given to us, does not conform to these things as they are in themselves, but that these objects, as appearances, conform to our mode of representation, *the contradiction vanishes* . . . we thus find that the unconditioned is not to be met with in things, insofar as we know them, that is insofar as they are given to us, but only insofar as we do not know them, that is insofar as they are things in themselves.
> —IMMANUEL KANT, *CRITIQUE OF PURE REASON*, PREFACE, B XX (1787)

While the preface inaugurates the long task of self-interrogation that is the destiny of and for the human species, the introduction of the *Phenomenology* addresses the reader/natural consciousness more directly in the specificity of his own historical moment as the man of "healthy common sense." Toward the end of the preface Hegel sarcastically dismisses both the conventions of common sense and the "sky-rockets of inspiration" of immediate intuition, as neither the man of common sense nor the man of insight and faith undertakes the arduous labor of unfolding (*Aufhebung*) that philosophy requires. The reader/natural consciousness, however, lives in the "casual dress" of common sense, not the "robes of a high priest," and it is in this guise that the introduction engages him (¶70).

Without naming him, Hegel undertakes a critique of Kant's *Critique of Pure Reason* as the narrative of the man of common sense. The man of common sense makes the "natural assumption" that philosophy must begin with some consensus on knowledge, implying that the singleton is primarily a knower and that perception is the paradigm of knowledge. The phenomenological analysis of the experience of the reader/natural consciousness will reveal the untruth of all of these assumptions.

The *Critique of Pure Reason* develops an anatomy of the act of perception in which determinations in the forms of intuition—space and time—are synthesized or unified according to categories in order to produce the perception of a thing. Cause and effect, unity, possibility and impossibility, the categories generate rules for the understanding that articulate the possibility conditions for the experience of any perceiving consciousness. In the course of his analysis Kant introduces a strict distinction between what can be known and what must be thought. A thing is always presented to the perceiver in perspective. While seeing the thing only from one perspective, the perceiver experiences the thing as having other perspectives that might be realized were he to move around it in space and time. A perceiver looking at a house knows that he can walk around it and see it from the other side. He assumes in his perceiving that there is another side. The perceiver, Kant argues, could not perceive in this way if his perception was not regulated by the idea of a completely determined object. The *thing for us* always appears in a determinate perspective, but the *thing in itself* comprises a totality of perspectives.

This perspectival character of perception opens it to error. Walking around the house, the perceiver may discover that it was only a façade. Perceptual knowledge is always delimited by or regulated by the idea of the thing in itself. The epistemological horizon of the idea of a totality of perspectives always reminds the perceiver of the possibility of perceptual error. Perceptual knowledge remains constantly subject to the possibility of being proved false, as it cannot in principle grasp the thing itself as a totality of perspectives.[1] Perception represents the thing as it is *for us*, not as it is *in itself*. Perception yields knowledge, but not truth.

This "fear of falling into error," Hegel argues, is "just the error itself," as it is based on a series of erroneous assumptions about knowledge

---

1. Merleau-Ponty, that latter-day Kantian phenomenologist, repeats Kant's phenomenology of the perspectival character of perception, but avoids the metaphysics of the thing in itself by demonstrating that the motility of the body addresses the problem of error. Perceptual error is corrected by more perception, as the body moves around the perceived thing. No speculative idea beyond perception is needed either to account for the reliability of perceptual knowledge or to address perceptual error. See Maurice Merleau-Ponty, *Phenomenology of Perception*, trans. Colin Smith (1945; New York: Humanities Press, 1962), esp. 102–6, 127n2, and 128–30. Merleau-Ponty criticizes "critical philosophy" for substituting a "non-temporal ghost" for the living perceiver as the subject of thought: "The Kantian subject posits a world, but, in order to be able to assert a truth, the actual subject must in the first place have a world or be in the world, that is, sustain round about it a system of meanings whose reciprocities, relationships and involvements do not require to be made explicit in order to be exploited." The "true subject of thought" is the one who "breathes his own life into the non-temporal ghost." "Living thought" depends on the body as an access to the world, not on "subsuming under some category" (128–29).

(*Erkennen*). When these false beliefs are dispelled, "what calls itself fear of error reveals itself rather as fear of truth" (¶74). While the critical philosophy purports to secure the domain of knowledge, in fact it dissembles by making truth inaccessible in principle.[2]

Critical philosophy's distinction between the thing for us and the thing in itself depends on the erroneous assumption that knowledge is either an "instrument" through which consciousness actively grasps the truth or a "medium" through which it passively receives it. If knowledge is an instrument, then "the use of an instrument on a thing certainly does not let it be what it is for itself, but sets out to reshape and alter it" (¶73). Similarly, if knowledge is "a more or less passive medium through which the light of truth reaches us, then again we do not receive the truth as it is in itself, but only as it exists through and in this medium" (¶73). In either case, the knower employs a means that produces the opposite of its aim: untruth, rather than knowledge.

Critical philosophy attempts to address the problem it has itself created "through an acquaintance with the way the instrument works" or by getting to know "the law of [the medium's] refraction." An understanding of the instrument would allow the knower to subtract from the representation of the thing what the instrument has contributed. Unfortunately, as Hegel notes, if the knower subtracts from the representation of the things what has been contributed by the instrument of knowledge, he will be back in the same position where he started, before the employment of the instrument. The thing would become for him "exactly what it was before this superfluous effort" (¶73). Similarly, getting to know the "law of refraction" of the "medium" of knowledge proves useless, because it is not the refraction of the medium, but the medium itself through which truth reaches the knower. If the medium were subtracted, "all that would be indicated would be a pure direction or blank space." If knowledge is a medium, subtracting the medium merely leaves the unknown.

The distinction between the thing in itself and the thing for us turns knowledge into a "ruse," as if the truth were "like a bird caught by a lime-twig" (¶73). The image comes from the ancient science of bird-catching. Like

---

2. Merleau-Ponty makes a similar diagnosis to Hegel's: the distinction between the transcendental and empirical in critical philosophy "conceals the problem [of thought] rather than solves it." Merleau-Ponty, *Phenomenology of Perception*, 129.

a hunter who wishes to trap small birds alive, the knower must use a series of strategies to bring the truth near enough to grasp it without denaturing it. To trap a goldfinch or sparrow the bird-catcher smears a sheaf of twigs with birdlime, an adhesive that will prevent the birds from flying off once they land on it. He must be sure not to use too much, as this will be "distasteful" to the birds, but he must also be sure to use enough, "for as too much will deter them from coming, too little will not hold them when they are there."[3] The bird-catcher places the bundle of lime-twigs in trees, hedges, or fields, as near as possible to the birds' usual haunts. Then, he employs his birdcall to bring them near. Sometimes he employs a living bird trapped previously as a decoy to attract other birds. When the birds alight on the lime-twigs, the birdlime will hold them down and prevent them flying off. The bird-catcher is advised to be patient and to wait until they are "sufficiently entangled" before attempting to cage them. The "little ruse" of the critical philosophy treats truth as if it were a bird to be ensnared by the knower's cunning. Such a take on truth, Hegel argues, is laughable.

Critical philosophy does not understand what it is doing. Thinking to act out of the fear of error, it actually installs the fear of truth. The fundamental delusion of the critical philosophy arises from two erroneous assumptions: first, that "there is a *difference between ourselves and this cognition*" and, second, that truth "stands on one side and knowledge on the other, independent and separated from it" (¶74). The first confusion stems in part from the attempt by the critical philosophy to think knowing *in general*, when there are "many different types of knowledge," each with its own appropriate object or domain of experience.[4] The critical philosophy treats knowledge as if it were a tool that the singleton could pick up or put down, as if the singleton is not always engaged in knowing the world. Apart

---

3. "Birdlime," in G. G. and J. Robinson, *The Sportsman's Dictionary, or the Gentleman's Companion for Town and Country*, 4th ed. (London: R. Noble, 1800). Shakespeare frequently employs the image: e.g., "you must lay lime to tangle her desires" (*Two Gentlemen of Verona*, act 3, scene 2, line 68). See also *Henry VI*, act 2, scene 4: "York and impious Beaufort, that false priest / Have all limn'd bushes to betray thy wings / And fly thou how thou can'st they'll tangle thee." Quoted in Robert Nares, *A Glossary: Or, Collection of Words, Phrases, Names, and Allusions to Customs, Proverbs, etc., Which Have Been Thought to Require Illustration in the Works of English Authors, Particularly Shakespeare and His Contemporaries* (Stralsund: Charles Loeffler, 1825), 453. Clearly, Hegel was familiar not only with the ancient practice but also with its use as an image in literature.

4. Moreover, knowing is not the singleton's primary relation to objects. As the phenomenologist will discover, desire is his first relation to objects, and knowing cannot be thought apart from that desire.

from his perceiving, the singleton would be a ghost, an abstraction, not a living being. To be human is to be engaged in knowing the world.

Similarly, the distinction between knowledge and truth is a "distinction which is no distinction." The distinction absurdly assumes that knowledge falls outside the truth yet is, nevertheless, true. Throughout this discussion Hegel has used the term *absolute* as another name for truth: "the absolute alone is true, or the truth alone is absolute" (¶75). It is necessary for the reader/natural consciousness to work through the different ways of knowing in their respective specificities in order to be able to think their belonging-together in the absolute as moments of truth. The delusion that the distinction between knowledge and truth is hard and fast introduces the idea that, though knowing is not capable of grasping the absolute or thing in itself, it is capable of some other kind of truth. This "hazy distinction" between absolute truth and some other truth is a symptom indicating that the man of healthy common sense really does not know what he is talking about (¶75). Reliance on these philosophical conventions—'knowledge,' 'absolute,' 'objective,' 'subjective'—gives the appearance of "working seriously and zealously" when, in fact, it amounts to an attempt to avoid "the hard work of science" (¶76). Science is the thought of the whole system of shapes of knowing and being. When confronted with a way of knowing that, just because it is a specific mode of experience and not the whole, is not yet science, science cannot merely "reject it as an ordinary way of looking at things." Much less can science put the reader/natural consciousness off with the mere intimation of "something better to come" (¶76). Science/philosophy requires of the reader/natural consciousness nothing less than the production of the absolute out of his own experience. This will require a long, arduous, and painful path of metamorphoses in the reader/natural consciousness.

The reader/natural consciousness can be engaged by Hegel's text and set upon this "highway of despair" only because he has been preceded by and embodies unconsciously the historical unfolding of all the possible shapes of experience. The complete system of shapes of experience has been lived and is now ready to be known. What the reader/natural consciousness lacks is the *concept* (*Begriff*) of his experience. Doubting himself at every turn, the reader/natural consciousness tests every shape and way of knowing to determine how it contributes to the truth of the whole. Neither the reader's own convictions nor the authority of others escapes the skepticism of science that repeatedly exposes the untruth of "natural ideas, thoughts, and opinions." Science/philosophy proceeds by a doubting that is neither a mere "shillyshallying" nor a methodological ruse so that "at the end of the process the matter is taken to be what it was in the first place" (¶78). This doubt produces a "state of despair" that drives the reader/natural consciousness forward in his philosophical education.

Discovering at every turn that he is not who he thought he was and does not know what he thought he knew, the reader/natural consciousness nevertheless progresses in his development, for the loss is also a gain. The skepticism that produces "the bare abstraction of nothingness" and is ready to throw everything "into the same empty abyss" is not the skepticism of phenomenology (¶79). The self-interrogation of the reader/natural consciousness not only dispels false confidence and mistaken identities, it also produces new figures of truth and new identities to be interrogated in turn. Just as the refutation of the boy is not a mere negation but the production of the man, so too in losing what he thought he knew and discovering that he is not who he was, the reader/natural consciousness reconfigures himself in a new identity and new commitment to truth. The negation of what has come before proves to be a "*determinate* negation," so that "a new form has thereby immediately arisen, and in the negation the transition is made by which the progress through the complete series of shapes comes about of itself" (¶79). The violence that consciousness suffers "at its own hands" drives the metamorphoses by which philosophical consciousness will emerge out of natural consciousness. Tested and interrogated at every moment, the reader/natural consciousness transforms himself into the narrator/philosophical consciousness who has "made himself into a moment" (¶53) and does not remain fixed to one shape or another but traverses the whole story of their unfolding.

Healthy common sense knows its objects to be its "antithesis": it distinguishes the object *in itself* from the object's relation to consciousness and itself from the object. Philosophical science, however, reveals that the everyday world where healthy common sense is "at home" is marked by "an absence of spirit" (¶26). At the same time, the truths of phenomenology—that the reader/natural consciousness is a "return from otherness," that he is both what he is and what he is not, that distinctions must be made only to be overcome—appear to natural consciousness to be contradictory abstractions that belong to a "beyond in which it no longer possesses itself."

Philosophical and natural consciousness each appear to the other as the "inversion of truth" (*das Verkehrte der Wahrheit*) (¶26). Taking up the phenomenological project, the reader/natural consciousness "makes an attempt, induced by he knows not what, to walk on his head too, just this once; the compulsion to assume this unwonted posture and to go about in it is a violence he is expected to do to himself, all unprepared and seemingly without necessity" (¶26). The reader/natural consciousness enjoys "the *immediate certainty* of himself" (¶26). He knows himself to be standing on his own. Thus, he has the right to demand that phenomenology or philosophical science provide him with a "ladder" to science. It is incumbent on philosophical science to show the reader/natural consciousness how science and philosophical consciousness already lie implicit in his immediate certainty, just as the oak is implicit in the acorn and the boy in the man.

As "unconditioned" (*unbedingtes*) being, the reader/natural consciousness is not merely substance, but also "explicitly the concept (*Begriff*) of himself" or self-consciousness (¶80). As such, he constantly goes beyond himself, in relation both to his objects and to himself. Just as the acorn "goes beyond itself" in the oak, so the reader/natural consciousness will constantly surpass himself in the course of his phenomenological education. "The series of shapes that consciousness runs through along this path is moreover the exhaustive history of the acculturation of consciousness itself to science" (¶78). Walking this path upright, but not without turnings, returns, inversions, and even perversions, natural consciousness arrives at the goal that is "as necessarily fixed for knowledge as the serial progression" (¶80). The reader/natural consciousness will know he has succeeded in the phenomenological project when he arrives at "the point where knowledge no longer needs to go beyond itself," because there is no longer anything that is other to it. All the possible modes of existence and ways of knowing, as well as all the possible shapes of objectivity, will have been run through in their genetic progression. "The necessary progression and belonging-together of the forms of the unrealized consciousness will by itself bring to pass the *completion* of the series" (¶79). Each shape will be a metamorphosis of those that have come before, until the reader/natural consciousness is transformed into the narrator/philosophical consciousness.

The method of the phenomenological project, like its goal, arises from the nonthingly, metamorphic existence of consciousness. Healthy common sense makes a distinction between knowledge and truth. On the one hand, natural consciousness relates himself to something, and this is called knowing. At the same time, he distinguishes this being-for-another from being-in-itself and calls the latter truth (¶82). The distinction between being-for-another and being-in-itself thus "falls within" consciousness itself. In the figure of being-in-itself consciousness provides its own "measure" of what it knows and what it takes to be the limit of knowledge. "Consciousness provides its own criterion from within itself, so that the investigation becomes a comparison of consciousness with itself" (¶84). Consciousness relates itself to its object and distinguishes itself from it. The in-itself or truth is posited as such by some shape of consciousness, and that shape can be interrogated—a philosophical opportunity that Kant fails to discern, because he fails to see that the distinction between the in-itself and the for-itself falls within consciousness. Phenomenology takes this double relation as its object:

> If we designate *knowledge* [*Wissen*] as the *concept* [*Begriff*], but the essence or the *true* as what exists, or the *object*, then the examination consists in seeing whether the concept corresponds to the object. But if we [philosophical consciousness] call the *essence* or the in-itself of the *object* the *concept*, and, on the other hand, understand by the *object* the concept, then the examination consists in seeing whether the object corresponds to its concept. (¶84)

The reader/natural consciousness thus interrogates his own knowing. By taking the concept as its object, consciousness has moved beyond the question of how the concept corresponds to the true or what exists. What will be tested in the course of the phenomenological interrogation is not only the moment of knowledge but also the moment of truth or the object. "Something is *for it* the *in-itself*; and knowledge or the being of the object for consciousness is, *for it*, another moment. Upon this distinction which is ready at hand the examination rests" (¶85). The difference between knowledge and the in-itself or truth falls within consciousness and generates a testing of both knowledge and the object. If the comparison of knowing with what consciousness takes to be the in-itself reveals that these two moments do not correspond to one another, then not only knowledge but also the object is revised. Consciousness discovers through the testing or comparison that what it took to be the truth or the in-itself "is not an *in-itself*, or that it was only an in-itself *for consciousness*" (§85). The object "does not stand the test" any more than does the way of knowing.

This self-interrogation generates a series of shapes or ways of knowing and a series of objects or figures of truth. This movement "is precisely what is called *experience* [*Erfahrung*]" (§86). Phenomenology or the "science of the experience of consciousness" requires that the analysis begin with natural consciousness of ordinary life in his "immediate certainty." The interrogation of that certainty inaugurates the generation of the series of shapes of knowledge and figures of truth. Hegel cautions the reader to avoid the temptation to import any of his own "bright ideas" into the analysis (§84). What appears in the course of the analysis must come forth from the interrogation of the immediate certainty of life. Each new shape or figure of truth must emerge from the shape that preceded it. Thus, when natural consciousness discovers that he is not who he thought he was and that what he took to be truth is not sustainable, he produces *at the same time* a new identity and claim to truth. The discovery is a matter not merely of showing something to be false, but of showing how it was not the whole or fully realized truth. As the truth of the acorn is the oak or the truth of the boy the man, so each shape will give way to another that realizes what was implicit, but unthought, in it.

Natural consciousness, however, repeatedly makes the mistake of focusing on a particular shape or figure of truth, rather than recognizing the movement or generation of shapes to be the truth. The reader/natural consciousness repeatedly thinks that when a shape and its figure of truth are found wanting, the new shape produced from this interrogation can be embraced as the truth. 'We,' philosophical consciousness, however, know that this is only one more in a series of shapes that will not be completed until consciousness arrives at the goal, that point at which knowledge need no longer go beyond itself because nothing is other to it. "*For us*," the moments—the ways of knowing and figures of truth or objectivity—belong to a "movement and process of becoming" that comprise the experience of consciousness (§87). While natural consciousness repeatedly embraces each new moment as the truth, philosophical consciousness/the narrator knows the whole series of shapes and the movement in which they are generated to be the truth. The truth of experience lies not in a particular shape, but in the "*reversal* [*Umkehrung*] *of consciousness itself*" that produces each shape from the one that came before (§87).

From the beginning, then, phenomenology is informed by this idea that the truth is only the fully realized series of shapes of knowing and figures of truth. As the "way to science," it is the practice of self-interrogation that will produce philosophical consciousness/the narrator out of the immediate certainty of the living natural consciousness/reader. Because it is already informed by the idea that the truth is the whole—the movement of reversal or becoming itself—and by the goal of a knowledge no longer "burdened with something alien," phenomenology or the way to science "is itself already *science*" (¶¶88–89). Science *will have been* the truth of phenomenology.

Phenomenology must show how philosophy or science arises out of life with the same necessity that the acorn gives way to the oak and the boy the man. Life gives birth to philosophy when the historical moment is "ripe to receive it" (¶71). All the possible shapes of life are to be given their due in this analysis, and nothing is to be *left behind* as if it were other to or alien to natural consciousness. On the one hand, though consciousness experiences many deaths of many selves in its progressive unfolding, nothing is to be lost. Every expenditure returns with an added value. On the other, it remains an open question what bodies will be required in this "birth-time," whose generativity will be spent, and how the living will fare under the regime of philosophical science.

Will everyone find a voice in the 'we' of philosophical consciousness, or will its appearance have depended in advance on exclusions that leave some behind, silent and invisible, after all? Does the phenomenology reveal excessive moments, which remain unresolved in absolute knowing, so that any termination of the interrogation would be indefinitely suspended? Perhaps, phenomenology will prove to have been the truth of science.

# THE BETRAYAL OF SUBSTANCE

# PART I

## EPOCHĒ

*Chapter One*

# CRITIQUE OF IMMEDIACY
## The Unreality of the Sensuous

> With [sense-certainty's] appeal to universal experience we may be permitted to anticipate how the case stands in the practical sphere. In this respect we can tell those who assert the truth and certainty of the reality of sense-objects that they should go back to the most elementary school of wisdom, viz. the ancient Eleusinian Mysteries of Ceres and Bacchus, and that they have still to learn the secret meaning of the eating of bread and the drinking of wine. For he who is initiated into these mysteries not only comes to doubt the being of sensuous things, but to despair of it.... Even the animals are not shut out from this wisdom ... for they do not just stand idly in front of sensuous things ... but, despairing of their reality,... they fall to without ceremony and eat them up.
>
> —G. W. F. HEGEL, *PHENOMENOLOGY OF SPIRIT*, ¶109

### 1.A. DETERMINATE NEGATION: INTERROGATION BETWEEN CERTAINTY AND TRUTH

> We learn by experience that we meant something other than we meant to mean; and this correction of our meaning compels our knowing to return to the proposition [*auf den Satz zurückzukommen*] and take hold of it in some other way.
>
> —G. W. F. HEGEL, *PHENOMENOLOGY OF SPIRIT*, PREFACE, ¶63

Only a philosopher or a madman would entertain any serious doubt about his existence or wonder whether or not the world exists as it appears to him. Ordinarily, humans live in a quotidian certainty that pervades experience and sustains agency. I do not ponder the ontology of the doorknob; I grasp it and open the door. I do not wonder if the bread is illusory; I slice it and eat it up. I do not hesitate in fear that the floor is not what it appears to be; I step on it with an absolute conviction that it will sustain me.

Any of these confident assumptions may be false. The doorknob may come off in my hand. The bread may turn out to be made of papier-mâché, a mere model meant to sit in the baker's window. The floor may be rotten and give way beneath my feet. In each case, however, further experience corrects the deception and restores confidence and certainty that my sensory capacities give me a reliable purchase on the world.

Some events in life may precipitate universal alterations. If I find myself betrayed by my lover or my friend, the very terms of my life may be threatened. The death of a child may make life itself seem unsustainable. War or domestic violence may make life almost unendurable. Still, the loss or suffering itself appears as *mine*. Experience always occurs in the first person, even when I experience myself as profoundly mistaken about who I was or deeply alienated from the conditions of my existence. I am still there suffering the contradictions between my assumptions and beliefs and what experience has taught me. For the most part, humans go about their business without doubting their existence or that of the world.

If phenomenology is to demonstrate how philosophical science lies implicit in life, it must begin here, where natural consciousness actually lives, with the "knowledge of the immediate or of what simply *is*" (¶90). Hegel reminds the reader that it would not be appropriate to import any "bright ideas" into the analysis. Sense-certainty must be allowed to speak for itself, and nothing alien can be introduced into the analysis without subverting the genetic logic that guarantees the systematicity and completeness of the series of shapes. 'We,' philosophical consciousness, must refrain from conceptualizing what is lived as sensuous immediacy. The truth of sense-certainty can only be found in the experience itself.

The question is, Can sense-certainty say what it means? Can it, in response to the interrogation of the phenomenologist, actually say its certainty or give voice to immediacy?

Given its "concrete content," sense-certainty appears to be the "*richest kind of knowledge*" (¶91). The horizons of space and time offer an "infinite wealth" of determinations. No matter how far we travel toward those horizons, there is always more sensuous material to be revealed. Similarly, if we take any of these contents and divide them up, we will always find more determinate content. Sense-certainty, however, precisely because it is an *immediacy*, can say no more than that "the thing *is*, and it *is*, merely because it *is*" (¶91). Of both the knower and the object, nothing more can be said than that each is given as an immediacy. To speak of the thing's qualities or its relation to a context of things—or to speak of the knower as more than mere sensuous apprehension, as if immediacy could include imagining, remembering, or thinking—would be to introduce a "complex process of mediation" into what was supposed to be "sheer *being*" (§91).

The simplicity of sense-certainty, its claim to be an immediacy, cannot be sustained. From the beginning there was always the difference between consciousness and the object, the 'I' and the 'this,' so not one simple being that merely *is*, but two, each a 'this' in its own right.

> When *we* [philosophical consciousness] reflect on this difference, we find [without importing any of our own bright ideas] that neither one nor the other is only *immediately* present, but each is at the same time *mediated*: I have this certainty *through* something else, viz., the thing; and it, similarly, is in sense-certainty *through* something else, viz., through the 'I.' (§92)

For sense-certainty, however, this difference appears not to undermine its immediacy, because only one of the terms appears to be essential. The object is posited as a "simple, immediate being" that simply *is*, while sensuous certainty itself exists only in relation to the object or is mediated by that relation. The object *is*, "while the knowing may either be or not be" (§93). The question is not what the object in truth might be, but whether or not it actually presents itself in sensuous certainty as what is essential. Is the truth of sensuous certainty a simple, immediate 'this'? Here is the test or comparison of consciousness with itself that inaugurates the phenomenological method.

Sense-certainty must be asked: What is the 'this'? The 'this' always presents itself to sensuous certainty in the twofold shape of the 'now' and the 'here.' The immediate being that is the object of sensuous certainty is 'this, here, now.' To address the question of what the 'now' is, Hegel proposes a simple experiment: he writes down, 'now is night.' The next day at noon he reads what he has written and discovers that this written truth has become stale or vapid (*schal*) (§95). It has lost its vitality, and the experience has taught us that the 'now' is not night, nor is it day either. The 'now' persists as the 'now' precisely because it is not a determinate moment of time or a simple immediacy. It persists in relation to what it is not; it is mediated by negation. The truth of the 'now' is not simple immediacy, but mediated simplicity (*eine vermittelte Einfachheit*). It remains the same with itself through the negation of determinate contents and is "indifferent to what happens in it" (¶96). Thus, the truth of sensuous certainty proves to be the universal, the 'now' as the universal form of experience. Sense-certainty meant to assert the object that merely *is* as the truth of its experience, but what it actually says in response to the phenomenological interrogation is that its truth is the universal produced by the mediation of determinate negation. The 'here' functions in the same way as the 'now,' as a universal form of experience that remains the same with itself through the negation of its determinate contents. The 'here' "abides constant," because it is not the house or the tree. In saying 'this,' sensuous certainty has given voice not to the richness of the sensuous, but to the emptiest of objects, the idea of a being in general.

Moreover, it is the motility of the living sensuous consciousness that demonstrates the universality of the 'this, here, now.' "'Here' is, e.g., the tree. *If I turn around*, this truth has vanished and is converted into its opposite: 'No tree is here, but a house instead'" (¶98, my emphasis). Thus, sensuous certainty's assertion that the immediately given object is the truth of its experience is "reversed" (*umgekehrt*) (¶100). Now it seems that the essential element of sensuous certainty is the moment of knowing. Experience has taught us that the true object of sense-certainty is the universal, but the universal is produced in the movement of sensuous certainty through the unfolding horizons of space and time. The truth of sensuous certainty lies in the object only as "*my* object, in its being *mine*" (¶100). The truth of the object depends upon what sensuous certainty means or intends as it moves from place to place. The universal 'now' and 'here' persist in the face of the changing determinations because sensuous certainty "hold[s] them fast" (¶101). What was supposed to have been a mere passive apprehending turns out to be an active knowing that produces the universal.

The truth of sense-certainty, then, would seem to depend not on the object that merely *is*, but just on the immediacy of its own seeing and hearing. This immediacy, however, when interrogated, proves no more sustainable than the immediacy of the propositions 'now is night' or 'here is the tree.' "I, *this* 'I,' see the tree and assert that 'here' is a tree; but another 'I' sees the house and maintains that 'here' is not a tree but a house instead" (¶101). The immediacy of seeing and hearing was to be the guarantor of truth, but these truths "vanish" into one another. The 'I' too appears to be not a simple immediacy but afflicted with an opposition between the 'I' as an empty form of experience and the many determinate I's that hear and see determinate things. The truth of sense-certainty, then, is not its immediacy, but that it is an *instance* (*Beispiel*) of a universal, as the tree or the house are instances of 'here' and day and night instances of 'now.'

As sensuous certainty moves from place to place, it learns by experience that the truth of its immediacy is neither in its seeing and hearing nor in the object, but in the "*whole* of sense-certainty." Sensuous certainty does not experience itself as an empty form, but as just this seeing and hearing now with the tree at noontime. If its truth is the immediacy of the whole experience, then it cannot be bothered by the fact that another 'I' is there at night in the house. It cannot "turn around" to notice the other seeing and hearing of another 'I'; it can only stick fast to what it immediately sees and hears—the robin in the tree or the creak of the stairs. As soon as it tries to respond to the phenomenological interrogation, to *say what it means*, it falls into the determinate negation that produces the universal and transforms any actual sense-certainty, any actual seeing and hearing, from an immediacy into an instance. Sense-certainty is, in principle, mute.

"We" phenomenologists, then, "must therefore enter the same point of time or space, point them out to ourselves, i.e., make ourselves into the same singular 'I' which is the one that knows with certainty" (¶105). As I point to the 'now,' I discover that it "has already ceased to be in the act of pointing to it" (¶106). Another 'now' has already taken its place. The truth of the 'now,' then, is that it has always already taken place or *has been*. The experience of trying to point to the being of the 'now' demonstrates that "*it is not.*" It is neither a being nor an immediacy, but the result of a movement of determinate negation.

Nor is the 'now' a mere empty form, because the form belongs together with its instances, as it is only produced in their negation. The movement of pointing out the 'now' reveals the belonging-together of the plurality of determinate 'nows' in and with the 'now' as the universal form of experience. So, this 'now,' this immediacy, always already belongs to this movement of mediation and negation.

Similarly, the 'here' to which I point always already belongs to a "simple complex of many heres" (¶108). This 'here' is always above or below, right or left, before or behind. When sensuous certainty tries to say what it means or to point to *this* 'here' as an immediacy, what it actually demonstrates is that the pointing out is not an "immediate knowing." It is a movement in which this 'here' is distinguished from many other 'heres' that all belong together as instances of the universal form of experience. The specificity of place turns out to be a result, not a given, and to depend on a movement of mediation and negation that sets it into relation to the complex of other 'heres' and to the universal.

The truth of sense-certainty, then, lies in the "history of this movement" (¶109). Natural consciousness knows this truth that it is taught by its own experience but continually forgets it. In its experience sensuous certainty moves happily from the tree to the house, from day to night, without losing either the determinateness of those moments or the capacity to surpass them. The philosopher, however, who asserts that the "reality or being of external things taken as 'thises' or objects of sense has absolute truth for consciousness" simply does not know what he is saying (¶109). Indeed, as experience has taught us, he is saying exactly the opposite of what he means. What is true for consciousness is not the sensuous 'this,' but the movement from here to there, from then to now, from this to that, a movement that generates both the complex of 'heres,' 'nows,' and 'thises,' each of which relates to its others as what it is not, and the universal in which they belong together as its instances.

In its effort to point out the 'now,' natural consciousness discovers that the truth of the 'now' is "to be no more, just when it is" (¶106). The 'now' that is pointed out always "*has been,*" and "it has not the truth of *being*" (¶106). Neither the 'now,' nor the pointing out of the 'now' appears as an "unmediated simplicity [*eine unmittelbare Einfachheit*]" (¶107). In the experiment of pointing out the 'now,' what is pointed out unfolds (*aufhebt*) in another 'now,' so that it might seem that natural consciousness has "turned back" (*zurückgekehrt*) to the first 'now.' But, this first 'now' is "not exactly what is was to begin with" (¶107). In the activity of pointing out, moving from 'here' to 'there' and from 'now' to 'then,' natural consciousness learns from experience that the 'now' unfolds (*aufhebt*) its truth as the belonging-together of the 'now' as the universal form of experience and the plurality of determinate 'nows' (day, night, noon). The truth of the 'now' results from this history of experience. Truth belongs to the movement of becoming, not to being,

Hegel invokes the "mysteries of Ceres and Bacchus," in which the meaning of eating the bread and drinking the wine lies precisely in the "nothingness" of sensuous things. Even animals, Hegel argues, understand this: "they do not just stand idly in front of sensuous things as if these possessed intrinsic being, but, despairing of their reality, and completely assured of their nothingness, they fall to without ceremony and eat them up" (¶109). The invocation of Bacchus should remind the reader of the image of the Bacchanalian revel from Hegel's preface: the sensuous thing is a stable moment of rest unfolded and surpassed by the movement of experience. Hegel avers to the instinctive insight of animals only to confirm the dangers of being misled by philosophers.

In the end, sensuous certainty cannot say itself because as soon as it speaks it utters the universal, not immediacy. This is not an error but a demonstration of the universalizing power of language. When consciousness says the sensuous 'this' and *means* what is immediately before it, it nonetheless utters the universal; for every object of sensation is a sensuous 'this.' "When I say: 'a single thing,' I am really saying what it is from a wholly universal point of view, for everything is a single thing; and likewise 'this thing' is anything you like. If we describe it more exactly as 'this bit of paper,' then each and every bit of a paper is 'this bit of paper,' and I have only uttered the universal all the time" (¶110). The interrogation of sense-certainty, the demand that it say what it means, transforms that certainty by "reversing" it (*verkehren*) in multiple ways. Through the interrogation the reader/natural consciousness learns that the "universal is the truth of sense-certainty" (¶97). Its certainty, which first seems to belong to the object as the essential moment—with knowledge being the optional or inessential moment—actually belongs to the complex of mediations that comprise both the 'I' and the 'this, here, now.' Far from being mere passive apprehension, the certainty of sensuous certainty requires that consciousness "hold fast" to the 'this, here, now.' The certainty of immediate experience turns out to be mediated, not only by the relation of and distinction between consciousness and the object, but also by the belonging-together of the 'I' and the 'this, here, now' as universal forms with the plurality of contents from which the persisting form is distinguished in a movement of determinate negation, as the 'now' is neither day nor night.

Hegel does not refute the certainty of sensuous immediacy; indeed, from the beginning he insists that it is just this certainty that must be addressed by philosophical science in order to show how that science is already implicit within it. The ladder of phenomenology stands on the ground of this certainty. "Science must therefore unite this element of self-certainty with itself, or rather show *that* and *how* this element belongs to it" (¶26). Moreover, at the end of the analysis, when the reader/natural consciousness has unfolded all the ways of knowing and forms of life that lie implicit within him in order to realize himself as the narrator/philosophical consciousness, we will find ourselves back at the beginning. The achievement of absolute knowing, the thought of the whole system of shapes, each one arising necessarily out of the one before, constitutes a return to immediacy and to its certainty, "the beginning from which we started" (¶806). The interrogation of sense-certainty, of natural consciousness, reveals nothing that was not already implicated in the beginning, just as the oak is implicated in the acorn.

Hegel insists twice that "it is just not possible for us ever to say, or express in words, a sensuous being that we *mean*" (¶97). He states outright that "the sensuous this *cannot be reached* by language" (¶110). As Derrida has argued, whenever I say 'I,' I mean to refer to myself in my immediate certainty. Yet, I inevitably utter something universal, for if my utterance is to make sense, it must be repeatable by other possible speakers, who displace me from the narrative position and speak for themselves; "my death is structurally necessary to the pronouncing of the I."[1] I mean to say my own living immediacy, but language reveals the truth of the universality of the narrative position.

Hegel does not mean, however, that the certainty of immediacy is lost to natural consciousness. Again, it is precisely on the ground of that certainty that the ladder of phenomenology rests. It is precisely that certainty that will be shown to be proper to science itself. Thus, when Hegel asserts that it is impossible for natural consciousness to say what it means or for language to "reach" the sensuous 'this,' he *means* that language cannot articulate the certainty of immediacy *immediately*, directly, or in a proposition. The whole narrative of the unfolding shapes of consciousness and objectivity will be required to give articulation to the beginning. Only then will natural consciousness, through the reversals of language, be transformed into philosophical consciousness, so that it is able to say what it means, its own immediate certainty.

Through the interrogation situated between certainty and truth, the self-certainty of sense-certainty has proved unsustainable, but the result is not merely negative. Through his active pointing, saying, and writing, the

---

1. Jacques Derrida, *Speech and Phenomena*, trans. David B. Allison (1967; Evanston, IL: Northwestern University Press, 1973), 96.

## 11
## CRITIQUE OF IMMEDIACY

reader/natural consciousness has learned that knowing and the object belong together in a distinction which is no distinction, a difference in which the two moments at the same time are necessarily related. As the site of the "little research," he has learned that, far from merely apprehending the object, he actively "takes the truth of it" (*nimmt er wahr*). And the object itself, like the 'I,' now appears not as a mere immediacy, but as a *singular being* of a form.[2] Thus, the interrogation of sense-certainty has produced a new shape of knowing, the perception (*Wahrnehmung*) of a thing, which is always an example of a form or kind.[3] Can perceptual consciousness sustain its claim to be the truth of experience?

### 1.B. CONTRADICTION: THE SOPHISTRY OF PERCEPTION

When 'healthy human understanding' tries to make [the abstractions of the universal and the single being] true by at one time making itself responsible for their untruth, while at another time it calls their deceptiveness a semblance of the unreliability of things, and separates what is essential from what is necessary to them yet supposedly unessential, holding the former to be their truth as against the latter, it does not secure them *their* truth, but convicts *itself* of untruth.

—G. W. F. HEGEL, *PHENOMENOLOGY OF SPIRIT*, ¶131

In the course of his experience, the reader/natural consciousness has learned that his object is not a simple 'this,' but a belonging-together of the single being and the universal: the *thing*. Every thing appears as a singular being of a certain kind. Natural consciousness has also learned to distinguish between the act of perceiving and the object perceived. Because these moments "are related to each other as opposites, only one can be the essential moment in the relation, and the distinction of essential and unessential moment must be shared between them" (¶111). The object appears to be the essential moment, as it appears to exist whether it is perceived or not, while the act of perceiving is the "unessential moment, the unstable factor, which can as well be as not be" (¶93). Hegel here contrasts the

---

2. One might be tempted to say an *instance* of a kind, but Hegel specifically distinguishes the singular or determinate being of perception from the mere (i.e., abstract) fleeting instances of the plurality of 'nows' (¶112).

3. The ordinary German word for "to perceive" is *wahrnehmen*, which literally means to take the truth of something or to take something as true.

apparent stability and substantiality of the object as being with the apparent instability of perception as a history or motion of pointing things out.[4]

Once again experience will prove deceptive: the truth of being will unfold (*aufheben*) in becoming. The relation (*die Beziehung*) between the moment of the object or perceived thing and the moment of the perceiving subject will turn out to be a movement (*Bewegung*) in which the two sides are both related and distinguished, a movement in which the two sides constantly exchange faces or determinations.

## The Difference Between the One and the Many: The Question of Abstraction

The difference between the one and the many that afflicted the 'this, here, now' reappears as internal both to the thing and to perception itself. Whereas the universal form of the 'now' stood *opposed* to the plurality of determinate 'nows' (day, night, noon), the relation between the perceived thing and the perceiving consciousness revolves around a *chiasm of differences*: between the one and the many, on the one hand, and the essential and inessential distinction, on the other. This sophistical "to-ing and fro-ing" will be managed by the sophistry of "aspects," or the "insofar as."

To be a thing is to be a singular being of a certain kind. This is a bottle. That is a tree. This is knife, and so on. The perceived thing, however, is not merely a type or kind but a specific and determinate object: this green bottle that I have before me, or the magnolia outside in my yard, or the 10" black-handled Sabatier chef's knife in the knife block in my kitchen that I will use later to chop vegetables. The "wealth of sense knowledge" belongs to perception rather than to the immediate certainty of sensation, because, as a "mediated simplicity" or an experience that is governed by the "universal as principle," perception "contains negation, that is difference or manifoldness, within its own essence" (¶112). Unlike the plurality of 'nows,' which are mere instances (*Beiherspielende*) arrayed alongside one another over against the form of the 'now,' the thing of perception displays itself as "*the thing with many properties*" (¶112). This knife is neither the tree nor the

---

4. The moments of rest and motion that compose the figure of the Bacchanalian revel reappear here in the perceiving of things. The apparently stable thing will prove unstable, just as perceiving will discover its own persistence and sustainability.

bottle, but it is also not the other chef's knife, the Wüsthof with the wooden handle. The thing of perception sustains its singular being through the belonging-together of the kind with "*differentiated, determinate*" properties (¶113). How do this unity and multiplicity belong together in the thing?

The thing is a unity, a one, but as such it is an abstract universal. Any or every thing can be said to be a one, and this moment does not yield the specificity of the thing of perception. The knife is sharp and *also* 10" long and *also* black-handled and *also* engraved with the mark of Sabatier and *also* of a certain weight. The binding thinghood (*zusammenfassende Dingheit*) inheres in the *also* as the "medium" in which the determinate properties appear together while remaining distinct from one another. They permeate (*durchdringen*) the thing without disturbing one another (*ohne sich aber zu berühren*). The length of the knife is not its sharpness, nor the blackness of its handle, nor its weight. The properties remain "indifferent to one another, each is on its own and free from the others," yet they inhere in the thing and distinguish it from other things (¶113). The thing is not only a 'this'—a simple unity—but also a medium of determinate properties: "the point of singularity [*der Punkt der Einzelheit*] in the medium of existence [*des Bestehens*] radiating out into plurality" (¶115). The thing's self-identity—its "self-standing," or being on its own—displays itself in the differentiation of its determinate properties. At the same time, the thing as a thing of a certain kind, or a "simple, self-identical universality," also remains on its own, "distinct and free from these determinate properties it has" (¶113). Identity occurs at the intersection of the general form and the determinate properties.

Moreover, the determinateness of the properties depends not on their "being free from the others," but on relating to other properties and to one another through "exclusion" or "negation."[5] Sharpness excludes length or

---

5. In the analysis of the thing with many properties, Hegel undertakes his first discussion of community (*die Gemeinschaft*). Each property is, like the thing, a belonging-together of a form and instances or singularities: red or redness is distinct from this red of the high-heel shoe. Each property comprises a belonging-together of universality and specificity. In pervading the thing while leaving one another undisturbed, the properties form a *community* (¶117). This prefigures how the successful political community will bind its members together in a universal will capable of acting as a whole, while at the same time preserving the singularity of each and all. In perception, however, the properties, as determinate properties, merely "oppose" and "exclude" one another, so the community "breaks up." The opposition between the one and the many, between the universal form and the singular instance, pervades every moment of perception: the perceiving consciousness, the thing perceived, and the property.

color, while it negates its opposite, dullness. Similarly, the unity of the thing is maintained by negating the multiplicity of properties, by negation of other things, and by its exclusion from its own concept. This knife is not sharpness, nor is it that tree, nor is it simply the concept of a knife.

The concept cannot be given in a *thing* to a perceiver without the "self-standing matter" (*die selbstständige Materien*). Yet, if concepts are manifest in sense, they remain mute and invisible until transformed by thought into language. Concepts are not perceived by the senses but instead thought in language. Here begins the long labor of the concept: to produce the conditions of its own actualization, the articulation of the concept not as a thing, but in its own proper element as something said or written.

It remains to be seen whether or not a concept articulated merely as a concept, as the opposite of its operation as an infrastructure of life, would be more than an empty distinction, alien to a phenomenology of experience. Perhaps the aims of transparency and completeness already betray the dense materiality, informality, and essential waywardness not only of life but of language too.

### Chiasmatic Effects: Movement, Deception, and the Assignment of Truth

How can the thing be at once a unity and a multiplicity? How can it be at once sharp and distinct from sharpness? How can sharpness and length belong together in the thing, while remaining distinct from each other? To natural consciousness seeking the essence of the thing in perception, the thing would appear to be inherently unstable. It appears to oscillate between the moments of the one and the many: between the simple self-identity of both the thing and each determinate property of it, "free and on its own," and the moment of negation or exclusion in which the thing distinguishes itself from the properties and the properties from each other. For perceptual consciousness, however, the "criterion of truth" is the "*self-identity*" of the object as something given and stable. If perceptual consciousness is "aware of the possibility of deception," then it cannot be "an untruth of the object—for this is the self-identical—but an untruth in perceiving itself" (¶116). Perception was supposed to "take" the truth of the object (*wahrnehmen*) as it is given. If the thing appears unstable and contradictory, it must be because perception has, by "adding or subtraction, alter[ed] the truth" (¶116). As the inessential moment of the relation, "*insofar as*" for the perceiving consciousness the thing *is* whether it is perceived or not, perception must have operated like an instrument or medium that alters the object. Of course, as Hegel argued in the introduction, to take cognition or perceptual knowledge as an instrument or medium, whose effect on the object must be subtracted from the experience, turns the fear of error into the fear of truth.

The thing is a 'this,' a simple self-sameness, but it is also determinate—this knife, that tree—only in virtue of its multiple properties. The sophistry of perception operates according to the distinction between essential and inessential "aspects" (¶120) and the logic of the "*insofar as*" (¶121). Truly, in itself, the thing is a simple self-sameness. The diversity of its properties is introduced by the diversity of the senses of consciousness. The thing appears both black and sharp because sight is "quite distinct" from touch. The diversity that undermines the unity of the thing, its simple self-sameness as this knife, arises "not from the thing, but from ourselves" (¶119). *Insofar as* the thing is in truth or in itself a simple self-sameness, it is the perceiver who is responsible for introducing multiplicity, the inessential aspect. Its unity as 'this one' only appears to be contradicted because it appears to the diversity of the senses of consciousness.

By saying 'this one,' however, natural consciousness does not say what he means, just as he failed in his attempt to speak the simple truth of sense-certainty. Any and every thing is a 'this one,' a simple self-sameness, but perception takes the truth of 'this knife' or 'that tree.' It means to give voice to its experience of determinate things, and a thing is only determinate through its multiple properties: the green bottle, not the red one. "The property [*Eigenschaft*] is the thing's *own* [*eigene*] property or a determination in the thing itself" (¶120). Without determinate properties, perception would take only an empty form of thinghood. Now, *insofar as* the determinate properties appear to be the essential aspect of the thing, consciousness "takes upon itself" the thing's unity. Truly, in itself, the thing is a multiplicity of determinate properties. It only appears to be a unity due to consciousness's own synthesizing, categorical activity. "Positing these properties as a oneness is the work of consciousness alone" (¶121).

Kant, the great phenomenologist of perception, describes cognition in just this way. Consciousness receives sensuous determinations in the forms of intuition—space and time—and synthesizes those representations into objective unities according to the categories and principles of the understanding. On its own, the thing morphs into "the broken up one" of the collected properties (¶117). Its unity as this bottle or that tree belongs to consciousness. This experience gives rise to the absurd effort to subtract the effects of cognition (sensation and perception) from the truth of the object, thus revealing the activity of consciousness in fabricating the object.

Kant demonstrates the necessary operation in experience of the idea of the thing-in-itself. You and I only see in perspectives. We do apprehend the thing as having aspects: texture, weight, shape, color, and so on. Yet, you and I do not perceive mere properties but determinate things: this knife and that tree. In any given moment of experience, you and I experience or perceive things from a certain perspective or line of sight and at a certain depth, as well as from a certain angle on particular aspects. (Perhaps, I am only looking at the glistening, bronzed turkey. Perhaps, I am only looking at the luscious lemon torte, though I can almost taste and feel the delicious contrast between the airy cream, the jelly of the lemon curd, and the thin, crisp layers of torte.) Yet, when I see these things given only in perspective or from a certain aspect, I *think* more than I *see*. The idea of a thing-in-itself given all at once in all its perspectives and aspects must be operating in my experience; otherwise I would mistake the perspective for the thing, the part for the whole. Every perception implies the movement of perceiving, led on by the regulative horizon of the thing-in-itself, unfolding the thing of perception in the display of its identifying sensuous properties.

It might seem that natural consciousness has reverted to the meaning of sensation, identifying the truth with "*sensuous being*" (¶117). Such a reversion does not occur, however, because the "holding on" to the 'now' that embodied the certainty of sensation unfolds (*aufhebt*) as the sophistical movement of perception. Perception constantly turns back to itself from the object in order to take on one of its "aspects." In sensuous certainty, natural consciousness discovered the truth of the object in his own "holding on," which produced the difference between the form of the 'now' and the multiplicity of 'nows.' In perception, to the contrary, natural consciousness itself takes on "the *untruth* occurring in perception" (¶118). If the thing is essentially a unity, and multiplicity is the inessential moment, then the *appearance* of multiplicity derives from the multiplicity of consciousness's own sense: "the eye is quite distinct from the tongue" (¶119). The bottle is green "only to my eyes"; it is cold only to my touch. Only my ears can hear the clink of the knife against it. Like the thing, consciousness appears to be a "universal medium" in which the different senses inhere, while being "kept apart to exist each on its own" (¶119). As with the thing, this universal medium thus seems to dissolve into its inherent properties and to "break apart." The distinctions of touch, taste, sight, smell, and sound stand opposed not only to each other but also to the simplicity of the one who says, "I perceive." At the same time, *insofar as* natural consciousness or the reader embraces this to-ing and fro-ing as his *own* return or movement, "self-identity" or "the truth of being a one" is preserved. Rather than locating truth in itself or in the object, then, perception moves back and forth between the two moments of self-identity and manifold determination, and it does so both in itself and in the object. It alternately makes itself as well as the thing both into a pure, many-less one and into an 'also' that resolves itself into self-standing matters (green, hard, and so on).

Through this movement, perceiving consciousness distinguishes itself from the thing while relating itself to it, distributing and redistributing the thing's "untruth" between the thing and itself.

### The Play of Differences in Perception: How the Difference Between Being-in-Itself and Being-for-Others Secures the Absolute Difference of the Concept from the Sensuous

The thing was supposed to be a simple self-identity, like perceiving consciousness itself, but only in distinction from other things and from the perceiver is it made determinate: it becomes 'this' and not 'that.' "The relation, however, is the negation of its self-standing, and it is really the essential property of the thing that is its undoing" (¶125). As a determinate 'this,' the thing depends on the manifold of its determinate properties and its distinction from the perceiver and other things, at the same time that it appears as a simple self-identity. Similarly, the simple self-identity of the perceiver, who says, "I see the bottle," depends on his distinction from the bottle and from the manifold of his own senses. Each is "*for itself, insofar as it is for another*, and [each] *is for another, so far as it is for itself.*"[6] Perception

---

6. Who is only 'for another' without the opportunity to be 'for itself'? Who are the others before whom the singleton appears *in itself* (or himself), as a self-standing, simple identity? Will another known in advance as the same be genuinely other? Will there be others for whom being for itself is not a possibility? Or will not these others have been reduced always already to the same?

or "healthy human understanding" is nothing more than the "play of *these abstractions*" (¶131). In place of the substantiality of both the thing and the perceiver, there now appears a play of distinctions.

By shifting restlessly back and forth from thing to perceiver according to the logical chiasm of the inessential/essential distinction, the 'insofar as,' and the strategy of 'aspects,' natural consciousness dissolves both itself and the thing into a constellation of moments that the perceiver endlessly navigates. Beginning with the abstract difference of the one, the 'this,' or the 'I' from the manifold of its determination, perception takes now one moment, now the other to be 'essential,' while taking the 'inessential' moment on itself, so that the perceiver and the thing are each a constellation of 'aspects.'

> When 'healthy common sense' [*gesunder Menschenverstand*] tries to make [the abstractions of the universal and the single being] true by at one time making itself responsible for their untruth, while at another time it calls their deceptiveness a semblance of the unreliability of things, and separates what is essential from what is necessary to them yet supposedly unessential, holding the former to be their truth as against the latter, it does not secure them *their* truth, but convicts *itself* of untruth. (¶131)

Natural consciousness relates to the moments as mere oppositions, and it does not grasp that the negative relation of a thing to the multiple properties or the negative relation of the thing to other things actually installs and preserves the moment of identity. This knife, *not* that one. Perception, rather, sticks fast to each moment as if it were the whole, only to shift to its opposite in utter forgetfulness, now taking the opposite to be the moment of truth. It restlessly navigates these oppositions, taking on itself with every shift the "inessential" moment or "untruth."

In the circuits of "healthy human understanding," both the thing and the 'I' appear as an unstable play of restless distinctions. Both the thing and the 'I' appear to be doubled or two-ed by the difference between the "*distinct moments of apprehension and return to self* [*in sich Zurückgehen*]" (¶122). Perception navigates this opposition of the 'in-itself' and 'for-others' by taking a necessary property—now this one, now that one—as inessential and only 'for another.' Under 'our' interrogation of sensuous certainty, "the sensuous singleton [*die sinnliche Einzelheit*] does indeed vanish" (¶130). 'We' found the empty universal in place of the richness of sensuous life. This universal *"originates in the sensuous, is essentially conditioned by it, and hence is not truly a self-identical universality at all but one afflicted with an opposition"* (¶129). This is the source of perception's instability and deceptive practices, but also of its ability to correct itself with further perceptions. In order to relieve this affliction, this instability, as well as natural consciousness's own self-deceptions, Kant proposes the great chiasm of distinctions between thinking and knowing, between the thing-in-itself and appearance or the thing-for-us:

> If, then, on the supposition that our empirical knowledge conforms to objects as things in themselves, we find that the unconditioned *cannot be thought without contradiction*, and that, when, on the other hand, we suppose that our representation of things, as they are given to us, does not conform to these things as they are in themselves, but that these objects, as appearances, conform to our mode of representation, *the contradiction vanishes.* . . . We thus find that the unconditioned is not to be met with in things, insofar as we know them, that is insofar as they are given to us, but only insofar as we do not know them, that is insofar as they are things in themselves.[7]

There are some aspects of sensuous experience that cannot be sensed or known but must be thought as the conditions of possibility for "our" experience. All knowledge originates in sensation, for the categorical apparatus must be put in motion by impressions, but, at the same time, not all aspects of thought are dependent on sensuous experience: "though we cannot *know* these objects as things in themselves, we must yet be in position at least to *think* them as things in themselves."[8] The idea of the completely determined object given all at once, in all its perspectives, must be operating in experience a priori, or 'we' would always take the perspective as the whole. If the sensuous thing seems inevitably to morph into the "broken up one" of the determinate properties, that is because the unity of the thing as a simple self-sameness or self-identity is an idea, not a sensuous

---

7. Kant, *Critique of Pure Reason*, trans. Norman Kemp Smith, revised 2nd ed. (1787; New York: St. Martin's Press, 1964), preface to the second edition, B xx (24).
8. Kant, B xxvi (27).

property—something thought, not known. The 'I think' that "accompanies all my representations," no less than the thing-in-itself, belongs to the concept, not to the matter of sense.[9]

'Our' interrogation of perception forces 'us' to admit that its operations and strategies have rendered the sensuous singleton a thought.

We have thus "entered the realm of the understanding" (¶129).

---

In his preface Hegel distinguished the Greek and modern ages as the inverse of each other. The "method of study" in the latter inverts that of the former. Given the density, intensity, and opacity of sensuous experience in ancient Greece, "instead of dwelling in this world's presence, men looked beyond it, following this thread to an other-worldly presence" (¶8). Only the sky and stars revealed, with mathematical precision, their regular truth. Only the heavens and heavenly bodies seemed to exist *in themselves*. Though the ancient Greek peoples lived under a "heaven adorned with a vast wealth of thoughts and imagery," managing bodily need would have overwhelmed each day for almost everyone.

> The eye of spirit had to be forcibly turned and held fast to the things of this world; and it has taken a long time before the lucidity which only heavenly things used to have could penetrate the dullness and confusion in which the sense of world things was enveloped, and so make attention to the here and now as such, attention to what has been called 'experience,' an interesting and valid enterprise. (¶8)

In the long working-through of culture and history by which humans turned sensuous being into concepts and laws, natural consciousness eventually penetrated the depth of sensuous being. "Putting itself to the test at every point of its existence, and philosophizing about everything it came across, it made itself into a universality that was active through and through" (¶33). By surveying a field of particulars, natural consciousness learned to

---

9. Kant assumes the self-sameness of healthy reason that authorizes the philosopher's "we" and "our." Hegel problematizes the "we" of philosophy, and the *Phenomenology of Spirit* is nothing less than its production out of the freestanding singletons.

abstract to the concept and its power of organizing beings into classes and kinds. The tables of the elements or of botanical kinds result from this descriptive power to recognize the one in the many.

The work required in ancient Greece transformed the profusion of the vegetal world into the mathematical regularities of the crystal:

> The concept strips off the traces of root, branches, and leaves still adhering to the forms and purifies the latter into shapes in which the crystal's straight lines and flat surfaces are raised into incommensurable ratios, so that the ensoulment of the organic is taken up into the abstract form of the understanding and, at the same time, its essential nature—incommensurability—is preserved for the understanding. (¶706)

Life, or the "organic"—determinateness, sensuous being, and the irreducibility of the singleton—comes to be managed by its difference from the form that inheres in it, by the difference between the sensuous 'this' and the abstract concept or law.

At the other end of history, in "our time," no domain of the sensuous remains unregulated by the concept and its powers. In Hegel's time, industrialization and state bureaucracy were already pervasive forces in the regularization of human life. In "our time" the infrastructures that manage human need, ensure security, and produce power and wealth have reduced the specificity of the singleton in the general images of person, citizen, worker, or consumer for the purposes of disposing of individuals as populations. At the same time, the universal as a form or law lies around "ready-made." Though the concepts of rights, laws, equity, and justice are familiar, they seem to be merely documentary rather than active as infrastructures of life. The task of philosophy is to make the familiar strange. The familiar, just because it is familiar, requires phenomenological critique (¶30). Natural consciousness tends to take the forms as a given and to remain fixed on or stuck to certain determinations. The modern subject must drive the abstract form back into the density and concrete richness of experience, so that its formative force in life can be owned, owned up to, and known as the reader's own.

Hegel writes the *Phenomenology* to show how from the beginning of history the modern political subject necessarily becomes who he is destined to be. In contrast, Foucault writes to make the familiar sufficiently strange, so that a man may have the opportunity *not to become who he is*. The general form of a population lays down probabilities, even as it makes it possible to dispose of classes of people—the poor, the undocumented, the migrant. A woman is destined to be paid less than a man. In many places she is fed less, receives less education, and has less say about whom she will marry (or if she will marry) than a man does, while she is more subject to domestic violence. No one wants to be disposed of in this way. Anyone would want the conditions of life to be otherwise.

As early as the moment of perception, one could append to the Hegelian text another text that would subvert the first, by unraveling the installation of the *Phenomenology*'s figures of truth. There will be other narratives, particularly in virtue of the gender division of labor and the bifurcation of life into family and state.

Here the issue is the relation of the concept and the sensuous, as it is throughout the text. Natural consciousness must come to see how all identity, while it might appear to be sensuous, can only appear as it does because of the labor and effects of the concept.

In insisting on the "purification" of the concept and the necessity that natural consciousness submit to a moment of risk and absolute detachment from life, Hegel appears to install the difference between phenomenology and logic. It remains to be seen, however, whether an abstract concept, a thought that is *itself* only a moment of a whole play of distinctions from which it can be extracted only for a moment, in a discrete performance of risk and self-negation, makes any sense on its own.

On the one hand, the abstract concept is merely a *result*, and the truth is not the result but the result and the process by which it came about. The concept cannot be freed from its generation. The concept makes sense of its sensuous origins and works as the sustaining infrastructure of actual life. Perhaps, the conceptual is the "lining" of sense, as Merleau-Ponty suggests. If the sensuous *adheres* to the concept, it may not be so easy to tear these membranes apart. Perhaps, however, it may be possible for women to shed their identity in relation to man as the "lining of his coat," as the keepers of the sensuous and the body, without morphing into an abstract concept.[10]

---

10. Luce Irigaray, "The Eternal Irony of the Community," in *Speculum of the Other Woman*, trans. Gillian C. Gill (1974; Ithaca, NY: Cornell University Press, 1985), 224.

# CRITIQUE OF IMMEDIACY

On the other hand, the concept must be forced absolutely from the sensuous, as the concept is not a being or a thing. As the no-thing of sensuous experience, the concept must be thought *in itself and on its own*, in *its own proper element: language*. As the bird is to air and the fish to water, so too is the concept or thinking to language. The reader/natural consciousness grasps the concept in itself through the universalizing power of language, or, more specifically, in *explanation*.

## 1.C. INVERSION: APPEARANCE, OR HEGEL'S CONCEPT OF EXPERIENCE

> Though we cannot *know* these objects as things in themselves, we must yet be in position at least to *think* them as things in themselves; otherwise, we should be landed in the absurd conclusion that there can be appearance without anything that appears.
>
> —IMMANUEL KANT, *CRITIQUE OF PURE REASON*, PREFACE TO THE SECOND EDITION, B XXVI (1787)

The reader/natural consciousness agreed to be the site of this research and to step in when necessary to animate the particular shape or moment under analysis. By stepping into the certainty of sense-certainty, the reader/natural consciousness discovered its truth to be the abstract form of the 'now' to which consciousness "holds on" amid the flux of a plurality of 'nows.' By stepping back down from this abstraction into the sensuous richness of perceptual things, the reader/natural consciousness attempted, through a sophistical to-ing and fro-ing, to negotiate the distinctions that comprise perceivers no less than perceptual things.

In perception, the perceiver and the thing appear to exhibit the same logic: each is bifurcated along the fault lines of a double difference—the difference between the one and the many and the distinction between the inessential and the essential. Both perceiver and thing exist in relation to the other, as a materiality that is "self-standing." Each is bifurcated by the difference between the simple immediacy of the singleton or singular being-in-itself, on the one hand, and its being-for-others, on the other. Perception cannot resolve these differences, and it remains fixed on the moments individually, even as it is impelled into to-ing and fro-ing among them. In its equivocation, perception dissolves into the "broken up one" of the "many matters." Perception experiences both the fixity of the moments as simple self-identities and the loss of reality in the "broken up one." Perception finds itself afflicted by differences that cannot be resolved within the narrative of perception: the difference between the oneness of the thing and the multiplicity of its properties (the "broken up one"), the difference between the unity of the perceiver and his multiple senses, the difference both in the thing and in the property between form and determinate being.

This orderly but restless fragmentation derives, in both the perceiver and the perceived, from the fact that the "universal" of perception remains adherent to sensuous being: "it *originates in the sensuous*, is essentially *conditioned* by it, and hence is not truly a self-identical universality at all, but one *afflicted with an opposition*; for this reason the universality splits into the extremes" (¶129). The concept must be "purged" and thought as absolutely distinct from sensuous being. It is as if the concept must be inverted and emptied of all its determination in order to come into its own as a concept by taking its determinate properties back, one by one. At the same time, the abstract concept is only an "empty husk." The truth or result is only articulated in the history of its generation. The concept only proves its truth as a "truly self-identical universality" by actually universalizing life, sustaining it with an infrastructure of forms and laws. The concept creates communities of knowledge and labor. Can the concept be thought as anything other than the infrastructure of life? What effects are produced in the concept by its adherence to the sensuous? Can the phenomenologist tear himself away from life and the sensuous and still speak the truth of experience? Is nothing lost in the transition from the 'I' to the 'we,' from the singleton to the species and history?

The understanding has internalized the differences of perception as its own. Here, these differences no longer distribute and redistribute themselves between two different substantial beings, i.e., between the perceiver and the object perceived. They belong instead to consciousness, to its object, and to the relation that sustains them. The understanding might say, as did perception, that truth lies on the side of the object (¶132), but his actions—his meaning—demonstrate that truth arises in the exchange between consciousness and its object as expressed in language, that is, in the *element* of the concept. A conceptual infrastructure adheres to the tissues of sense to produce the law and order of the perceptual world. The understanding knows the object to be a thought—as a simple identity, as an instance of a

# CRITIQUE OF IMMEDIACY

kind—yet, it continues perversely to locate truth in what 'we' cannot know. Kant embraces this stance: "we thus find that the unconditioned is not to be met with in things, insofar as we know them, that is insofar as they are given to us, but only insofar as we do not know them, that is insofar as they are things in themselves."[11] Thus, has the fear of error turned into the fear of truth.

## The New Object: Solicitation or the Play of Forces

Once again "*we* must step in for consciousness," making ourselves the site of the little research, in order to say for consciousness or the healthy human understanding what it could not say for itself in the abstract language of the concept (¶133). 'Our' task will be to drive the ready-made form back into the rich density of experience (¶33). Hegel prefigures here the length of the education required in modern times (*die neue Zeit*): the phenomenological analysis of the "fully acculturated object" will require a commitment reflective of the depth of history that produced it. Only by making transparent the dense history of this object's production does consciousness morph from mere apprehension (*Auffassung*) into understanding (*Verstand*), the consciousness that knows its object to be a thought. The feminine capacity of receptivity and adhesion to the sensuous gives way to the masculine power of the constitutive concept (¶721), which tears the concept away from the sensuous to create what Merleau-Ponty calls a "second positivity."[12]

Consciousness no longer merely "holds on," nor does it spend itself in "to-ing and fro-ing," restlessly navigating the fixed moments of perception. The understanding knows the truth of the sensuous to be the concept. The reader/natural consciousness reappears in the understanding as the conceptualizing consciousness (*das begreifende Bewusstsein*). Under the explanatory force of the understanding, everything, in the end, will be reduced to a form or law, and consciousness will recognize his own thought in the object.

---

11. Kant, *Critique of Pure Reason*, preface, B xx (24).
12. Maurice Merleau-Ponty, *The Visible and the Invisible*, ed. Claude Lefort, trans. Alphonso Lingis (1963; Evanston, IL: Northwestern University Press, 1968), 146. Merleau-Ponty offers a critique of thought's tendency to produce abstract generalizations or norms that are then used to judge the experience from which they have been abstracted. Foucault's project carries forward this analysis to show how identity is determined by a culture of possibilities, an infrastructure that determines who can speak, what can be said, and who is spoken about.

The object of understanding is no longer this moment or that, as it was for perception, but the whole constellation of moments and the exchanges that bind them. 'We' can see already that the object is no longer simple. The truth of experience now appears as the relation between two in which each moment is already bifurcated like the other. In every moment, division "has already taken place" (¶162). Consciousness is both a being-in-itself and a being-for-another, and so is his object, or the other. Consciousness is a one in a many, and so is his object and the other. And so on.

The concept of force incorporates the differences of perception as its own proper logic. A force exists only in relation to another force. It is "equally in its own self what it is for another" (¶136). It appears as a being-in-itself that is just as much a being-for-others. I push against my desk, and only the counterforce of its resistance allows me to move the chair, gliding across the rug on its smooth wheels. Every event or identity is an effect of an interplay of forces. I push against the desk and "solicit" its resistance, and it replies by expressing itself in the force of my motion. No force exists on its own, but only in relation to the others that solicit it to express itself. From vast cosmological events across the horizon of the sky to the teeming activity in the interior of substance (fermions, leptons, bosons), what can be said to be is a play of forces, in which the identity of bodies and events is an effect.

Insofar as force exists only in relation to another force, the play of forces, as a logic of soliciting and solicited, unfolds the substantiality of the forces as vanishing moments, as the desk's expression of resistance vanished along with the chair's motion. As the object turns into an effect of the play, so too does the subject; both moments vanish in the play. The conceptualizing consciousness (*das begreifende Bewusstsein*) subjects both the thing and the perceiver to the play of forces, rendering experience an "absolute flux" of differences and vanishing moments (¶148). The linear flux of the 'nows' in sensuous experience has been reconceptualized as the solicitations of force amid the vanishing moments.

With the realization that the truth of the object is the concept, consciousness experiences a further "loss of reality" (¶141). As the essential moments of reality unfold, they vanish in the play of becoming. Seeing and hearing are "lost" to this conceptualizing consciousness (¶132). The concept of the play of forces implies the difference between force in itself and force expressed, which transforms the world of things into the world of appearances. The sensuous world becomes a "totality of show," insofar as its truth is to be the expression of the "inner being of things" (¶143). Hegel distinguishes three worlds: *immediacy*, the sensuous world of seeing and hearing; the world of *appearance*, or the sensuous taken as appearance; and appearance qua appearance, or the *supersensible* world, the "beyond" or the "inner being of things." The truth of appearance is the supersensible world.

A double inversion will be required if consciousness is to say what he means: insofar as the truth of appearance is the "inner being of things," it will be necessary for healthy human understanding to turn things inside out to expose the conceptual lining of the sensuous, as one might turn a dress inside out to expose the seams that hold it together. Insofar as the truth of the thing is thought as the horizon of experience or the "beyond," however, the understanding will need to turn an already-inverted world right-side-out again, with the conceptual lining back on the inside. On Hegel's view, the former has been the task of history from the Greeks to modernity (*die neue Zeit*); the latter is the "driving forth of the universal" back into the sensuous that Hegel assigns to "our time" (¶33).

In isolating the conceptual element in experience, "purging" itself of any "antithesis" to the singleton, the understanding "opens up above the *sensuous* world, which is the world of *appearance*, a *supersensible* world which henceforth is the *true* world; above the vanishing *present* world there opens up a permanent *beyond*" (¶144). The generation of the concept of appearance as the truth of the sensuous world produces a new interiority within both the object and consciousness. In the thing, consciousness finds the difference between being-in-itself and being-for-others. This distinction opens up the incommensurability between experience and its truth or essence. In both consciousness and the object, an interior horizon marks the unreconciled difference between the singleton and the form, between the event and the law, between appearance and truth. Here, in this difference within itself, self-consciousness first appears. This new figure emerges with the distinction between a consciousness that sees and hears and one that thinks. Across this difference and at this distance, the conceptualizing consciousness looks at himself with his sightless eyes.

Hegel leaps ahead from this initial prefiguration of self-consciousness to the unfolded figure of reason (¶144). Reason happily sets about making sense of the world as it works through its armamentarium of concepts, and it subjects every realm of life to conceptual analysis. Maps and schedules, the architect's schematic drawing, grids of communication and transportation—such representations take on the density of flesh and blood. The world comes to reflect back to reason, more and more, reason's own activity or power of thought, so that, by being conscious of the world, reason is also self-conscious.

In place of the sensuous thing, a new object has arisen in the phenomenological analysis: *appearance*. The idea that the sensuous world is a world of appearance installs, at once, three figures: an interrogating consciousness, a field of experience or appearance to be interrogated, and the truth as the beyond or inner being of things. 'We' have learned from perception that *"our object"* now embraces the understanding, the inner being of things, and the world of appearance as their mediating term (¶145). From the critique of appearance, healthy human reason will produce the law to stabilize the flux of appearance and manage the chiasm of differences.

### The Bacchanalian Revel: First Critique of Law

Any physicist will confirm that the events of the physical world are summarized in and transcended by the laws of physics. The vanishing of any particular present leaves those laws untouched. Any body and its motion can be reduced to them. The law supplies the "*stable* image of unstable appearance" (¶149). The understanding will treat the vertigo it feels while awash in the flux of experience by abstracting from it a "static kingdom of laws." The permanent and stationary laws supply the truth or the in-itself for appearance. In the play of forces, the two moments of soliciting and solicited prove inherently unstable and adhere to one another as an "absolute inversion and mistaken identity [*absolute Verkehrung und Verwechslung*]" (¶148). In the Bacchanalian revel, "no member [*kein Glied*] is not drunk" (¶47). The moments or members morph into one another. What remains still, what does not "arise and pass away," is "appearance," or the "arising and passing away itself" (¶47). The restlessness of appearance first comes to rest in the immobile laws formulated by reason.

The law, however, remains "afflicted by an opposition," or rather by a whole chiasm of oppositions. First, it does not include within itself an account of how it provides the lining of the sensuous. The stable law stands apart from the flux of experience. Having insisted on the absolute difference between the concept and the sensuous, the understanding finds itself

## CRITIQUE OF IMMEDIACY

left with a logic that may not be about anything real. Law is undone by the stability that is its essential property. The law lacks the mobility of the concept and fails to articulate its necessary adherence to the sensuous.

Second, there is a difference between the concept of law or law *as such* and the "indefinitely *many* laws" of, e.g., physics or engineering. Law is no less afflicted with the difference between the one and the many than the sensuous thing. The law is afflicted by the opposition between the unity of the law and its many cases, by the difference between the law and other laws, and by the distinction between the law and the form of the law, or law *as such*.

Finally, law's parts do not seem to derive necessarily from law's own unity as a whole. "In the law of motion, e.g., it is necessary that motion be split up into time and space, or again, into distance and velocity.... But now these parts do not in themselves express this origin in a one; they are indifferent to one another" (¶153). It is precisely in its stability and fixity that law remains distinct from the plurality of 'nows' and the multiplicity of properties in the flux of experience, so as to provide a counterforce to the loss of reality. Yet, just because of its immobility, law remains "afflicted with an opposition." Both in the multiplicity of its parts and in its relation to a multiplicity of laws, the concept of law seems to repeat the logic of the 'one' and the 'also': an empty self-sameness, on the one hand, and a broken up one, on the other. Law will not be sufficient to reach the truth, to touch the "beyond," or to unfold the inner being of things.

Law requires explanation as a supplement.[13] Like holding on to the 'now' and the sophistical to-ing and fro-ing of perception, explanation is a movement that negotiates the difference between the sensuous and the concept, or, more precisely, between the world of appearance and the formality of the law. In stable laws, explanation generates an orderly redescription of the flux of forces. Law repeats all the distinctions and differences that defined force—the difference between the one and the many, the difference between force in itself and force expressed or before others, and the difference between the concept of force and the play of forces that is the actual life of substance. "*Force is constituted exactly the same as law*" (¶154). Explanation, however, abstracts the laws from the flux that characterizes forces, and it

---

13. The *Phenomenology* unfolds four critiques of law and four supplementary practices that it requires: explanation, testing, meaning, and forgiveness.

redeploys those laws as its truth. This "tautological movement" on the part of the understanding "gives rise to nothing new" (¶155). It means to add nothing to the thing-in-itself and means only to explain how the in-itself appears as the sensuous world. Distinctions are made only to be unfolded [*aufgehoben*]. The determinate moments stand only to be unfolded in the flux of experience. The dispersal of the understanding in its essential distinctions will have always already taken place. "In the process, then, of explaining, the to and fro of change, which before was outside of the inner world and present only in the appearance, has penetrated into the supersensible world itself" (¶155). These passages restlessly negotiate this difference between motion and rest.

Contrasting the flux with the stable law, Hegel works through the essential distinctions that make up the difference between appearance and the in-itself. "The understanding thus *learns* that it is a *law* of *appearance itself*, that differences arise which are no differences" (¶156). The knife is and is not its properties. The knife is and is not its relation to other knives. The knife is a knife because it is not these other things. The knife is and is not the concept of a knife. Consciousness learns to "eliminate the sensuous idea of fixing the differences in a different sustaining element" (¶160). These distinctions—between the one and the many, the thing and its properties, the thing and other things, the thing and consciousness—all fall within consciousness and inscribe an "inner difference." These differences place consciousness in relation not merely to any other, but to its opposite to which it belongs: "the opposite is not merely *one of two* ... but it is the opposite of an opposite, or the other is itself immediately present in it" (¶160). The opposite is that other in relation to whom consciousness itself comes into being. Identity appears as an effect of that chiasm of differences from the other and as an effect of the inner differences it creates. As that chiasm of differences unfolds within it, consciousness takes a distance on itself, just as a hiker, having reached after many stages a place of sufficient elevation and advantageous perspective, looks back across his own path and labor. Consciousness thus reappears as self-consciousness.

### Inversion and the Fate of the Sensuous

Hegel turns again to the figure of the Bacchanalian revel to invoke this belonging-together of self-sameness and change in the identity of the singleton. In "this absolute unrest of pure self-movement" (*diese absolute Unruhe des reinen Sichselbstbewegens*), the singleton remains the same with himself; the human being remains self-identical even as the boy becomes the man. The concept appears retrospectively through a turning back. It will have been the logic of appearance as becoming. It will have sustained the unfolding of being in becoming according to the logic of the organism: in the becoming of Earth as the "imperishable individuality" (¶452), in the becoming of the singleton as the irreducible site of thinking, and in the becoming of history as the unfolding necessity of the concept. Just as the boy grows into the man, so too the seed of Greek culture grows into the mighty oak of the modern nation-state. The concept will have a *narrative* existence, unfolding in time, marking and extending the interior horizons of natural consciousness/the reader and the chiasm of distinctions.

Through an absolute loss and dismemberment, consciousness produces out of experience the difference between the sensuous and the abstract form. By dispossessing itself at every moment, the conceptualizing consciousness frees itself from the sensuous and knows every moment as vanishing. He lets go of himself, of the mortality of the singleton. He embraces the "imperishable individuality, Earth." He embraces the species and history as *his* truth and "expects less for himself." He appears as himself only as a member of a community, first figured in the community of properties in the thing and the play of forces. Here begins the domestication of death in the "inverted world."

From here on in, the *Phenomenology* locates the real issue (*die Sache selbst*) in the problem of articulating communities that respect the irreducibility of the singleton, while embodying a general or universal will sufficient to enable the community to act as a community. This strategy assumes, however, that the singleton *has already reduced himself.* He already identifies with the species and with history wherein he is only a *vanishing moment.* His death counts for little against their truth. Spirit sustains the loss of the singleton, your death, as if, by being unfolded as life in the next generation, it were erased without remainder. The singleton in Hegel's telling seems satisfied by the funeral rites that manage his mortality. The urgency and freedom of spirit no longer awaken in him, as he no longer comes face to face with death. The man of healthy human understanding busies himself with utilities and satisfactions, and he enjoys his ability to dispose of singular beings all at once as kinds or populations.

If truth is the lining of the sensuous, then the understanding must invert the world, turning it inside out to reveal its "inner being"; the healthy understanding seeks to touch the "beyond" with his own hand. If the task for history from ancient Greece to Kant was to extrude the sensuous and produce the concept as abstract form, for Hegel—and in "our time"—the task is the reverse or inverse: to revivify the abstract concept, to remember how it sustains life.[14]

The figure of inversion introduces the themes of dissemblance and self-deception. Knowledge proves deceptive, intention appears inscrutable, and speech exposes its hypocrisy and insincerity. Nothing is what it seems, and natural consciousness/the reader cannot say what he means. If 'we' take seriously the idea that a property can only be determinate in relation to other properties and to its own proper opposite, then, in some sense, yes, the truth of sweet is sour (¶159). If 'we' intend to punish someone who commits a crime, we discover that the intention inverts itself in actually carrying out the punishment. A criminal must "pay for" the crime by being punished, yet, by undergoing the prescribed punishment, he is restored to his membership in the body politic. Thus, what was meant to be "bad" for him turns out actually to be "good" (¶158).

These storylines will course throughout the narrative, as the reader/natural consciousness negotiates this logic of inversion, of self-sundering and remembering. As a logic of exteriorization/interiorization, natural consciousness/the reader turns himself inside-out only in order to turn himself right-side-out again by taking everything back as his own.

The reader/natural consciousness has learned that the real issue—the matter at stake in the phenomenological analysis—is not the truth of the object alone, for the object is always presented to some shape of consciousness. Objectivity falls within self-consciousness as a moment. Having learned that the in-itself or truth always appears as it does for some shape of consciousness, the reader/natural consciousness discovers too that "consciousness provides its own criterion from within itself" (¶84). The difference between being-for-another and being-in-itself "falls within the knowledge which we are investigating" (¶84). Self-consciousness tests itself, testing the moment of knowledge against the moment of truth, by

---

14. See ¶26, where natural consciousness and science each appear to the other as the inversion of truth.

attempting to say what it means. In his self-interrogation, the reader/natural consciousness performs this staging of self-consciousness and earns the right to walk behind the curtain of appearance: "*we* go behind it ourselves" (¶165). This cannot be accomplished "straightaway," as it requires the working-through of all the distinctions and differences composing this self-consciousness. Through the interrogation, self-consciousness takes shape by taking on the series of shapes of consciousness and of forms of objectivity. The "inner being" or "undifferentiated self-sameness" that "gazes" into an equally undifferentiated "inner world" proves to be only the abstraction of an actual knowing that will reproduce itself in a world of culture as an acculturated self.

*Chapter Two*

# SELF-CONSCIOUSNESS
## The Fate of the Singleton

> There is for self-consciousness another self-consciousness; self-consciousness has come *out of itself*. This has a double significance: first, it has lost itself, for it finds itself as an *other* existence; secondly, in doing so it has unfolded the other, not as *other*, but as *itself* in the other.
>
> —G. W. F. HEGEL, *PHENOMENOLOGY OF SPIRIT*, ¶179

## 2.A. STRUGGLE UNTO DEATH: THE MYTH OF ORIGINARY VIOLENCE

> The Passions that incline men to Peace, are Feare of Death; Desire of such things as are necessary to commodious living; and a Hope by their Industry to obtain them.
>
> —THOMAS HOBBES, *LEVIATHAN*, CHAPTER 12 (1651)

> Amongst masterless men, there is perpetuall war . . .
>
> —THOMAS HOBBES, *LEVIATHAN*, CHAPTER 21

> Man is an animal who, if he lives among others of his kind, *needs a master*. . . . One cannot fashion something absolutely straight from wood as crooked as that of which man is made.
>
> —IMMANUEL KANT, *IDEA FOR A UNIVERSAL HISTORY WITH COSMOPOLITAN INTENT*, 6TH PROPOSITION (1784)

> Each seeks the death of the other . . . and the former involves the staking of his own life. . . . It is only through staking one's life that freedom is won.
>
> —G. W. F. HEGEL, *PHENOMENOLOGY OF SPIRIT*, ¶187

## SELF-CONSCIOUSNESS

In the state of nature, prior to the social contract and the institution of the law of property, all men have an absolute right to the goods of nature. No natural differences among men are sufficient to distinguish one from all the rest. At the same time, this absolute right of one is compromised by the absolute right of every other man. Nothing secures a man's possessions except his own might, for any other man has a right to claim them and make them his own. Thus, every man lives in a constant state of dread, for there will always be a stronger force or one sufficiently clever to breach all defenses. Each man's possession of generative space—land, women, children, chattel—remains insecure. Even when he is not actually in battle, he exists in a state of war, for there is no way other than violence or treachery to adjudicate this claim of all against all.

Hegel finds this Hobbesian fable familiar and ready-made. The discipline of sovereign power has already secured the contract, the law of property, and the division of the body politic into classes of labor. The bureaucracy of the modern nation-state already exists under sovereign power—in the military, the financial apparatus, educational institutions, commercial guilds, and the apparatus of public health. The laterally dispersed disciplinary power of the nation-state originates in the same mythology and adheres to the same institutions of property and security that sustained sovereign power.

### Life as the Object of Desire

At this moment in Hegel's text, the reader/natural consciousness encounters an absolute break and a new beginning: he has learned that he was attending to the wrong object. Experience has taught him that all along what he "meant to say"—what he took to be the truth of his experience—was self-consciousness, which includes, as a moment, knowledge or consciousness in relation to objects. From here onward, consciousness or self-consciousness has a "double object": first, the "immediate object, that of sense-certainty and perception," and, second, knowledge or the being-for-another of consciousness and its objects (¶167). Self-consciousness is no longer afflicted with the oppositions of consciousness—of perception and understanding—because self-consciousness stands related to and distinguished from an other that is like himself. Self-consciousness makes a distinction within himself, a distinction that immediately dissolves in the certainty of his self-identity. At the same time, self-consciousness relates himself to another who also makes a distinction within himself, which is in turn resolved in *his* own self-identity. The logic of distinction and self-identity that determines each member also determines their relationship or being for one another. In this doubled double relation of two, each one being in-himself and for-another, "certainty loses itself in truth" (¶166). The immediate certainty of existence will find its security and confirmation through membership in a community of others constituted like himself, with each, like himself, dissolving the 'I' in the 'we.'

Hegel again invokes the image of the Bacchanalian revel with its metamorphic logic of rest and motion, dismemberment and remembering. Self-consciousness is a "movement" of being reflected back to itself from the other, a "return from otherness" (*die Rückkehr aus dem Anderssein*), but at the same time, "it is only the motionless tautology of: 'I am I' " (¶167). This chiasm of restless motion and tranquil stillness defines the identity of self-consciousness.

Hegel's introduction of *desire* may seem sudden: "self-consciousness is *desire* in general" (¶167). At this first "turning point" (*Wendungspunkt*), where the reader/natural consciousness will finally set himself upon the right path, Hegel identifies consciousness as desire and "life" as the "object of desire" (¶175). As the desire for life, Hegel's self-consciousness will not turn out to be very different from Hobbes's man of self-interest and self-preservation. The relation of humans to objects is first and foremost one not of knowledge, but of need. The analysis of truth in the object has led to self-consciousness, or to the recognition that desire is the real issue.[1]

Desire, as the movement of self-consciousness, removes the difference between what self-consciousness is in himself and what he is for another. For self-consciousness the object is primarily a "negative element": when a man is hungry, he eats, thereby annulling his difference from the object and restoring the tranquility of self-identity. Self-consciousness first comes on the scene as need, and he sets about consuming things. Initially, man's reflection back to himself from the object takes the form of sensuous appetites, like hunger or thirst. This unstable self comes and goes with the

---

1. Hegel marks the difference between need and desire. Need arises as a sensuous lack, with hunger, thirst, or some other appetite or stimulus. Desire, on the other hand, directs need in the attachment to a specific object. Nearly a hundred years before psychoanalysis, Hegel deploys the method of reading the identity of man in his object choices and in what he makes of the object.

upsurge and satisfaction of appetite. Self-consciousness will come into his own only when he "learn[s] through experience that the object is independent" (¶168). If the object of consciousness is not independent like himself, self-consciousness keeps vanishing along with the consumable things.

"*Self-consciousness achieves its satisfaction only in another self-consciousness*" (¶175). He can be reflected back to himself in such a way as to sustain his self-identity only when "the object of immediate desire is a *living being [ein Lebendiges]*" (¶168). Faced with another desiring self-consciousness like himself, the reader/natural consciousness will learn from experience that the other exceeds his desires, just as the reader/natural consciousness is himself excessive to the desires of the other. This will take time. The actual realization of the idea of contract will have taken a long history of labor and the negotiations and collaborations of men, as well as the installation of institutions that sustain them.

In the phenomenology of knowing, Hegel insists on the necessity of thinking the concept as the abstract concept, "purged" of the sensuous and peeled off from its adherence to sensuous being, so that the concept is no longer "afflicted with an opposition." In the phenomenology of self-consciousness as desire, the reader/natural consciousness, in order to realize or prove himself as the freedom of thought, must similarly detach himself from life. He does so by risking it absolutely.

Hegel takes up Hobbes's narrative line but draws it into a long detour. Hegel's myth of origin does not issue directly in a contract among equals but gives birth to the figures of the master and the slave. Having become a slave because he failed to risk his life, the slave loses it anyway to the master. Only the long history of the slave, as he reclaims his freedom in every register of life, will yield something like a community of equals, for whom the state apparatus will play the role of sovereign power.

This formation of the master and the slave takes place when each self-consciousness *puts his life "at stake"* (¶187). Life must be risked absolutely in order to establish self-consciousness as *more than life*, more than substance. Self-consciousness will peel himself away from his adherence to sensuous being in order not to be made an object by the other, who deploys, like himself, a sovereign gaze.

Hegel's confidence in the immortality of Earth and the species allows him to discount the death of the singleton. He prefigures here the coming engagement with the concept of spirit in chapter 6 of the *Phenomenology*.

Chapters 1 through 5 produce only the abstract concept of spirit as a free-standing agency unfolding in itself. With chapter 6, it becomes necessary for Hegel once again to turn back to the beginning. Once again, the reader/natural consciousness will experience a metamorphosis in the object. He will learn by experience that the real issue is how to produce the " 'I' that is 'we' and 'we' that is 'I' " (¶177). Self-consciousness will create the conditions for its own identity by producing in history the material communities necessary to sustain it. Self-consciousness belongs only to the living being, but its truth is the species in its historical unfolding. How can the essential form also be a vanishing moment? Only the singleton can think substance as subject. Does the 'we' of community belong to an abstract discourse that no longer adheres to the sensuous? Can the 'I' be at once dissolved in the 'we' and remembered as living, as a vanishing moment?

### Life and the "Trial by Death"

> Whatsoever therefore is consequent to a time of Warre, where every man is Enemy to every man; the same is consequent to the time, wherein men live without other security, than what their own strength, and their own invention shall furnish them withall. In such condition, there is no place for Industry; because the fruit thereof is uncertain; and consequently no Culture of the Earth; no Navigation, nor use of the commodities that may be imported by Sea; no commodious Building; no Instruments of moving, and removing such things as require much force; no Knowledge of the face of the Earth; no account of Time; no Arts; no Letters; no Society; and which is worst of all, continuall feare, and danger of violent death; And the life of man, solitary, poore, nasty, brutish, and short.
> —THOMAS HOBBES, *LEVIATHAN*, CHAPTER 13

Hegel returns yet again to the image of the Bacchanalian revel to articulate the logic of life. Self-consciousness exists as restless motion and motionless rest. Its "essence" is the "pure revolutionary movement" of becoming, "its self-repose being an absolutely restless infinity" (¶169). Within the genus "life," Hegel distinguishes between "life as *process*"—the "movement" of becoming in a series of shapes—and "life as *the living*," that is, the living self-consciousness, the reader/natural consciousness (¶171). The former presents itself in the survival of the species and in history, while the latter appears in itself as motion and rest, a process of becoming and a simple self-identity. The boy will become the man while remaining the same with himself against the others. Self-consciousness is the moment of substance that thinks for itself.

In Hegel's first three chapters, the reader/natural consciousness has worked through his relationship to objects of knowledge. Under the phenomenological interrogation, reality morphs into the play of forces, and consciousness is presented with a "loss of reality," with the idea of substance as thought. With the understanding's grasp of substance in the concept, consciousness confronts itself (the thinking subject) in the other (the object) and is returned to itself or reflected back in itself from the other. Consciousness learns by experience that the object is permeated through and through by the concept and can be grasped in and as concept. Thus, the abstract figure of self-consciousness emerges from knowing as a self who is returned to himself from the other. The difference between two is also internal to each one.

Chapter 4 stages the dramatic transformative encounter between two, in which self-consciousness emerges out of animal life: one self-consciousness faced by another self-consciousness. Consciousness will find itself reflected back to itself as self-consciousness only by the look of the other. The reader/self-consciousness will learn by experience the difference between knowledge of objects and the acknowledgment that can occur only in relation to another self-consciousness. Violence will be required in the course of this education. From the very beginning, humans are already enshrouded by the Oedipal atmosphere: two men at either end of a bridge, neither of whom will give way, can only fight. They fight not for the bridge, but for acknowledgment.

Each one is a *living being*. All animals have a sense of self that arises with bodily need but is limited by the object of consumption. The human desire for acknowledgment arises in the difference in each one between self-consciousness and consciousness. Each one recognizes himself in the gaze of the other, at the same time that he finds himself an object to the other. "A self-consciousness, in being an object, is just as much 'I' as 'object.' With this, we already have before us the concept of *spirit*" (¶177). Each self-consciousness is just as much subject as substance. The struggle for recognition ironically produces a detachment from life and a transubstantiation of self-consciousness in the concept, at the same time that it inflicts regimes of violent discipline and mastery on living bodies.

In his discussion of the emergence of self-consciousness in chapter 4, Hegel summarizes (¶¶179–81) the three moments of the narrative that will unfold from there to the end of chapter 6, the narrative of spirit becoming itself. Each moment is doubled twice: first, the experience is reflected in the other self-consciousness—i.e., it is an experience of two—and, second, each moment has a double meaning for each self-consciousness.

### 1. THE ENCOUNTER

The epochal unfolding of spirit in the individual and in history is initiated when two men encounter each other (¶179). The satisfying objects within each one's reach now appear threatened by the possessive gaze of the other. Prior to this encounter, each grasped the things of the perceptual world as turning their faces toward him. Now, they seem to have turned away from him to face the other. The other's very look seems to dispossess. In Sartre's telling,

> Suddenly an object has appeared which has stolen the world from me. Everything is in place; everything still exists for me; but everything is traversed by an invisible flight and fixed in the direction of a new object. The appearance of the Other in the world corresponds therefore to a fixed sliding of the whole universe, to a decentralization of the world which undermines the centralization which I am simultaneously effecting.[2]

With the look of this other, he makes self-consciousness into an object among the other objects. Self-consciousness has thus "lost" himself in/to the other. But, at the same time, in looking at the other, consciousness sees *himself*, not the other; he has thereby also enfolded the other in himself. The other is just as much an object for him as he is for the other. The first double meaning is that I have lost myself in the other, even as I have also erased the other, insofar as I see only myself in him, and not the other as himself.

---

2. Jean-Paul Sartre, *Being and Nothingness: An Essay on Phenomenological Ontology*, trans. Hazel Barnes (1943; New York: Washington Square Press, 1969), 343.

## SELF-CONSCIOUSNESS

### 2. THE STRUGGLE UNTO DEATH: MASTERY AND SLAVERY

The encounter evolves into a struggle unto death (¶¶180, 187). Each one fights the other to prove that he is not an object. Each one fights to prove that he is a proprietor of the world, not property in it. Each one fights for the position of desiring subject, not desired object. Each one fights to recover his narrative position that was destabilized or lost in the first moment of encounter. Hegel insists that the detachment from life must be absolute—that, in its formative education, natural consciousness/the reader must pass through a moment of absolute detachment of the concept and of thinking from adherence to the sensuous and to the singleton. Self-consciousness demonstrates through his absolute risk that he is "not attached to any specific *existence* [*Dasein*], not to the universal singularity of existence in general, not attached to life" (¶187). He who risks life absolutely becomes the master; he who gives in to his adherence to life becomes the slave.

Experience will expose the ironic reversals that compose this relationship. It might seem that the master has installed his will as the prevailing power, but his freedom will prove illusory. He fought to win the other's acknowledgment, but, by reducing the other to a possession, the master makes the slave incapable of giving that acknowledgment. The slave, conversely, will recover his freedom and detachment from life through his own labor, reappearing to himself in the purity of the concept as he gives form to the thing.

### 3. MUTUAL RECOGNITION

A long history of struggle and invention will have been required to reach the moment when material infrastructures exist adequate to sustain the 'I' that is a 'we.' Laboring with others, the singleton will reproduce himself as a member of a community, at the same time that he produces the institutions and spaces to sustain that community. The theme of work takes center stage in the phenomenological theater. Through these productive collaborations, the singleton recovers his desire from the other and lets the other go free, as the other lets him go free (¶181).

Each must risk life absolutely to effect a complete detachment from adherence to life. It is as if only death would be revelatory of the truth of experience. To prove that he is more than life, more than material substance, more than the object caught by the gaze of the other, self-consciousness requires a transformative risk. Only in this gesture can he prove to himself and to the other that his truth is to be the desiring gaze and the self-standing freedom of thought, not the mortal flesh and blood. Hegel here prefigures the critique of the person in chapter 6, where the term is said to be an "insult." "The individual who has not risked his life may well be recognized as a *person*, but he has not attained to the truth of this acknowledgment as a self-standing self-consciousness" (¶187).[3] To say of someone that he is a person is to dissolve the singularity of the singleton in the generality of a generic form. Conversely, the "trial by death" individualizes the singleton through the negation of *his* life, as he confronts the face of his own death. Death is never faceless; it always individualizes and makes each its own.

Self-consciousness fights for acknowledgment; thus, it does no good to kill the threatening other. Experience teaches self-consciousness that "life is as essential to it as pure self-consciousness" (¶189). 'We,' philosophical consciousness, recognize that both moments are essential, but natural consciousness makes its usual mistake of breaking the moments apart and fixing them in two different substances (¶191). Natural consciousness then tries to navigate the dichotomy he has erected by deploying the essential/inessential distinction.[4] The master appears to be the essential moment of the relation, as he is self-standing and self-conscious for himself, while the slave merely lives or exists for another (¶189). Hegel reminds the reader that he has here reached another turning point in the text, for the master is not merely a concept, but "a consciousness existing *for itself* that is mediated with itself through another self-consciousness" (¶190). The real issue (*die Sache selbst*) has revealed itself as no longer a way of knowing, but a mode of existence.

### Inversion and the Thing

The master exists as the subjection of the slave, and the thing mediates their relation. In the phenomenological interrogation of the *formed thing*, the

---

3. I am indebted to my colleague Marcus Brown for pointing out this passage during a discussion of the later analysis of the "legal person" in chapter 6 of the *Phenomenology*.

4. Note that natural consciousness here employs the same strategy he deployed in perception to treat the dichotomy in the thing between its unity and its multiple properties, as well as in consciousness, between his unity and his multiple senses and selves in the flux of becoming—the ruse of the essential/inessential distinction.

relation between master and slave undergoes an inversion. For the slave, life was an irresistible object of desire. His attachment proved to be "his chain from which he could not break free in the struggle" (¶190). The master desired something else more than life, something intangible like the awful transparency of another's gaze.

The master desired acknowledgment, but he has produced a relationship mediated by things in two ways. First, he has reduced the slave to the status of a satisfying object, an existence conditioned by "thinghood in general" (¶189). The subjection denies the slave desire and the narrative position from which he might give acknowledgment. Second, the relation of the master to the slave is mediated by the thing, a material object. As the independent consciousness, the master relates to the thing as an object of desire available for his consumption. He regresses to that complacency prior to the encounter with the other, in which self-consciousness arises with appetite and subsides with its satisfaction: "this satisfaction is only a fleeting one, for it lacks the side of objectivity and permanence" (¶195). For the master, the master/slave relationship sustains only this regression to a relationship to things and a self-consciousness borne on the tides of appetite. Thus, mastery "turns out to be something quite different from an independent consciousness" (¶192). The master proves to be dependent on the thing he desires, and, as he remains unacknowledged, "he is, therefore, not certain of *being-for-self* as the truth of himself" (¶192). The slave acts for the master, making the master the "dependent" and "unessential" consciousness. Here is the moment of inversion: the truth of the master is "the servile consciousness of the slave" (¶193). Once again, experience proves deceptive. Mastery proves to be "the reverse of what it wants to be" (¶193). The phenomenological interrogation reveals an inverted intention.

While the master consumes, the slave works. He is related mediately to the master through the thing on which he works: he belongs to the master as labor. While the master regresses to the intermittent self-consciousness of appetite and satisfaction, the slave's work amounts to "desire held in check." In his work the slave gives a thing form, and his thought becomes visible to him. Ironically, his work, by which he appeared to be subjected, is exactly the activity through which he "acquires a mind of his own" (¶196). He does not consume the formed thing but relates to it as a reflection of his own "formative activity" (¶196). The slave appropriates the independence of the object in working on it (¶195). The truth of the master here turns out to be the truth of the slave, for it is the slave that externalizes himself, displaying himself in the formed thing as the independent power of thought.

The slave, however, would not discover and recover himself in his work had he not experienced "absolute fear" (¶196). Just as the concept must be detached completely from its adherence to life in order to be thought as the concept, so too the slave's "whole being" must have been "seized with dread" for him to regain actualization (¶194). The "substance" of self-consciousness must have been "infected through and through" by the fear of death (¶196). This "absolute fear" is distinguished from ordinary fear in two ways. First, it is not of something but of nothing. It has no particular object. Second, it is transtemporal, not of a particular moment. It runs through life, through and through. The fear of death precipitates the "dissolution" of this self-consciousness.[5] Everything "stable" is made to "tremble." What was fixed becomes fluid. And this detachment from life and identity constitutes, at the same time, "the simple essence of self-consciousness, absolute negativity" (¶194). This "absolute fear" demonstrates to the slave *what is left when he has lost everything substantial*. The fear of death reveals what is excessive to life: self-consciousness as the power of the negative. The production of identity through differentiation—the ability to say, "I am not that object," or, "I am not that man"—has been, from the very beginning, bound up with the fear of death, the inverse of the master's absolute risk.

The absolute fear of death replaces the merely contingent fear of the master. It provides the necessary existential atmosphere for the slave's labor. Through the "discipline of service and obedience" (¶196), the slave transforms fear into his own self-mastery. Under this discipline, self-consciousness learns to delay and defer his desires and to sustain these distances within himself. He unfolds and is unfolded in the landscape and history of his labor. He acquires mastery over the physical world and his own appetites. He learns to follow rules in preparation for one day giving himself his own rules. He develops associations with others that sustain his membership in the 'we' of community, so that its rules are his.

Freedom first appears in the stubbornness of "having a mind of one's own" (¶196). All the forms of hardheadedness and hardheartedness that will

---

5. Hegel uses here the same word he uses to describe the dissolution of members in the Bacchanalian revel: *auflösen*. "*Sich in Rauch auflösen*" is to dissolve in smoke or to disappear without a trace.

appear in the interrogation are prefigured here, from the tenacity of the law of the heart and the howls of the spiritual zoo to the self-confidence of judging consciousness, the arrogance of terror, and the hypocrisy of the moral "world view." For the slave who has not enacted absolute dread, "self-will" remains tied to particular affairs. He exhibits a "freedom that is still enmeshed in servitude" (¶196). It will take a long time for the conceptualizing consciousness to work through all the registers of life, giving form to substance so that he finds himself reflected back in it. It will take a long time to elaborate the infrastructures of community that can sustain each member's specificity, while embodying a general will.

How is the specificity of the singleton to be preserved in his detachment from life as the universal power of the negative? How is the singleton or living being preserved as the "essential form," if the 'I' is dissolved in the 'we'? Can the singleton be irreducible, if the community is to act as a community?

Two unstable relationships decussate here at the fear of death: the relation within the singleton, between the specificity of his substance and the formality of his self-consciousness, intersects the relation between each specific singleton and the unity of the 'we.' On the one hand, the specificity of the subject depends on his substantiality, on all that having a body entails. On the other, his self-consciousness depends on his detachment, on the transparency of the gaze, and on the fear of death. Writing with two hands, Hegel insists on the necessity of detaching from life, of peeling the concept away from the sensuous, at the same time that he advances life as the very object of phenomenology, as the *real issue*. It will take a long time and powerful narratives to strip natural consciousness away from the sensuous, so that he knows himself to be in truth "only an instance," fully absorbed in the 'we' of the species and in history as a vanishing moment.

## 2.B. SLAVE NARRATIVES: FREEDOM IN DETACHMENT FROM LIFE

The Stoic . . . trains himself to swallow stones and worms, slivers of glass and scorpions without nausea; he wants his stomach to become ultimately indifferent to whatever the accidents of existence might pour into it. . . . He, too, enjoys having an audience when he shows off his insensitivity.

—FRIEDRICH NIETZSCHE, *THE GAY SCIENCE*, §306 (1886)

## SELF-CONSCIOUSNESS

*Ultimate skepsis*—What are man's truths ultimately? Merely his *irrefutable* errors.

—FRIEDRICH NIETZSCHE, THE GAY SCIENCE, §265

There are as many species of Joy, Sadness and Desire, and consequently of each affect composed of these (like vacillation of mind) or derived from them (like love, hate, hope, fear, etc.), as there are objects by which we are affected.

—BARUCH SPINOZA, ETHICS, BOOK 3, PROPOSITION 56 (1677)

In the first three chapters of the *Phenomenology*, the interrogation of the reader/natural consciousness produces the difference in the thing between being-in-itself and being-for-another and the transformation of being into appearance or becoming. These chapters outline the three essential moments of the relation of consciousness to its objects, or three essential moments of knowledge: the certainty of sensuous being, the self-regulating movement of perception, and the apprehension, through understanding, of the present, or being, as a vanishing movement in a movement of becoming that has its own logic. Traversing this epistemological terrain reproduces consciousness as self-consciousness and the object as something *thought*.

Ironically, at the very moment that Hegel requires of the reader/natural consciousness a pervasive detachment from life, the real issue (*die Sache selbst*) appears clearly as a living being. What is at stake in the phenomenological interrogation shifts from the question of objective knowledge to the possibility of the slave's recovery of his freedom. This will take a long time. Just as consciousness tried to say what it meant about sensuous objects, so too self-consciousness will try to say what he means about himself. He will tell himself stories that represent his future and destiny. These philosophical narratives negotiate the difference between life and thought and articulate a future where the slave has reclaimed his agency and self-standing.

At this point in the interrogation, a complex of differences, each chiasmatically related to the others, marks the open distances of self-consciousness: one/many, in-itself/for-another, saying/meaning, certainty/truth, inner/outer, rest/motion, being/becoming, essence/appearance, consciousness/self-consciousness, life/thought, slavery/freedom, self-standing/dependence.

The slave narratives negotiate these differences to develop the identity of self-consciousness as a being that thinks. But "*to think* does not mean to be an *abstract* 'I' but an 'I' which has at the same time the significance of *intrinsic* being" (§197). These narratives address the difference and belonging-together of the freedom and spontaneity of thought with the contingency and determinateness of the living body. Just as Hegel's first three chapters articulate the three essential moments of knowledge or consciousness in relation to its objects, so too the fourth chapter unfolds the three essential moments of self-consciousness or the relation of thought and life. Just as it was necessary for consciousness to risk life "absolutely" and for the slave to experience an "absolute dread," so too the narratives of stoicism and skepticism install an absolute difference between life and thought.

Affectivity suffuses the concept and negotiates between the horizon of purity and the profusion of life, even as the negative power of the understanding alienates the one from the other. The sense-certainty that knows and thinks was from the beginning a man of desire and violence.

## Stoicism: Indifference to Life

Stoicism repositions the slave as "a being that *thinks*" (§197). The stoic posits himself in the empty universality of self-sameness or identity—I = I—as the "*immediate* unity of *being-in-itself* and *being-for-itself*" (§197). The stoic thus acknowledges only the concept. Something is "essentially important, or true and good only in so far as he thinks it to be such" (§198). The stoic thinks his freedom and nullifies the "manifold self-differentiating expanse of life, with all its detail and complexity . . . on which desire and work operate" (§199). For the stoic the specificity neither of the object nor of consciousness commands attention. Affect and desire are of no "essential importance" (§199). The stoic's relation to himself is purely conceptual, and he remains "simply and solely in communion" with himself (§197). This purity and isolation are essential to stoicism, for any contact with life and with others would contradict his claim to freedom. The stoic's freedom, or "self-will," requires a "lifeless indifference which steadfastly withdraws from the bustle of life" (§199). The stoic claims the place of the master, of the self-standing consciousness, but his purity and isolation may prove as unproductive as the master's triumph. As Nietzsche remarks, the stoic too wants to be *acknowledged*.[6]

Stoicism, precisely because it establishes itself in thinking as the negative of life, offers only the concept of freedom and not "the living reality of freedom itself" (¶200). Stoicism dismisses the stoic's own enslavement, along with all the perturbations of life. A freedom deployed only in thought "has only *pure thought* as its truth, a truth lacking the fullness of life" (¶200). The subject of the phenomenological interrogation, however, is a living being, and "individuality in its activity should show itself to be alive" (¶200). Stoicism, by alienating life, deprives itself of any determination and is capable only of "contentless thought" (¶200). The abstract concept "cut off from the multiplicity of things" cannot produce its own content and remains afflicted with an opposition. The "self-identity of thought" as a "pure form" leaves determination aside, as if it were not an essential moment of individuality. What stoicism *meant* was the "absolute negation" of its existence, but by "withdrawing from existence into itself," this self-consciousness merely opposes the determinateness that is essential to it and to the concept. The concept itself is always a determinate concept. The concept of the concept, the abstract concept, is no more the concept's "living reality" than the concept of freedom is the "living reality of freedom itself." Stoicism cannot sustain itself on a meager diet of "general terms." A man who is offered apples, pears, berries, and so on but will have only *fruit* goes hungry.[7] Like sense-certainty, the stoic finds himself holding no more than an empty form that cannot sustain the living individuality.

Stoicism consists in a kind of hardheadedness that will not compromise its attachment to the pure concept. It remains fixed on this moment of experience at the expense of the specificity of existence. This purity also constitutes a hardheartedness, as it cannot sustain the affectivity of the concept. Nietzsche notes the "indifference and statue coldness against the hot-headed folly of the affects which the stoics advised and administered."[8] Yet, there is no more a consciousness in general than there is a thing in general.

---

6. Friedrich Nietzsche, *The Gay Science*, trans. Walter Kaufmann (1887; New York: Vintage, 1974), 245 (§306).

7. G. W. F. Hegel, *Encyclopedia of the Philosophical Sciences in Basic Outline*, part 1, *The Science of Logic*, trans. Klaus Brinkmann and Daniel O. Dahlstrom (1827; Cambridge: Cambridge University Press, 2010), 42 (§13).

8. Friedrich Nietzsche, *Beyond Good and Evil*, trans. Walter Kaufmann (1886; New York: Vintage, 1966), 109 (§198).

## SELF-CONSCIOUSNESS

### Skepticism and the Annihilation of the World

In stoicism thought appears as a negative power, distinguishing itself from life and setting aside the alienating determinateness to produce the pure concept. The skeptic realizes what in stoicism is only a concept (¶202). If "stoicism corresponds to the *concept* of the *self-standing* consciousness that appeared in the master and slave relationship, skepticism corresponds to its *realization* as a negative attitude toward otherness, to desire and work" (¶202). Just as the slave makes the other or the object his own through desire and work, so too the skeptic "annihilates the being of the world in all its manifold determinateness, and the negativity of free self-consciousness comes to know itself in the many and varied forms of life as a real negativity" (¶202). Testing existence at every point, skepticism appropriates the determinateness that remained alien to stoicism. "Through this self-conscious negation it procures for its own self the certainty of its freedom, generates the experience of that freedom, and thereby raises it to truth" (¶204). The determinate other does not merely vanish in the flux of experience but is *made* to vanish by skepticism itself. In its activity of negation, skepticism "procures for its own self the certainty of its freedom" (¶204). Through its work the alien determination has been made its own.

Skepticism repeats the sophistical to-ing and fro-ing of perception, just as stoicism repeated the holding-on of sense-certainty and produced an empty form. Skepticism's "unrest" constantly undermines its "self-identity." Its voracious negative power deploys itself in a "medley of sensuous and intellectual representations" and produces a bifurcated subject (¶205). Though the skeptic takes the determinate object to be nothing, his own freedom nonetheless depends on the negation of that object. Thus, skepticism appears to "take its guidance from what has no reality for it" (¶205). On the one hand, skepticism engages determinateness and knows itself "to be a single and separate, contingent, and, in fact, animal life, and a *lost* self-consciousness" (¶205).[9] In perception the singleton experiences himself in the stability of the 'now' as the form of experience, at the same time that he

---

9. Recall that Hegel figures phenomenology as a "highway of despair" and a path along which the traveler seems to lose his way, even as he approaches ever closer to his goal (¶78). This "lost" self-consciousness subjects even his own existence to the negative power of thought, but that negativity will give rise to reason, who in his "happy" activity in the world has forgotten this path altogether.

loses himself in the flux of determinations. On the other hand, the skeptic is just the power of the negative and the inverse of all singularity, "a consciousness that is universal and self-identical" (¶205). Just as perception consists in a restless, sophistical movement between the one and the many, so too skepticism ceaselessly rambles "back and forth from the one extreme of self-identical self-consciousness to the other extreme of the contingent consciousness that is both bewildered and bewildering" (¶205). Skepticism turns its negative power upon itself and produces the irresolvable difference between the unchangeable 'I' of the negative power and the manifold determinateness of life. Lacking the resources for this resolution, skepticism "keeps the poles of this contradiction apart" and spends itself in an endless to-ing and fro-ing that "bewilders" (¶205).

Skepticism consistently fails to say what it means. It takes the determinate content to be inessential yet busies itself with it. It dismisses sensation yet relies on it. It proclaims absolute negation but in doing so exists positively as the consciousness that makes the proclamation. "Its deeds and its words always belie one another" (¶205). Skepticism's "purely negative activity" devolves into mere opposition: "its talk is in fact like the squabbling of self-willed children, one of whom says *A* if the other says *B*, and in turn says *B* if the other says *A*, and who by contradicting *themselves* buy for themselves the pleasure of continually contradicting *one another*" (¶205). Skepticism, too, is a kind of hardheadedness and, even, hardheartedness: it only says, "no," and it sticks to its negative power. The squabbling, self-willed children prefigure the human inhabitants of reason's spiritual zoo, each one squawking and howling at the others.[10] This squabbling can provide neither an infrastructure of mutual recognition nor a context for effective or collaborative action.

Skepticism is a "doubly contradictory consciousness," riven by the difference between "unchangeableness and sameness," on the one hand, and "utter contingency and non-identity with itself," on the other (¶205). It perversely insists on the absolute opposition of the two poles, and, thus, "truly experiences itself as internally contradictory" (¶206). The experience of the contradiction demonstrates that both moments are essential to consciousness. Skepticism "is in fact *one* consciousness which contains within itself these two modes" (¶206). It is at once "self-liberating, unchangeable, and

---

10. See ¶¶397–418 and ¶537. See also my discussion of the spiritual zoo, I.3.b.

SELF-CONSCIOUSNESS

self-identical, and ... self-bewildering and self-perverting" (¶206). Out of skepticism emerges a new shape of self-consciousness that knows himself to be this duality. The difference that was formerly distributed between the master and the slave has now been internalized in a "single undivided consciousness" of a "dual nature" (¶207). This *unhappy consciousness* experiences itself as "disrupted" and dreams of its reconciliation with itself.

## 2.C. MASTERING LIFE: UNHAPPY CONSCIOUSNESS AND THE BEYOND

> There are *master morality* and *slave morality*—I add immediately that in all the higher and more mixed cultures there also appear attempts at mediation between these two moralities, and yet more often the interpenetration and mutual misunderstanding of both, and at times they occur directly alongside each other—even in the same human being, within a *single* soul.
> —FRIEDRICH NIETZSCHE, BEYOND GOOD AND EVIL, §260 (1886)

> The duplication which formerly was divided between two individuals, the master and the slave, is now lodged in one.
> —G. W. F. HEGEL, PHENOMENOLOGY OF SPIRIT, ¶206 (1807)

> Unhappy consciousness is the fundamental theme of the *Phenomenology*.
> —JEAN HYPPOLITE, GENESIS AND STRUCTURE OF HEGEL'S PHENOMENOLOGY OF SPIRIT (1946)

With the analysis of the unhappy consciousness, Hegel changes registers. The result of the phenomenological interrogation of the experience of unhappy consciousness will be a metamorphosis so significant that it will be necessary to begin the book again with a different object and project. Natural consciousness, undergoing the phenomenological analysis, will have discovered that he did not know what the "real issue" (*die Sache selbst*) was. Out of this discovery unfolds (*aufhebt*) a new attachment or truth, a new identity, and a new object for the reader/natural consciousness.

After the two beginnings of Hegel's preface and introduction, which, strictly speaking, are attachments to the body of the text, there have already been two moments of inauguration in the phenomenological analysis. First, in the inversion of the understanding, who, while conceptualizing the object as "outer" and inaccessible in itself, regularly demonstrated in his own actions and in his narratives the unsustainability of the inner/outer distinction as a mere contradiction. Each determines the other, and the truth of the understanding is this movement of inversion (*Verkehren*), of othering (*Entaüsserung*) and remembering (*Erinnerung*).

Learning this in the phenomenological analysis, the reader/natural consciousness unfolds as self-consciousness, and the book begins a second (or fourth) time. The first three chapters of the *Phenomenology* articulated the essential figures of knowing. The fourth chapter, heavy with the hand of Hobbes, unfolded the mythology of the originary violence at the heart of social life. In an experiment of the imagination, this narrative revealed what *must have been* the case for self-consciousness to emerge as it has, as *desire*.

A second metamorphic inversion takes place in the working-through (*Durcharbeitung*) of the unhappy consciousness. The unhappy consciousness is doomed to be unhappy, because even when his action is efficacious in treating the gap between himself and the unchangeable, he does not own his action as his own. Committing the usual error of natural consciousness, the unhappy consciousness fixes his own transcending activity in a being outside himself. The unchangeable, a being situated beyond the flux of experience, is for the unhappy consciousness the truth, the being on whom everything, including the natural consciousness himself, depends. Overcoming the error of unhappy consciousness, the book will begin again a third (or fifth) time with the emergence of happy reason, the agency that owns his activity and knows himself in making the world his own.

Hegel's critique of the "moral insolence" of reason in chapter 5 will effect a third inversion, in which the contradiction between intention and action—and its entire nest of contradictions: virtue/vice, self/other, heart/action—can no longer be maintained under the phenomenological interrogation. The book will begin a fourth (or sixth) time, and only then will the reader/natural consciousness address *die Sache selbst*, "the real issue." The book, the *Phenomenology of Spirit*, finally begins there.

Throughout the analysis, Hegel appears to be committed to what Alasdair MacIntyre calls the "ultimacy of concreteness."[11] For Hegel, the project of philosophy does not consist in the articulation of abstract concepts

---

11. Alasdair MacIntyre, "Hegel on Faces and Skulls," in *Hegel: A Collection of Critical Essays*, ed. Alasdair MacIntyre (Notre Dame, IN: University of Notre Dame Press, 1976), 230.

or general laws, but in the demonstration of the universal's power to realize itself in the singular individual and his world. This universalization happens only through the individual's own self-critical activity, as he experiences the inadequacy of his own representations to articulate his experience. Scientific progress responds to the *inadequacies* of theories and concepts, just as political communities either evolve or implode when their theories and concepts, their narratives of right and justice, no longer serve or sustain them. The human organism realizes itself through this activity of attempting to "say what it means," the very activity that the interrogation of phenomenology makes conscious and visible. In the *Phenomenology* Hegel repeatedly identifies spirit with life, and more than once sneers at any attempt to conceptualize the absolute as an abstraction not immanent in experience.

At the same time, there courses throughout the text an unrelenting insistence on an absolute detachment from life, as a necessary moment of experience in the transition from natural to philosophical consciousness. The point is not so much the existentialist one, that humans are separated from other animals by the *knowledge* that they will die.[12] What distinguishes humans from other animals with regard to death for Hegel is, rather, their willingness to risk their lives and to detach from life in their commitments, putting abstract principle before the living person, not only to defend themselves and their property, but also frequently, as Hobbes notes, for "glory."[13] Having insisted on the *untruth* of the abstract concept, Hegel nonetheless makes its embrace *affectively* necessary. The risk and detachment must be absolute, unto the death. Only such an absolute abandonment of life, which Hegel appears to suggest must be both practical and conceptual, will secure the "purity" of the concept and "purify" natural consciousness of the attachment to sensuous existence. If the singleton is to be transformed into the individual who knows and acts as a member of a community, he must detach absolutely from all his own attachments. As Hegel demands later on, the leaves must be stripped from the branch, and substance betrayed as

---

12. Elaine Miller, *The Vegetative Soul: From Philosophy of Nature to Subjectivity in the Feminine* (Albany: State University of New York Press, 2002), 142–43. Miller cites the knowledge of death as the basis of knowledge in both Hegel and Bataille, but for Hegel, as I imagine Miller would admit, the production of the philosophical subject requires the annihilation of the *affective* attachments to life. The "purifications" of the concept involve more violent acts than knowing one is going to die.

13. Thomas Hobbes, *Leviathan* (1651; Cambridge: Cambridge University Press, 1991), 88.

subject (¶706). Both conceptually and metaphorically, Hegel thus advances a countercurrent against the phenomenological commitment to concreteness that may prepare the way for the abstractions of the logics or the reversion—against the radical politics of confession and forgiveness in *Phenomenology of Spirit*—to a Hobbesian state based on the right to property in *The Philosophy of Right*.[14]

This countercurrent emerges in the analysis of unhappy consciousness, where the themes of purification intensify in the "fight against the fiend." Here, the body and everything associated with it—women, Earth, sensuous experience—will require discipline and regulation. Desire will be reshaped and redirected through good works, penances, and rituals of obedience and devotion. Like all the forms of slave consciousness, unhappy consciousness unfolds as a specific form of labor that takes as his own truth the gap between himself and the being that he has made both necessary and inaccessible.

Whereas stoicism established its self-consciousness by negating life, skepticism negotiated ceaselessly and fruitlessly between the purity of the concept and the determinateness of life. These two moments—thought and life—fell within skepticism, but in its "lack of thought about itself," the skeptic held the two moments apart. From this thoughtless contradiction, a new form emerges, "one which *knows* that it is the dual consciousness of itself, as self-liberating, unchangeable, and self-identical, and as self-bewildering and self-perverting" (¶206).[15] Rather than the restless to-ing and fro-ing of skepticism between the moments of an opposition, the unhappy consciousness absorbs that opposition as his very substance.

As a "single undivided consciousness," the unhappy consciousness knows himself to be a "dual-natured" and "contradictory" being (¶206). On the one hand, he is attached to life and conscious of his alienation from his own freedom; on the other, he has detached from life and knows the truth to lie in the "beyond" of the pure concept. The unhappy consciousness repeats within himself the double relation of the master and slave; he is the

---

14. While, unlike Hobbes, Hegel disperses sovereignty in quasi-democratic institutions, he nevertheless retains the basic infrastructures of the law of property and the gender division of labor.

15. This figure repeats the initial figure of sense-certainty: the persistence of the 'now' as the form of experience amid the changing flux of the contents of experience. Through the phenomenological analysis, the figure has been enriched to include both knowing and desiring and to reposition the singleton among others as an active agent engaged in practical activities that are meant to treat the dichotomy that constitutes him.

"gazing of one self-consciousness into another, and he himself *is* both, and the unity of both is also his essential nature" (¶207). The singleton here knows himself to be subject to change and loss, and the repose of simple self-identity seems inaccessible. At the same time, he knows himself to be *in truth* the unchangeable that has left the flux of determinations behind. The unhappy consciousness experiences within himself the distinctions of the Bacchanalian revel: he exists as the difference between the absolute motion of the flux of appearance and the absolute rest of simple self-identity. As the contradiction of the double moments, unhappy consciousness seeks the resolution in which each moment of the opposition comes to rest in the other.

Hegel outlines here the narratives and infrastructures that will have been necessary to the emergence of self-consciousness. Self-consciousness is a historical artifact, produced through human labor. The narratives of stoicism and skepticism begin the ingestion of the opposition between the master and the slave, the opposition between thought and life, and the opposition between rest and motion, the unchangeable and the changing. For unhappy consciousness, these moments are no longer to be divided between different beings but embraced as his own essential contradictions. This doubling within consciousness "is essential in the concept of spirit" (¶206). It depends not only on the slave narratives, but also on the work, discipline, and service that will address the difference between the unchangeable and the changing. The unhappy consciousness knows himself to be alienated from a truth beyond life that is his own truth, and he works hard to overcome that alienation. The massive edifice of religion serves this purpose.

This shape prefigures all the shapes of virtue that are legislated by reason and deployed in the narratives of spirit. So far, all the thought-positions have been mere representations. The unhappy conscious emerges in concrete practices—religious rituals, penances, good works—as a form of life.

Desire manifests itself as a gap or difference within the self, between a current state of affairs and some end. Object choices that demand the deferral of satisfaction open up the distances and differences of identity or self-consciousness, at the same time that these attachments motivate the overcoming of these very diremptions. If life is desire, then there is from the very beginning something altogether morbid about Hegel's aim: that point where knowledge need no longer go beyond itself because nothing is other to it (¶80). There seems no reason to assume, even in the register of the pure concept, that the image of the ouroboros should reign: whatever conceptual terminus may be located in the return to immediacy of absolute knowing, the existential resolution of this difference would be nothing less than the extinction of self-consciousness, of desire. As Derrida remarks in a different context,

> What's needed . . . is that *in*adequation should remain *always possible* in order that interpretation in general, and the reply, be *possible* in its turn. Here is an example of this law linking the possible and the impossible. For a faultless interpretation, a totally adequate self-comprehension, would not only mark the end of a history exhausted by its very transparency. By ruling out the future, they would make everything *impossible*, both the event and the advent of the other.[16]

Hegel emphasizes incessantly that the impetus for his growth and development arises immanently within each man. Each suffers the violence of many transformations at his own hand. How would the closure of the concept, turning back on itself, treat the difference between its transparency and the density and vagaries of existence? Hegel imagines himself, like Plato's philosopher, at the outside of heaven, looking on at the circle of celestial shapes. Hegel's phenomenology of self-consciousness, however, describes a creature situated in life and history and marked by differences, spanning delays and detours. Attempting to touch the horizon with his hand, the philosopher would erase just those distances and differences on which self-consciousness depends. Perhaps life always undermines the aim of closure.

Stoicism and skepticism represent the relation of life and concept as contradiction but cannot prescribe any resolution other than abnegation. The unhappy consciousness, although unhappy, sets about *working on the difference*. No mere representation, the unhappy consciousness elaborates practices and institutions that treat his bifurcation. His works, discipline, and obedience address the belonging-together of the singleton and the universal and begin to create a genuine community of recognition. Rather

---

16. Jacques Derrida, *Paper Machine*, trans. Rachel Bowlby (Stanford, CA: Stanford University Press, 2005), 89, translation modified.

than merely representing or entertaining picture-thoughts, unhappy consciousness *acts* in a community of others. With this figure, spirit first appears as spirit, a singleton living among others in the horizon of a world (¶210).

Though as the narrator of the phenomenological analysis, 'we' recognize the emergence of spirit in life, the unhappy consciousness repeats the usual error of self-consciousness, mistaking the part for the whole and taking now one moment and now the other as essential. The experience of this unhappiness traverses three distinct moments in relation to the unchangeable, figured as rest or the simple self-sameness of self-identity. The Bacchanalian revel of rest and motion takes place between the unhappy consciousness and the unchangeable.[17] "The *experience* through which the divided self-consciousness passes in its wretchedness" will produce, in the end, a "reconciliation of its singularity with universality" and even "joy" (¶¶210–11). Yet, the unhappy consciousness will remain unhappy, for the efficacy of these works and experiences belongs to the unchangeable and not to himself.

The life of unhappy consciousness is devoted to an "elevation to the unchangeable" that is also the "struggle against an enemy" (¶208). The resolution of the contradiction between the flux of determinate properties and the stillness of simple self-identity—I = I, or "I am that I am"—will require an alienation from the body and regimes of discipline and work applied to it. This is the first moment. In this double "movement," singularity emerges in the unchangeable (¶210), while the unchangeable emerges in singularity (¶211). The initial opposition of the changing singleton and the unchangeable gives way to a second moment: the moment of incarnation, in which the body and world are sanctified by the penetration of the divine, while the divine is singularized through an actual embodiment. The unchangeable, however, will have always already transcended this embodiment: the incarnation remains a hope or a memory. One is always waiting for the messiah or bearing witness at the tomb. Through discipline and work, however, the church emerges as the third moment of resolution in which the incarnation of the unchangeable and the spiritualization of the

---

17. As Hegel notes, the transformations that take place in unhappy consciousness are reflected in the unchangeable. The unchangeable undergoes a metamorphosis along with unhappy consciousness (¶211).

changing singleton actually take place. This institution supports a community of collaboration that prefigures the political and social communities of mutual recognition in which spirit is realized.

First Attitude of the Double Relation: Contradiction or Judgment

> The greater the opposition from which spirit returns into itself, the greater is the spirit.
>
> —JEAN HYPPOLITE, *GENESIS AND STRUCTURE OF HEGEL'S PHENOMENOLOGY OF SPIRIT*

Initially, each moment, the unhappy consciousness and the unchangeable, appears to be merely the opposite of the other.[18] The unhappy consciousness identifies himself with the protean flux against the simple self-identity of the unchangeable and takes himself to be the inessential moment. The unchangeable belongs to an inaccessible beyond, and its relationship to the singleton takes the form only of *judgment*. The unchangeable is "alien" to the living singleton (¶210). As the mere opposite of the "true reality"—i.e., the unchangeable—the "protean changeable" or the unhappy consciousness discovers through his own experience that he is an inessential moment to be "put aside" (¶208). He discovers "his own nothingness" (¶209). As the true reality, the unchangeable—formless, yet a singular being—commands absolute submission from the inessential or dependent consciousness. The lord is "he who may not be named." He gives the law and can command the absolute submission of absolute sacrifice: the sacrifice of the son.

Abraham demonstrates his absolute submission to Yahweh by raising a knife to plunge into the heart of his son Isaac. Putting aside for a moment the rights of the child, Abraham could sustain no greater loss than that of the son who represents Abraham's potency and his future; yet, Abraham raises the knife. He does so not because he has faith that the god will

---

18. The unhappy consciousness comprises a relation of two moments, each of which is doubled: as the changing singleton, the unhappy consciousness also experiences himself as a simple self-identity in saying "I." At the same time, the unchangeable, *from the very beginning*, appears as a singular, if absolute and universal, being. It is, *from the very beginning*, incarnate in the (world of) the singleton, as his very truth. The relation of these two double moments itself traverses three attitudes (*Verhältnisse*) in its evolution: contradiction, reciprocity, and resolution. Paragraph 210 articulates the three moments from the side of singularity, as, through its "elevation," the unchangeable emerges (*hervortreten*) in it. Paragraph 211 articulates the three moments from the side of the unchangeable, as, through its incarnation, it takes command of the singular.

# SELF-CONSCIOUSNESS

suspend his decree, but because Abraham knows he counts as nothing in relation to this absolute and invisible being. As the father wields absolute power over his son—even bringing the knife to his breast—so too the judging paternal figure of the universal unchangeable wields absolute power over the singleton.

The god of judgment issues commandments on the "struggle against the enemy," or the management of flesh and desire. Desire must be deferred and delayed, subjected to a complex logic of substitutions and transformations. But the god of judgment supplies only the injunction and punishment. Life, even the life that means everything, must be put at nothing relative to the unchangeable as absolute master. In the "struggle against the enemy," the unhappy consciousness repeats the negation of life prefigured in the mythology of the originary violent encounter, which yielded the shapes of master and slave. Here, however, the detachment from life takes the shape not of mere representation, but of forms of actual practice deployed on living bodies.

### Second Attitude of the Double Relation: Reciprocity or Incarnation

In the movement or experience of the "elevation" or "struggle against the enemy," the singleton experiences himself affectively, if not conceptually, as belonging to the unchangeable. At the same time, the unchangeable enters into and becomes the truth of singularity, thus itself taking on the figure of singularity. The unchangeable takes on just that dimension of embodiment that elicited the campaign or "struggle against the enemy." This second attitude of incarnation itself traverses three moments in the movement of experience by which the singular and universal will be resolved. Each moment reflects the internal contradiction that determines both the singleton and the unchangeable, the opposition between the motility of determinations and the stability of the indeterminate universal. The Bacchanalian revel—motion and rest—reveals itself again.

In the first moment of this second attitude, the incarnation remains only a hope. Any actual incarnation would introduce into the universal unchangeable the determination of form in time and space, but this seems unattainable: it is in principle impossible to say that the universal unchangeable is 'here' or 'there.' The embodiment of the universal unchangeable would present consciousness with "an opaque sensuous *unit* [*Eins*]" with which it could not possibly become one, which could not possibly embody the universal as one among others (¶212). Consciousness anticipates the incarnation of the universal unchangeable, while such an incarnation "has not yet come into existence" (¶215). Moreover, were the incarnation actualized, so that consciousness could "lay hold" on the unchangeable universal as one among others, consciousness would grasp only the inessential, not the "unattainable *beyond* which, being laid hold of, flees, or rather has already flown" (¶217). The universal unchangeable cannot be tied to a sensuous body. The "event" (*Geschehen*) of the incarnation cannot take place, or it will always already have taken place.

Unhappy consciousness advances beyond the abstract negation of stoicism and the restless self-contradictions of skepticism by "bring[ing] and hold[ing] together pure thinking and singularity" (¶216). The movement of elevation and struggle will teach consciousness what it *experiences* but does not yet *know*: that the unchangeable itself has the form of singularity or "is itself the singularity of consciousness" (¶216). As this essential singularity, the universal unchangeable manifests itself in each and all: everywhere and nowhere, it will have been. Where would "pure thinking" be without the first-person singular? It remains to be seen, however, how "pure thinking" might incorporate the specificity of the singleton while remaining "pure."

Looking for an "*actual* existence" beyond mere hope, unhappy consciousness finds only "the *grave* of its *actual* unchangeable being" (¶217). This is the second moment of the second attitude. In confusing the universal unchangeable with sensuous being, unhappy consciousness discovers the unchangeable is always already dead, or rather, that the unchangeable has already transcended the body and life as pure thinking. Death particularizes, but the spirit that has left the tomb can be among each and all, everywhere and nowhere. The impossible event of the incarnation opens a way for each and all to overcome alienation from the universal unchangeable. The empty tomb turns away the unhappy consciousness and turns him back on himself. The "*return of the feeling heart into itself*" teaches consciousness that his singularity is something real, not inessential (¶218). Despite the alienation of the unhappy consciousness from the essential unchangeable, this "*pure heart*" longs for nothing and is "inwardly satiated," as if consciousness could be at once living and without desire. The unhappy consciousness experiences a "pure feeling" that produces a "feeling of *self*" (¶218). This purification of the heart, of feeling, and of the relation of the unhappy consciousness to the universal unchangeable aims to transcend life in the universal form of singularity.

Having taken place, the event (*Geschehen*) of the incarnation will have prescribed the way for each singleton to restore his belonging-together with the universal unchangeable. "I am the way, the truth, and the life. No man cometh unto the Father but by me" (John 14:16).[19] Despite his "purity" and "inward satiation," the unhappy consciousness "*finds* himself *desiring* and *working*" (¶218). Through these actual activities, in which he imitates the vanished life of the incarnation, the unhappy consciousness transforms himself from a singleton (*der Einzelne*) into a member (*das Glied*) of the whole.[20] In this way, the unhappy consciousness "overcom[es] and enjoy[s] the existence alien to" him (¶218). Piety or feeling manifests itself only in the mere representations of devotion, in the "chaotic jingling of bells, or a mist of warm incense, a musical thinking that does not get as far as the concept" (¶217). The reconciliation of the changeable and the unchangeable in the unhappy consciousness requires actual work on real bodies. Through the practices of discipline and obedience, adherence to regimens of self-regulation, and good works, the unhappy consciousness undergoes a metamorphosis that is reflected in the universal unchangeable itself.

Whereas the figure of the unchangeable as the judge or absolute master demanded the sacrifice of the singleton's son, in incarnation the unchangeable at once sacrifices itself to the protean changeable and renounces its

---

19. Bible quotations and citations are from the Authorized (King James) Version.

20. Alexandre Kojève correctly notes that this Christian shape repeats the figure of mastery and slavery: "And if the Slave accepts this new divine Master, he does it for the same reason that he accepted the human Master: through fear of death. He accepted—or produced—his first Slavery because it was the price of his biological *life*. He accepts—or produces—the second, because it is the price of his *eternal* life. For the fundamental motive of the ideology of the 'two worlds' and the duality of human existence is the slavish desire for life at any price, sublimated in the desire for an eternal life." He adds in a note, "there is no human (conscious, articulate, free) existence without Fighting that implies the risk of life—i.e., without death, without finiteness. 'Immortal man' is a 'squared circle.'" Kojève's description affirms Hegel's account of the origin of self-consciousness in violence and the fear of death. However, his analysis of the unhappy consciousness, though correct, is too general and somewhat premature. The unhappy consciousness focuses specifically on the theme of purification and the institutions and practices that produce a *detachment* from life. The fear of death is specifically addressed by more ancient funerary practices, and this mastery of death—the absolute lord—is specifically analyzed in Hegel's chapter 6 through the figure of Antigone. What is at stake in chapter 4 of the *Phenomenology* is not only the general issue of mastering (the fear of) death, but more specifically the achievement of the purity of the concept and the installation of the absolute difference of the concept from bodies. See Alexandre Kojève, *Introduction to the Reading of Hegel: Lectures on the* Phenomenology of Spirit, trans. James H. Nichols, Jr. (1947; Ithaca, NY: Cornell University Press, 1969), 56.

embodied self. "For God so loved the world, that he gave his only begotten Son, that whosoever believeth in him should not perish, but have everlasting life" (John 3:16). The gesture demanded by the judging god of Abraham as a demonstration of piety, the sacrifice of the son, reappears in the generous descent of the universal into the sensuous and its subsequent "*surrender*" of its embodied form. Only by "*relinquishing*" life can the universal unchangeable prescribe the belonging-together of itself with the protean changeable, of the concept with life (¶220). Its absence holds open the space for and prefigures the works and regimens of the unhappy consciousness. Through those practices unhappy consciousness transforms himself; no longer awaiting or mourning the messiah, unhappy consciousness works at the difference between himself and the unchangeable to produce a third moment, a new figure of reciprocity.

Those works and regimens measure not only the difference between the singleton and the unchangeable, but also the singleton's efficacy in addressing that difference. The pious consciousness of pure feeling is only a "musical abstract moment" (¶223). Action, in contrast, demonstrates the capacity to overcome particularity and realize a relation to the other beyond mere contradiction. The unhappy consciousness remains unhappy, however, because he takes the efficacy of his actions to belong not to himself but to the alien unchangeable. On the one hand, his actions can be efficacious only because the world has been "sanctified" through the incarnation (¶219). On the other, the efficacy of the actions depends on the "faculties and powers" that consciousness has received as a "gift from an alien source" (¶220). Instead of finding in his works and regimens a confirmation of himself and of his self-certainty—instead of returning to himself out of this activity—consciousness projects that agency onto the alien other and "gives thanks" for theses talents and capacities.

Thus, the singleton and the unchangeable exist in a new attitude toward each other: the one is no longer the mere opposite of the other. Rather, each expresses itself and realizes itself in relation to the other.[21] Each one confronts the other as a "freestanding singularity [*eine fürsichseiende Einzelheit*]" (¶222). Though the unhappy consciousness remains unhappy, he has nonetheless demonstrated his capacity to "elevate" himself and has, through

---

21. Here the figure of the play of forces reappears. A force is only in being solicited by another force, just as the two extremes exist only in their "reciprocal self-surrender."

his *actual* desire, work, and enjoyment, obtained "*actual* satisfaction" (¶222). Even in giving thanks, which marks his difference from the universal unchangeable, the unhappy consciousness demonstrates reciprocity and belonging-together with the universal.

### Third Attitude of the Double Relation: Resolution, or the Church

The movement of the reciprocal self-surrender renders a transformation in each extreme. The universal unchangeable becomes immanent in sensuous being: "where two or three are gathered together in my name, there am I in the midst of them" (Matthew 18:20). At the same time, the singleton overcomes particularity as a member of a community of collaboration. In action, the singleton makes himself into something before others and, thereby, re-creates himself as more than a particular. Shared practices and rituals render his action both his own and something universal. In the religious community, each one repeats the creed or the prayer for himself but with all the others, and agency proves efficacious only in the context of a community of desire and action.

Despite this actual satisfaction and the productivity of his works, the unhappy consciousness remains unhappy, as he still does not own the efficacy of his actions as his own and remains essentially divided in himself. His actions both treat this gap and reaffirm it. The real resolution of his internal contradiction lies in an inaccessible "beyond," and he abnegates authority over his own actions and enjoyment to a "mediator" or priest, who has an "immediate relationship [*unmittelbare Beziehung*]" with the unchangeable. By following the dictates of the priest, the singleton relieves himself of the responsibility for his own actions. By divesting himself of the "fruit of his labor," the singleton denies the "actuality" that he achieves in work. Through his "fastings and mortifications," the singleton takes as nothing his own enjoyment (¶229). These "sacrifices" secure "relief from his misery," but only "*in principle*" (¶230). He remains fractured and unhappy.

And "here, now, is where the enemy is met with in his most characteristic form" (¶223). What particularizes must be combated.

The body that acts—that fasts, prays, and tithes—proves to be the enemy. The "animal functions," ingestion and elimination, particularize consciousness (¶225). There can be no substitutions by the other in these acts. These universal needs inhere in the singularity of each body and in them self-consciousness—the reader/narrator—comes to know himself "as *this real singleton [als dieses wirklichen Einzelnen]*" (¶225). If he had written the *Phenomenology* otherwise, Hegel might have reminded us here that this "absolute self-standing" (*absolute Selbstständigkeit*) is precisely the origin of certainty. He might have reminded us that the "individual [*Individuum*] is the absolute form" (¶26). Insofar as they eliminate the possibility of generalizing bodies in a concept of the body, the bodily functions might seem to have a positive philosophical effect. Insofar as they inhibit the tendency to reduce the singleton in a general image, however, the bodily functions reinscribe a singular face on every universal concept.

Instead, Hegel pursues the theme of shame. In his subjection to the "bodily functions," the unhappy consciousness is set apart from the others as a singleton, and the power of the other's gaze reappears. Bodily functions cease to be performed "without embarrassment" (¶225). Instead of being dealt with expeditiously, as "trifles," they become the focus of elaborate regimens and institutions of regulation and concealment. As Foucault demonstrates in *The Care of the Self*, the emergence of Christianity is coterminous with an emerging complicity of medicine, morality, and philosophy in policing the body and in a "characterization of the ethical substance based on finitude, the Fall, and evil."[22] While sexual desire for the Stoics might have required careful management due to its effects on health, under Christianity sexual desire (concupiscence) becomes something evil in itself—something that requires not only medical but also moral and religious intervention. By the nineteenth century, medicine, public health, moral and religious institutions, and economists all approached man as a being thoroughly subjected to sexual desire. The more thoroughly sexuality was objectified and studied, the more dangerous it appeared to become; "inquiry is joined to vigilance."[23] By the time of Freud, sexual desire and

---

22. Michel Foucault, *The Care of the Self*, vol. 3, *History of Sexuality*, trans. Robert Hurley (1984; New York: Random House, 1986), 239. Cf. Terry Pinkard, *Hegel's Phenomenology: The Sociality of Reason* (Cambridge: Cambridge University Press, 1994), 69ff. Pinkard explicitly cautions against confusing the unhappy consciousness with the understanding, but, like most readers, he analyzes the shape largely in epistemological terms as "the way in which the skeptic must live his life." Pinkard emphasizes the discontinuity between the beliefs of this consciousness and the sense of inability to ground or justify those beliefs in any way. While he mentions religious practices and their formative power in passing, Pinkard's discussion of unhappy consciousness does not focus on the themes of purification and mortification or on the violent application of the concept to the body.

23. Foucault, *Care of the Self*, 239. See also Foucault, *The Use of Pleasure*, vol. 2, *History of Sexuality*, trans. Robert Hurley (1984; New York: Random House, 1985), 253.

sexual activity provided an "inexhaustible causal power" in morality and medicine and had provoked a "purifying hermeneutics of desire" across multiple disciplines.[24] As Hegel notes, the more the unhappy consciousness seems to subjugate the enemy through his observations, regulations, and mortifications, the more powerful and commanding the enemy's hold on him: the unhappy consciousness, "far from freeing himself from [the enemy], really remains forever in contact with him, and forever sees himself as defiled" (¶225). His attentions elevate what should have been "trifles" into "the object of serious endeavor" and "matters of the utmost importance" (¶225). This elaborate care of the self focuses on what is "meanest" and "the merest particular," producing a self that is no more than a "personality confined to its own self and its own petty actions, a personality brooding over itself, as wretched as it is impoverished" (¶225). Further vigilance, more regimens, stricter purifications only intensify the command of the enemy and the subjugation of unhappy consciousness to the "evil fiend."

Hegel's fictions of "pure thinking" and "pure feeling" impose upon the philosopher the imperative to tear himself away from animal life and from the sensuous body. This gesture, however, is no different than the attempt to get at the truth by subtracting consciousness, as the instrument or medium, from the event of knowing—the very self-defeating strategy whose dismissal began the phenomenological analysis. To absolutely detach thought and feeling from animal life—from the profusion of life and from the living, breathing, ingesting, defecating, seeing, hearing, feeling, thinking body—would be to subtract the openness to the world that consciousness is. This would leave, well, nothing, instead of the knowing and thinking of which objectivity is a moment. "*Here, then we have a struggle against an enemy, to vanquish whom is really to suffer defeat*" (¶209).

The specificity of determinate content and the identity of the perceptual thing are absorbed in the logic of appearance as the "protean changeable" against which the purity of the unchangeable is inscribed. Unlike gesture or speech, which, as soon as they are deployed, can be taken up by others, activities tied to bodily need remain particular and unavailable for substitution. The body or animal life must be risked absolutely in order that thought might appear in its purity. The stoic negates life in order to

---

24. Michel Foucault, *Abnormal: Lectures at the Collège de France 1974–1975*, trans. Graham Burchell (1999; London: Verso, 2003), 240.

demonstrate the freedom of thought. The skeptic, in his shillyshallying, demonstrates the unsustainability of a thought (*not yet*) purified of life. The unhappy consciousness inaugurates the work and desire that will produce ethics, culture, morality, and religion as institutional infrastructures sustaining the self-transcendence of the singleton in the 'we' of a community. This long historical labor will involve extensive regimens of "mortification" and "obedience" to master the body and purify the concept or the freedom of thought. With the installation of incommensurability as the essence of the organic and, thus, of self-consciousness or desire, this work fills the gap with infrastructures of transcendence and commences the long transformation of experience into language. Through his own "obedience and service," self-consciousness will "work off" (*abarbeiten*) every element of particularity, every "unconscious existence and fixed determination" (¶703). In this way, substance will be "betrayed" and "made subject" (¶703). Through this long mortification and management of the flesh, self-consciousness will be "purified" and reborn, no longer a particular (body), but a member of the body politic. "Out of this night of the pure certainty of the self, the ethical spirit is resurrected as a shape freed from nature and its own immediate existence" (¶703). The *Phenomenology* stages a series of abnegations: the abandonment of the sensuous, the dissolution of the thing, the "loss of reality" in the play of forces, the absolute imperative to risk life absolutely, the abstract negation of life, the self-negation of living thought, the absolute detachment from the body, and the long purgatory of labor, discipline, and obedience that will purify consciousness and transform it into the purity of the concept. "*Here, then we have a struggle against an enemy, to vanquish whom is really to suffer defeat . . .*"

Experience teaches the unhappy consciousness that his action, insofar as it is his, is not universal; however, his renunciations turn that action back to the unchangeable, just as his dispossession of himself in his offerings and alms repositions the unchangeable as the source of his work's productivity. Through this experience, the "self-will" (*der Eigensinn*) of skepticism transforms itself into the self-negating will that transcends itself in its renunciations. What appears to be an abnegation actually achieves the very resolution of the contradiction that was sought, though not *for* this self-consciousness, who continues to defer to the priest and to practice his rituals of mortification, fasting, offerings, and good works. He experiences these acts as efficacious, even if he credits another with their agency. Indeed, by crediting the other with its productivity, his action—the action of a particular individual—becomes something public and for others. "Action is only really action when it is the action of a singleton" (¶230), but the singleton morphs into a member of the community and a moment of the universal will. The absolute risk of life, the absolute alienation from life and the body, produces a self-consciousness that is "freed from nature and its own immediate existence," at the same time that it reveals action to be the point of resolution for the nest of contradictions: self/other, inner/outer, particular/universal, and so on.

In the midst of this experience, there will appear a self-consciousness that knows his own action to be something universal—not as a sacrifice to be taken up by the other but as his own effective action in the world. Pleasure and enjoyment, as well as utility, call forth his activity, and he will set about making sense of the world and remaking it to suit his needs and desires. Experience teaches self-consciousness that, rather than being the enemy, the body and the world constitute the means and scope of his own self-realization. He knows his action to be not only his own but for others. His truths reflect not merely himself but a community of actors, just as the judgment of a scientist becomes something universal when confirmed by his peers. Action produces in the "pitiful misery" of unhappy consciousness his own foil: the happy, smiling face of reason. While the unhappy consciousness works over the absolute difference between the unchangeable and himself, reason gets busy in the world where it regularly reveals the regularity of the concept. Reason will replace the particular with the regularity of form and law. Through his abstractions, classifications, and generalizations, reason will master the protean changeable, turning the particular into a mere instance, and reason's own self-will into a universal agency. In the products of reason—concepts, forms, and laws—the specificity of the particular, this body and its need, will at once be deployed, reduced, and transcended.

Only the singleton acts, but in acting for himself according to reason, he acts for each and all. As Hobbes remarks, "all men by nature reason alike."[25] Experience teaches the unhappy consciousness that his own

---

25. Hobbes, *Leviathan*, chapter 5, ¶16. Cf. Hans-Georg Gadamer, *Hegel's Dialectic: Five Hermeneutical Studies*, trans. P. Christopher Smith (1971; New Haven, CT: Yale University Press, 1976): "What we have here is something truly universal in which you and I are the same. It will be developed as the self-consciousness of reason" (72). Gadamer does not appear troubled by the specific

particularity, not the unchangeable, is the alien extreme, and this "superseded singleton is the universal" (¶231). The universal consciousness of reason or the understanding can come to exist only in the singleton, yet its emergence will erase his specificity or singularity. In reason the singleton's self-certainty will become a universal truth.

Yet, reason, however pure, acts only in a world of bodies. These themes—the adherence of the sensuous to the concept, the necessity of affectively embracing death as detachment from the attachments of life, the unsentimental sacrifice of the singleton to contingency and the tides of generations—motivate Hegel's identification of a mother's love as the most dangerous force with which the state must contend. It becomes clear in Hegel's analysis of the gender division of labor in chapter 6 of the *Phenomenology* why her attachment to the son makes her incapable of the detachment necessary to the citizen. While the husband enjoys both the "right of desire" and the freedom from it, women fail on both counts (¶457). On the one hand, because of her attention to the particularities of the family, she "perverts" the "universal activity" of the community or state into "the work of some singleton" (¶475). Her ethical life is not "pure," because it remains suffused by affect and particular attachments.

On the other hand, her particular attachments are abstract, based not on "feeling, but on the universal" (¶457). She would love any husband or any child. She is the "eternal irony of the community," the "inner enemy" (*Feind*), because she remains "impure." She does not detach from her natural attachments, at the same time that these attachments fail to recognize the specificity of the other. To maintain itself, the community must "oppress" the "spirit of her singularity," even as it "creates it" through its "hostile posture toward it as a principle of the enemy" (¶475). Hegel has reminded us from the preface onward that *in principle* no "essential moment" can be left behind; otherwise, philosophical consciousness would not have reached its goal where "nothing is other to it." Hegel attempts to finesse a transgression of his own principle, when he explicitly decrees that women must be "left behind" in the family, contained in domestic space, when man leaves the family to continue his evolution into a participating member of the public life of political, economic, and scientific community. Whether Hegel

---

exclusions on which this sameness depends. Hegel will explicitly mark it masculine. Sexual difference either excludes women from the universal or marks the universal with a singular face.

succeeds in his attempt to write with both hands—to purify the concept of the sensuous and to erase sexual difference—remains to be seen. Perhaps, the affective singularity of a mother's love, which is always a love for *this* child, and which Hegel dismisses with little attention in his discussion of the family, in fact turns out to exhibit just how the singular and the universal belong together in experience.

*Chapter Three*

# HAPPINESS

## Reason at Work

> Reason is the certainty of consciousness that it is all reality; thus does idealism express its concept.
>
> —G. W. F. HEGEL, *PHENOMENOLOGY OF SPIRIT*, ¶233

The unhappy consciousness did not realize that his sacrifice of his will was in and of itself his universalization. Abnegating the credit for the efficacy of his actions, he cannot count on even his successes to yield satisfaction, which remains in principle *beyond* his own experience. Yet, this negation of his singularity is just the gesture that transforms him into a moment of the universal. As active reason, this unhappy consciousness will learn by experience that the universal is realized in his action.

At the beginning of the analysis of reason, the *Phenomenology*'s third beginning, Hegel trumpets the thesis of idealism: "reason is the certainty of consciousness that it is all reality" (¶233).[1] The activity of reason will transform nature or substance by appropriating it in the concept, and in doing so, it will generate the infrastructures necessary to sustain the belonging-together of the singletons in the universal. Though Hegel condemns abstract

---

1. As Adrian Johnston argues, Hegel hardly puts forward here a "monad-like Mega-mind devouring and digesting the entire expanse of non-mental being," as he is often accused of doing. Hegel is focused, rather, on the way in which reason makes sense of the world, paradigmatically in this discussion, through scientific practice, so that what can be said to *be* always appears in relation to the activity of self-consciousness. See Adrian Johnston, *Prolegomena to Any Future Materialism*, vol. 2, *A Weak Nature Alone* (Evanston, IL: Northwestern University Press, 2019), 30–43.

idealism and any kind of intuitionism that would try to circumvent the hard labor of phenomenological analysis, the effect of human activity will turn out to have been the transformation of substance into subject. Hegel's pronouncement is not a wild speculation; rather, it constitutes the measure of the effects of human activity on nature, including its transformative force on human nature.

The proclamation results from the progress of self-consciousness "*along the path*" of his education—his movement through the forms of objective knowing (meaning, perceiving, and understanding) and through the forms of self-relation that comprise the slave, the stoic, the skeptic, and the unhappy consciousness (¶233). *Along this path*, consciousness learns that the in-itself is the in-itself for some shape of consciousness, while what is for consciousness is also independent and has "*intrinsic* being." Reason "has this path behind it and has forgotten it" (¶233). Reason sets about making sense of the world, but it acts without understanding itself as a result of that sense-making activity. Reason's activity mediates between a self-making and a remaking of nature. It is only "*along that forgotten path*" that the identity of reason and reality can be understood. In the slave ideologies consciousness maintains a negative relation to otherness and establishes itself in opposition to the world (¶234). Reason, conversely, realizes itself in engagement with the world. This shape figures the inversion of the unhappy consciousness, who remains, along with the other shapes, haunting reason as its unconscious content.

Unlike the unhappy consciousness, the man of reason owns his actions as his own. Through his action, a man makes public something that was in the beginning a thought for him alone. Observing reason—the first shape taken by reason—works this difference between the inner and the outer, while virtue negotiates the difference between a man and the others. This working-through transforms unconscious substance into self-conscious subject. It unfolds the horizons of self-consciousness, to expand the inner landscape of the singleton.

Observing reason approaches the real as a field of "sensuous things opposite to the 'I.'" However, "what it actually does, contradicts this belief, for it apprehends them *intellectually*; [reason] transforms their sensuous being into *concepts*, i.e., into just that kind of being which is at the same time 'I'" (¶242). While reason maintains the hard and fast distinction between the "in-itself" of the sensuous thing and the "for-consciousness" of appearance, or reason's "representations,"[2] it nonetheless sets about remaking the real in concepts, transforming substance into subject.

While observing reason may have forgotten his path, 'we' have not. Reason will transform substance or the real into its own concept, but 'we,' philosophical consciousness, will limn the essential features of consciousness itself (¶242). We have learned already that cognition cannot be subtracted from truth, as if it were a medium or instrument. We have learned how the instability of perception can be stabilized in the thing only through the operation of ideas and conceptual distinctions. So, far from being a wild speculation, Hegel's idealism merely advances good phenomenology of perception. Reason will extend its sense-making activities throughout all the regions of life. The body, the thing, and the world are transfigured by reason's activity of *"appropriating"* reality as his own (¶237). Life in all its dimensions is so thoroughly analyzed, theorized, codified, and disciplined in our time that it is hard to contest Hegel's claim about the power of reason to master life—to remake the sensuous suffused by the idea. After centuries of effort, reason "plants the symbol of its sovereignty on every height and in every depth" (¶241). No experience, no object resists the categorial and legislative powers of reason.

Throughout this chapter, Hegel repeatedly invokes the violent image of the Bacchanalian revel (¶¶237, 265, 285, 380). On the one hand, the singleton knows himself in the stability of self-sameness, in the pure self-certainty of simple identity, I = I. On the other hand, he finds himself in the restless motion of determinations. Reason repeats the restlessness of perception and the unhappy consciousness, for whom satisfaction is in principle impossible: "this reason remains a restless searching and in its very searching declares that the satisfaction of *finding* is a sheer impossibility" (¶239). Unlike the unhappy consciousness, who can only repeat over and over the rituals and works that address but never reach the unchangeable beyond, reason's restlessness deploys itself upon a wealth of content, so that reason

---

2. As in his introduction, Hegel here does not spare Kant in his criticism of the epistemology of reason. Reason condemns itself by rendering its own knowing an untruth. It installs between knowing and the object an unbridgeable gap, and it then proceeds to produce and engage with representations of this unrepresentable object. Reason, the faculty that represents the real in concepts, reproduces this relation between itself and its inaccessible object in relation to itself. Reason's own truth lies in the unrepresentable, unknowable "unity of apperception." Reason "condemns itself of its own knowledge and volition to be an untrue kind of knowing" (¶242). It will repeat all the contradictions, ruses, and disappointments of "meaning" and "perceiving."

advances in transforming substance into subject against an infinite horizon. Only reason's own self-actualization will be adequate to negotiate the gap between what reason knows and what he thinks, between the for-us and the in-itself. Far from being a passive perceiver, reason "*makes its own* observations and experiments" (¶240). A scientist performs an experiment. Others repeat it and confirm the truth of his conclusions.[3] Through the publicity of action, reason produces communities of truth.

To draw the limit of observing reason and its failure to achieve the "consummation of itself," Hegel reaches again for the gruesome disembowelments of the Bacchanalian revel: "even if reason digs into the very entrails of things and opens every vein in them so that it may gush forth to meet itself, it will not attain this joy" (¶241). However the categorial and legislative activity of reason might divide and dismember the body of life, reason will need to submit himself to the same conceptual knife. If reason would experience the joy of the Bacchanalian revel, he must not only submit himself to the same observational and experimental study as the rest of nature; he must also come to know himself as the spiritual, nonnatural creature of action who appropriates nature and his own nature. Reason discovers through his own activity his identity with spiritualized substance, at the same time that he discovers the necessity of *working on himself*. Man, unlike the acorn or the puppy, does not become who he is without owning up in some determinate way—not without decision, will, and labor.

## 3.A. INNER/OUTER: HUMAN EXCEPTIONALISM AND THE MASTERY OF NATURE

Though all the distinctions and differences of self-consciousness are operative in every shape, within each thought-position some distinction rules. In its conceptualizing activity, observing reason negotiates the difference between inner and outer, a distinction that reason has himself instituted as irresolvable within the horizons of experience. Observing reason does

---

3. That there are women scientists in our time does not inhibit the masculine logic of Hegel's figure of reason. To participate in reason, the sexually specific body is left behind, even as that body must be sustained and cared for by women's labor. For the woman who would be a scientist of reason, her femaleness is an accident that must be left behind in favor of a universal always already marked masculine, while other women continue to serve the body's needs that she leaves unfulfilled—caring for her children and elderly parents, cleaning her house, and so forth.

not merely enumerate the disposition of things in space, as if all he had to say were "this penknife lies alongside this snuff box" (¶244). Rather than merely reporting what he sees, he observes in order to divide the field of being into classes and kinds and to subjugate the sensuous to law. "What is perceived should at least have the significance of a *universal*, not of a *sensuous particular*" (¶244). What observing reason finds in the particular body is the concept of the class or an instance of law. Instead of merely perceiving "this thing" before him, through his representations of sensuous particulars observing reason "transforms their sensuous being into concepts" (¶242). He converts the living being into an instance of a kind or law, betraying substance as subject and discovering himself or his own ideas in the real (¶242). Thus is reason "all reality."

While reason's activity demonstrates this truth, observing reason displays in every moment—in law, in the sensuous being, in itself—the contradiction between what it is in itself and what it is externally for others, or as appearance (of the inner). Law is in itself an immaterial concept, yet "it is valid as a law because it is manifested in the world of appearance" (¶250). To reason, the sensuous particular is "in truth" merely the manifestation of an immaterial concept. A man's act may or may not realize his intentions. Indeed, in Hegel's analysis, restless reason constantly "seeks" himself in seeking to overcome the difference between his ideas and their realization before others, between inner and outer.

Observing reason "finds itself . . . *as a life*" (¶258). Hegel likens the "instinct" of reason to the instinct of the animal that "seeks and consumes food." Just as, in eating, the animal produces nothing but himself, so too the instinct of reason drives it only to its own self-realization. The analogy echoes Hegel's reminder to the reader of the truth of the Eleusinian mysteries, a truth reflected in the innate wisdom of animals: animals are instinctively aware of the unreality of sensuous things, and, thus, they do not hesitate to "fall to without ceremony and eat them up" (¶109). In the same way that, in eating, animals turn other substances into themselves, reason appropriates all reality through his conceptualizing activity. The concept of law "has destroyed within itself the indifferent subsistence [*das gleichgültige Bestehen*] of sensuous reality" (¶248). Yet, it is this same "indifference" of "simple substance" that constitutes the "absolute freedom" of the organism (¶285). The irreducibility of the singular individual as the form of life resists reason's generalizing force. Life comprises genus and species but appears only in the singular individual. Between the motionless taxonomy of genus and species and the restlessness of becoming, the singular individual embodies both the stable identity of the species and the flux of determinations.[4]

What distinguishes organic from inorganic being is its ability to maintain itself in relation to its other. Whereas one chemical in contact with another might transform into a new substance, organic being unfolds and reproduces only as itself. The inorganic is subject to change, while the organism is subject only to its own development or self-differentiation. Hegel repeatedly emphasizes the "fluidity" of the organism. This "universal fluidity" realizes nothing but itself or "returns only to itself." As a *"prius"* or "going before," the organism takes place in the future perfect: what appears through its activity will have been the case from the beginning. "The organism does not produce something but only preserves itself; or, what is produced is as much already present as produced" (¶256). In negotiating the difference between "what *is*" and "what it *seeks*," the organism arrives through its activity "only at itself" (¶257). The distinction between what it is in itself and what it is for itself will be dispelled inevitably by the organism's own becoming. An organism "has its end within itself." It unfolds in its determinate moments according to an internal principle of otherness, or, rather, through self-othering. It constantly "becomes other" to itself in the course of its self-development: the boy is not the man any more than the acorn is the oak.

Once again, the figure of the logic of rest and motion in the Bacchanalian revel reappears. On the one hand, the organism is the *"simple, unitary soul"* (¶265). On the other, it is the "action or movement" of its own self-development or becoming (¶265). The essence of an organism is "just this: to be a simple universality in which all determinations are dissolved, and to be the movement of this process" (¶278). Its fluidity contrasts with the hardheadedness and hardheartedness of stoicism and skepticism. Taking the organism as its object, observing reason repeats the movements of sense-certainty, perception, and the understanding, with the difference that the

---

4. Here freedom appears as number. The "actual life" of the singleton is a "simplicity," into which difference is introduced by his appropriation as his own of the "actual structured shape" of the species. As a singleton, he is essentially *one*, an "inner" simplicity, but that simplicity is expressed in the "outer" as a "multiform actuality" in terms of all the properties that comprise sensuous experience (¶285).

oppositions between universal and particular, essential and inessential, and inner and outer, which were *acted out* by the shapes of consciousness, have become for reason the object of observation. For observing reason, the "real issue" (*die Sache selbst*) is the determination of the relation between universal and particular as manifested in the observable properties of the singular individual.[5]

Deploying the difference between essential and inessential properties, reason identifies what is "*distinctive*" and definitive of a kind of being—plant or animal.[6] The "essential" properties are not only those by which consciousness "distinguish[es] one thing from another," but also the characteristics "whereby the things themselves *break loose* from the general continuity of being as such, *separate* themselves from others, and are explicitly *for themselves*" (¶246). The *differentiae* mediate between the pure concept of matter or being and the particularities of the sensuous to define discrete identities within the organic.

The distinguishing marks are not mere properties, but "weapons." It is only through "their claws and teeth" that "each animal itself *separates* itself from others . . . [and] maintains itself in its independence and in its detachment from the generality" (¶246). The division of the genus into species happens against the horizon of the "universal individual, *the Earth*," and comprises a scene of "unchecked violence" (¶294). The destiny of the eagle is embodied in its talons and beak, just as the fate of the rabbit is written in its large haunches and ears.

While the being of an organism cannot be reduced to an anatomical system, within the context of its becoming even the anatomical parts have meaning (¶276). The difference between humans and other animals, however, lies precisely in the *differentiae*: while the destiny of other animals can be read in their *differentiae*, so that it would make no sense to hold the eagle responsible for eating the rabbit, the plasticity of the human brain, hand, and foot leave human destiny in question. The human organism cannot rely

---

5. While Hegel certainly respects the projects and results of Linnaeus or Lamarck, he also anticipates Foucault's critique of the element of convention and historical determination that attends any classification of life. The taxonomy of organisms is not like the periodic table. The diversity of species "conflict[s] with any conformity to law" (¶275, see also ¶282).

6. Hegel insists that the plant only "touches the boundary-line of individuality" (¶246). Perhaps, this is true for plants like loosestrife or monkshood that in their natural habitats spread via rhizomes in vast indefinite fields, but even these plants form fields or stands that have a distinct identity. The claim seems even less certain for great trees or my mother's camellia. Plants, too, have identity.

on a passive principle of development; rather, his actions are experienced, both by himself and by others, as his own and as subject to critique.[7] His "absolute freedom" appears initially in that he is "indifferent [*gleichgültig*] toward and secured against being-for-other" (¶285). Unlike the chemical that may be absorbed into a new compound, animals and at least some plants occur only as individuals distinct from others. Moreover, the human animal is conscious of this distinction and realizes his freedom as an 'I' that means and acts in the world.[8]

Reason, however, repeats the usual error of natural consciousness by fixing the two extremes of inner and outer, as if consciousness and action were mere *things*. Rather than thinking through the self-development of self-consciousness in the history of its moments, observing reason takes both consciousness and external reality as an "*otherness already given.*" Each appears before it as a determinate thing. The "speaking mouth" and the "working hand" appear to observing reason as "organs of performance and actualization" (¶312). Reason attempts to identify these members with thought via a logic of "expression," a logic that proves unsustainable. On the one hand, the words and deeds *are* the inner and not merely an expression of it. On the other, in the words and deeds the inner is no longer inner, but something "at the mercy of the elements of change" (¶312). Words and deeds may be "twisted" by others into something other than what was meant. Or the singleton himself may misrepresent his intentions in his actions and speech, either purposefully or because he is "clumsy." Observing reason adduces a variety of laws to explain the relation between the two given things—both laws reflecting the influence of the environment on the individual (¶255) and laws reflecting the influence of the

---

7. Hegel's phenomenological analysis does not deny that there may be instances where an individual's agency is usurped, such as by delirium, torture, or abject fear, but these experiences appear precisely against the individual's sense of himself—and others' sense of him—as the narrator of his own experience. These are scenes of violation, of the violent displacement of the singleton from the narrative position.

8. Though he is speaking of the organic rather than the specifically human, Hegel is surely wrong to equate this freedom with an undifferentiated life. "This concept or pure freedom is one and the same life, no matter how many and varied its shapes or its being-for-other; it is a matter of indifference to this stream of life what kind of mills it drives" (¶285). Recognizing the continuity of life does not imply that the force of generation is indifferent to what it drives. Indeed, Hegel's analysis argues otherwise. Is not his entire analysis devoted to an account of how the whole comes to self-awareness in the human singleton? Hegel cannot here sustain the difference between life and the mill it drives. Humans—and other animals who possess memory and deliberation—are those moments of the stream that care very much about which mills get driven.

individual on the actual world (¶307). Just as the explanatory activity of the understanding produced a redescription of reality in the law that "gave rise to nothing new," so too observing reason produces "a double gallery of pictures, one of which would be the reflection of the other" (¶306). The "gallery of external circumstances" would completely circumscribe the individual, while the second gallery depicts the reflection of those circumstances in the individual.

By holding apart the two aspects of inner and outer and fixing them in separate things, observing reason cannot comprehend a "being in and for itself," which is to say that it cannot comprehend its own self-making, self-reflecting activity (¶308). Rather than speculating laws about the "great influence of the environment" or dividing life into categories determined by fixed properties, 'we,' philosophical consciousness, know that the *real issue* is not the content of reason's observations—the specific laws or concepts—but reason's own self-appropriating activity, through which he realizes himself by acting in the world, a world that reason makes "its own." Misunderstanding action as expression and as distinct from what was "meant," observing reason fails to see how action negotiates the difference between inner and outer, as well as the difference between the genus or species and the living singleton. As observation, reason can apprehend self-consciousness only as a thing with properties, so that the issue seems to be the identification of its essential properties or the laws that govern its relations to other things.

However, "the true universality takes its stand on the side of the single individual" (¶293). This specificity escapes observation; for reason it can appear "only as *life in general*" (¶295). Hegel again asserts here what Alasdair MacIntyre names the "ultimacy of concreteness."[9] What is at issue for Hegel is not the articulation of abstract concepts or general laws, but the demonstration of how the universal realizes itself in the singular individual. This universalization happens only through the individual's own self-critical activity, as he experiences the inadequacy of his own representations to articulate his experience. The human organism becomes itself through this activity of attempting to "say what it means"—the very activity that

---

9. Alasdair MacIntyre, "Hegel on Faces and Skulls," in *Hegel: A Collection of Critical Essays*, ed. A. MacIntyre (Notre Dame, IN: University of Notre Dame Press, 1976), 230.

the interrogation of phenomenology makes conscious and visible. As Terry Pinkard argues, human agency implies both that the agent is self-conscious—that is, that his actions have the character of being *his own*—and that they reflect his situation in a "social space."[10] Understanding the actions of another requires that one have "some idea of how he *takes* himself to be, and that 'taking' is not a matter of correlating 'inner' things with 'outer' things."[11] Whatever forces or causes may beset the individual, whether they be external or internal, the human is still faced with the necessity of appropriating them as his own.

Thus, general causes—from poverty to low blood sugar—find only *specific* appropriations in *specific* individual histories. In medicine, for example, the general concepts of disease and laws of physiology are insufficient to explain the differential outcomes of specific cases, where the appropriation of the disease by the individual remains decisive. The individual does not merely suffer the disease but makes it his own in some way. The patient embraces his treatment or fails to follow through. He lives with disease by continuing the habits that produced it or he changes his mode of life. He succumbs to illness with a sense of helplessness or is motivated to become an activist. These differences only make sense within the context of the history and social relations of a self-realizing agency; they cannot be derived from the general concepts and laws of medical science. Similarly, the stories of children who grow up in poverty are irreducibly specific and readable only in relation to how those children understood themselves and in relation to their social resources. The ability of the social sciences to observe trends (e.g., that children whose parents read to them are more likely to be academically and socially successful) does not imply that it is possible to predict the individual case, as the laws of physics prescribe physical events. What distinguishes the human is the irreducible singularity of his experience. In Hegel's telling, the critical self-reflection that comprises self-consciousness means that the singleton is always asking and answering the question of who he is, not merely as a representation but in the body of action and history. Observing reason, however, makes his observation of

---

10. Terry Pinkard, *Hegel's Phenomenology: The Sociality of Reason* (Cambridge: Cambridge University Press, 1994), 91.

11. Pinkard, 91.

the singleton as a thing in isolation comprising parts that are external to one another, as the properties of a thing are distinct within the thing as an entity. The animating narrative of self-consciousness, which supersedes all the distinctions, remains invisible.

At the extreme, observing reason identifies self-consciousness immediately with a material thing—whether it be a bone, as in phrenology, or "brain fibers," as in neurology—as if human agency were reducible to material causes manifest in a thing. As MacIntyre argues, "the thesis that there are biochemical or neural states of affairs, processes, and events, the occurrence and the nature of which are the sufficient causes of human action,... wore phrenological clothing in 1807," but Hegel's rebuttal of phrenology holds against that reductive thesis, "whatever its scientific clothing."[12] In contemporary cognitive neuroscience, one repeatedly encounters statements like "the brain reads," the "brain decides," or the "brain distinguishes," as if the language of brain states and brain activity were adequate to describe self-conscious experience.[13] Hegel diagnoses here a fatal category mistake. Without denying that some actions may have physiological causes, Hegel shows why the rhetoric of neurophysiology, like that of phrenology, is logically inappropriate to describe self-conscious experience. As Hegel famously remarks, "organic nature has no history" (¶295). The species immediately particularizes itself in the individual. Human experience, however, is fundamentally historical and can only be articulated through the temporal modes of narrative. It takes time to realize the universal in human experiences. It takes time for reason to find the laws of physics or the table of botanical kinds in sensuous particulars. It takes time for the infrastructures to be articulated that will transform the isolated singleton into a member of a community. This history, not brain fibers, constitutes the objective body of self-conscious spirit. As MacIntyre notes, "being aware of what I am is conceptually inseparable from confronting what I am not but could become.... Action springs not from fixed and determinate dispositions, but from the confrontation in consciousness of what I am by what I am not."[14]

---

12. MacIntyre, "Hegel on Faces and Skulls," 225.

13. For a philosophical ascription of intentionality to the brain, see, e.g., Jeffrey S. Holtzman, "Normative Moral Neuroscience: The Third Tradition of Neuroscience," *Journal of the American Philosophical Association* 4, no. 3 (2018): 411–31: "It seems clear that the brain is largely responsible for producing moral cognition, emotion, motivation, and behavior—though partial responsibility for these functions may also lie in other areas of the nervous system" (411).

14. MacIntyre, "Hegel on Faces and Skulls," 232.

It is that difference that comprises self-conscious reason and makes sense of his action.

Observation apprehends reason only as if it were the effect of given causes, not a self-critical, self-negating becoming that produces a history of metamorphoses. Self-consciousness—and philosophical cognition too—always operates in the future perfect and only apprehends what will have been the case. Self-consciousness has for its "objective existence" not merely a body, but world history (§295). Observing reason will have its own history of error and self-correction and its own historically determined social forms, which cannot be rendered in the language of brain fibers or the description of any other material thing but only through the temporality of narrative.[15] Neurology yields the "double gallery" of pictures, but discounts the necessity for a rhetoric appropriate not to things but to experience (§306).[16] Neurology regularly assumes a rough-and-ready phenomenology of experience, as it correlates brain states with affects and dispositions taken as given—anger or despair, for example. Either the scientist takes the report of a subject or assumes from some observable properties that he can identify these states. Yet, neurology proceeds without subjecting what it *means* to the rigorous interrogations of phenomenology. Hegel's position in no way denies that an intact nervous system is a necessary precondition to the full exercise of human capacities, nor need he deny that there are cases in which action is determined by brain events that lack the self-awareness of action. Observing reason, however, whether in phrenology or neuroscience, continually runs up against the problem that self-consciousness is not observable, because *consciousness is not a thing*. It cannot be weighed or measured or described in terms of its textures and colors, as a brain or its electrical activity can be. If you want to understand a friend's experience, you ask for a story. Even if the story involves some material cause—a stroke, for example—you will want to know how your friend appropriated it or whether he is still capable of the appropriating activity that made him your friend, the singular individual, not an effect of a material cause.

---

15. See Maryanne Wolf, *Proust and the Squid: The Story and Science of the Reading Brain* (New York: Harper Perennial, 2007).

16. If Oliver Sacks is an exception, it is because he is a clinician who understood that the truth of his patients could only be rendered in a narrative, not a lab scientist trying to find explanations in the brain.

From the beginning of his chapter on reason, Hegel has reminded the reader repeatedly of the difference between perception and observation. While the perceiving consciousness experiences the thing and its properties as if he were merely passive and acted upon by the thing, observing reason actively tests and interrogates experience to produce its representations. Reason in this way *"makes its own observations and experiments"* (¶240). While observing reason acts as if truth lies on the side of the thing, which he merely observes, his own activity displays his constitutive role. Science will have its own social history and depend on its own infrastructures of sociality. The real issue, then, is not to identify the material thing that embodies self-consciousness, but to analyze phenomenologically the agency or self-making that comprises the human singleton.

### 3.B. I/OTHERS: THE STRUGGLE BETWEEN VIRTUE AND THE MAN OF THE WORLD

> The *depth* which spirit brings forth from within—but only as far as his *representing consciousness* [*vorstellendes Bewusstsein*] where he lets it stand—and the *ignorance* [*Unwissenheit*] of this consciousness about what he is really saying [when he identifies self-consciousness with "brain fibers"] are the same conjunction of high and low which, in the living being, nature naively expresses when it combines the organ of its highest fulfillment, the organ of generation, with the organ of urination. The infinite judgment, *qua* infinite, would be the fulfillment of life that fathoms itself; in the consciousness that remains at representation it is but pissing.
>
> —G. W. F. HEGEL, *PHENOMENOLOGY OF SPIRIT*, ¶346

Were there still any doubt about the sex of the narrator of the *Phenomenology*, the transition in reason's unfolding from observation to action should surely eliminate it. The complexity of female sexuality, with its multiple lips and orifices, its nipples and mounds, remains invisible, while the single member of the penis takes the phenomenological stage. In citing the penis as the "organ of [nature's] highest fulfillment," Hegel identifies it as the organ of generation, arrogating generativity to the male as if Aristotle were right that women were only a kind of medium or soil for the unfolding of the form of man's seed, a nutritive element that could be erased from the generative logic. At the same time, the penis in this passage embodies the "conjunction of high and low" that characterizes reason himself. Both the continuation of the species and the most immediate bodily need find their realization in the penis. Similarly, reason enacts, in every register of life, the truth of the idea that he is identical with all reality. At the same time, he opposes himself to his object as something merely given, a merely given substance, of which he can produce only representations. Hegel reprises here the critique of Kantian reason launched with understanding and unfolded in the unhappy consciousness, each of whom did not yet recognize the truth of becoming or appearance and still fixed truth in a substance that could only be represented and never known in itself. This is true also for reason's own relation to himself.

Reason remains afflicted by the opposition between subject and object, and he sticks to perception as the form of knowledge. Reason represents himself to himself in images, as if these images could substitute for the "fulfillment of life" that has fathomed its own depths and knows itself through and through. Reason does not reproduce experience in the concept but sticks to his oppositions and distinctions, pissing himself away in a sophistical to-ing and fro-ing among the moments, each one in turn taken as the essential substance against the inessential others.

Hegel's meditation on the penis introduces the figure of a reason that represents himself as a thing but, at the same time, demonstrates himself to be self-making and self-actualizing. Hegel sarcastically derides the stupidity of identifying experience with a thing: those who make such pronouncements simply do not know what they are saying. The "brain fibers," which represented the "disgracefulness of the irrational, crude thought" of a materialism that would attempt to reduce self-consciousness to a substance, have been displaced by the belonging-together of high and low in the organ of desire. The penis embodies the immediate relation of need and the concept. The text will ceaselessly negotiate this difference between the particularity of need and the conceptual arc of desire. This anatomical substitution in the argument continues Hegel's critique of immediacy and installs the philosophical or conceptual tense of the future-perfect 'will have been.' Unlike the brain fibers, the penis has a history.

Reason has found himself in the thing: in the formed thing of his own labor and in the observation of nature. The things he has made and observed reflect back to him his own concepts. In the figure of virtue, reason makes himself the object of his activity, as he takes up as his own the long "struggle against the enemy" pursued by his religious twin, the "unhappy consciousness." Reason's activity already occurs in a world and in relation to others, and even though this world and these others remain only images or abstract ideas for reason, his concepts and principles will authorize real practices of discipline and education on actual bodies. Reason will reproduce himself as self-regulating by giving himself his own law, a law that is for each and all, or universal. All of life will be rationalized, including the penis.[17]

As in the experience of mastery and slavery, active reason must detach from life absolutely and with respect to every determination in order to embrace as his own the law of each and all. The penis also represents this substitutability of one for the other, in the tide of generations and in the universal law. What first appears most intimate, most particular, most *his* to any man, turns out to be a universal trope. The penis represents reason's labor of detaching desire from *his* life in order to reattach it to the child (the species) and the concept (the 'we' of science, politics, and philosophy). The affectivity of knowing continues to haunt reason's aspirations toward conceptual purity.

What is at stake from now on in the *Phenomenology*, indeed what has been at stake from the very beginning, is nothing less than the life of the singleton, that is, of the reader himself. How can the singleton and singularity "perish" (¶374), be "sacrificed" (¶¶350, 359), and be "smashed to pieces" (¶365) by the phenomenological interrogation only in order to be remade as a moment of a universal will? Hegel tells us that singularity in *all its depth* must be sacrificed, so that the sacrifice itself can be abandoned in favor of a transformed natural consciousness/reader who embraces the universal as his own.

### The Emergence of Agency from Custom

Each singleton finds himself already following a universal law. Every singleton from the beginning finds himself as a member of a people bound

---

17. The phenomenological interrogation makes self-conscious what already will have been lived unconsciously. Psychoanalysis will take up this task of making the unconscious conscious. Like Hegel, Freud valorizes the penis and the Oedipal narrative of male competition in the project of converting the unconscious languages of dream, parapraxes, and symptoms into a self-conscious knowledge of the identifications, displacements, and sublimations that produce character and culture.

together by custom. The phenomenological interrogation has revealed that the knower's relation to the world was already one of desire and that his own agency has already been situated within the "realm of ethical life." The "life of a people or a nation" constitutes the "fluid universal *substance*" (¶350). This substance is "simple" and "unchangeable," yet "bursts asunder into many completely independent beings, just as light bursts asunder into stars as countless self-luminous points" (¶350). Through a "sacrifice of their particularity" each independent being participates in the production of the universal and the reproduction of themselves as moments of it.

The customs and laws (*Sitten und Gesetze*) of a nation comprise the "universal language" within which the singular individual can express himself. The "ethical substance" (*sittliche Substanz*) of custom prescribes the culture of possibilities in which the singleton's agency is situated.[18] Insofar as his activity is "purely particular," it relates to the "needs he has as a natural creature" (¶351). Even the satisfaction of these needs, however, depends on the "universal sustaining medium" of the nation (¶351). Spirit comes on the scene as a "practical" consciousness seeking his own satisfaction, who "steps into a world he finds already *given*" (¶356). The skills and customs through which the singleton satisfies his needs belong to the nation, and, in laboring for himself, this practical consciousness necessarily becomes involved with the needs and labor of others. The labor of one satisfies the needs of others, as his own satisfactions depend on the labor of others. The laws of the nation "are *particularized* in his own individuality and in each of his fellow citizens" (¶351). Each knows the others to be like himself: "he is as certain of the others as he is of himself" (¶351). Whereas the singleton might first have seemed to be opposed to the "unchangeable essence" or "universal substance," in fact only the "universal language" of custom and law "expresses" his individuality. Rather than existing as a separate "unit," this practical consciousness understands himself as existing in "reciprocity" with others *like himself.* The others face the same task of realizing themselves within the possibilities prescribed by custom and law. The reproduction of the singleton as a member of community depends on this sameness, an identity in which the only difference is number: of the others this practical

---

18. For discussion of "cultures of possibilities," see Mary C. Rawlinson, "Liminal Agencies: Literature as Moral Philosophy," in *Literature and Philosophy: A Guide to Contemporary Debates*, ed. David Rudrum (London: Palgrave Macmillan, 2006), 129–41.

consciousness states, "I regard them as myself and myself as them" (¶351). The exclusions necessary to maintain this fiction of sameness remain invisible. Soon in Hegel's narrative, women will be excluded explicitly and will remain "the enemy" of political community precisely because the irreducibility of sexual difference threatens the logic of the same on which the community relies.

The "happy state" of the practical consciousness in a "free nation" turns out to be, like the messiah, something that has either not yet come or already flown (¶353). In custom the ethical exists as something merely "*given*" (¶354).[19] Reason, Hegel insists, "*must* withdraw from this happy state," so that through the interrogation of unconscious custom, reason will produce self-conscious law. This practical consciousness takes up the task of realizing his own happiness by achieving "the unity of its own actuality with the objective being of the world" (¶356). For reason, this truth already exists in principle, or the world appears to him as available for his satisfaction—a satisfaction to be achieved through his own labor. The singleton inevitably rebels against custom in seeking his own happiness, and this *must* be so if his unconscious reciprocity with the others is to be transformed into the self-legislated mutual recognition of citizens in a modern nation-state. A community that is merely *given* is only a community in the abstract, one in which the singleton is a "vanishing quantity" (¶355). As the "desire for life," the individual necessarily seeks his own happiness and in doing so comes into conflict with custom. Perhaps he wants to marry outside the tribe, to settle in new territory, to change the stories and rituals, or to hunt or farm in a new way. The customs and laws seem arbitrary and alien against his sense of himself as "this particular 'I'" (¶355). The customs and laws may be ignored, he believes, but he is certain of himself as this existing being, and it is his own activity that will reconcile him with the world in truth and happiness. From the point of view of this consciousness, happiness appears to be lost and only his activity will regain it. *For us*, however—for philosophical consciousness—his activity is no more than the self-conscious

---

19. See also ¶357, where Hegel contrasts the consciousness for whom the happy state is not yet attained, who is "pressed forward" by a "natural impulse," with the consciousness for whom the happy state is something lost to be regained. From the former perspective, the "forms" or the "coming to be of ethical substance" precede consciousness and must be realized; for the latter, they arrive after the fact, after this consciousness purges itself of particularity, "setting aside his own ends" in favor of the species and the state.

re-creation of his reciprocity with the others and his rediscovery of the truth that he exists only as a moment of community (¶357). Just as life had to be risked absolutely in order to establish that self-consciousness is not a thing and to detach the singleton from his particularity, so too the singleton particularizes himself in his rebellion against custom so that this very particularity can be reappropriated by the universal 'we' of science, politics, and philosophy, in which he is only a moment.

You, dear reader, have a sense of yourself as *this one* who is different from the others, this 'I.' In the Bacchanalian revel of life (or appearances) this constitutes the moment of rest against the flux of determinations and particular beings.

It is this sense of independence or standing on your own (*Selbstständigkeit*) that the phenomenological interrogation will detach from the specificity of your body and history and reattach to the 'we' of the concept in politics, science, and philosophy. The citizen finds his independence in the laws and institutions of the modern nation-state, against which the individual's desire and happiness appear very small. The scientist finds his independence in the truths confirmed by a community of researchers, without whose reproduction of his results the scientist would know nothing. The philosopher finds his independence in the community of readers created by the circulation of the book. Without the book, his thought would remain a "thought for him alone" (¶71).[20] Against the state, science, and the book, the desire and death of the particular individual mark only a "vanishing moment." Members can "drop out "of the revel, but the species and the historical unfolding of the concept will go forward against the horizon of the "immortal elementary individual, Earth" (¶452). Recall that, at a time when the universal gathers such strength, the particular individual must "expect less for himself," just as "less can be expected of him" (¶72). The emergence of the corporate forms on which the flourishing of human life depends requires this detachment from need and impulse, from that initial sense of being 'this one,' independent and standing on your own, and a reinvestment or reattachment of that affect in the 'we' of the communities of science, politics, and philosophy.

---

20. In our time, two extreme forces impede this circulation: violent censorship in large parts of the world and in others a cacophonous media environment in which the truth seems not to matter. In 2016, China is a good example of the former, and the United States of the latter.

To inaugurate the long negotiation between particularity and universality, need and desire, affect and concept, heart and law, Hegel invokes Faust and the perverting influence of the "spirit of the Earth." Against the "heavenly-seeming spirit of the universality of knowledge and action," this earthly consciousness "has given itself to the devil and must be put to ground" (¶360, Hegel quoting Goethe). He "plunges into life" and "indulges himself to the full" (¶361). Hegel resorts again to food metaphors to articulate the activity of reason, who "takes hold of life much as a ripe fruit is plucked, which readily offers itself to the hand that takes it" (¶361). Devouring life in seeking his own happiness, this practical consciousness "attains to the enjoyment of pleasure," but in so doing he contradicts his own claim to be "this particular 'I.'" He acts only because he is conscious of a difference within himself, between desire and satisfaction. Even within himself, immediacy is only a moment. Moreover, without the mediation of forms and laws, his desire and the pleasure he attains appear, ironically, as an alien *necessity*. Nothing can be said about it except that it *is*. Sticking to the immediacy of his being, this consciousness thus effects an inversion that converts the living being into a "*dead* actuality" lacking the narrative development of life (¶363). In adhering to his own particularity, this consciousness meant to "take hold of life," but "in doing so he really laid hold of death" (¶364). This consciousness remains opaque to himself and cannot even comprehend his own desires without some mediation between aim and end. Otherwise, he is himself the effect of an alien necessity, not self-unfolding but merely given.

The tenacity of this self, who sticks to his own sense of independence as something absolute, is "pulverized on the equally unrelenting but continuous world of actuality" (¶364). The abstract necessity that emerges in his experience represents the "uncomprehended power of universality, on which individuality [*Individualität*] is smashed to pieces" (¶365). The emergence of a community of self-conscious individuals who know themselves to be real only as its members will require not only the originary violence of the state of nature and the rebellion of the individual against the given of custom, but also an unrelenting "pulverizing" and "smashing" of the individual's sense of independence. If the concept is only concretely realized in the thought of a living individual, it remains to be seen how it will fare after this violence has been inflicted.

# HAPPINESS

### The Law of the Heart

In pursuing his satisfactions, consciousness learns by experience that he is himself the principle of necessity, or he has discovered necessity within himself. The law of the heart immediately joins the immediacy of the particular consciousness with the universality of the law of reason. The law appears as given to consciousness immediately in his own feeling, while that feeling is no longer spontaneous and opaque but lawful. Once again, Hegel requires the reader to step into the place of this consciousness and to answer the phenomenological interrogation into whether he can say what he means (¶368). His own experience will teach him the impossibility of sustaining the law of the heart.

"The heart is confronted by a real world" (¶369). As the law of the heart, this law exists only in principle and is not yet realized in the world. Reality appears to be governed by a cruel and alien necessity that "contradicts the law of the heart." Under the "violent ordering" of this alien law, the singleton is "oppressed," and humanity suffers. The "levity" of the practical consciousness that sought only his own pleasure gives way to the "earnestness of a high purpose that seeks its pleasure in displaying the excellence of its own nature, and in promoting the welfare of mankind" (¶370). This earnest consciousness experiences with certainty the immediate identity of singularity and necessity. He takes the law to be immediately given in his heart. His "undisciplined nature" has not been shaped by the works and activities that might mediate between singular and universal. Hegel regularly turns his sarcasm on any consciousness that represents himself as a moral savior in a corrupted world, a theme that commences here with the law of the heart.

For this earnest consciousness, what is important is not merely following the law, but "that in the law it has the consciousness of *itself*, that therein it has satisfied *itself*" (¶371). Just as phenomenology must demonstrate how the immediate certainty of natural consciousness already has implicit within it all the shapes of consciousness and the 'we' of philosophy, so too the phenomenological interrogation will produce a law that is no longer alien, but in which each singleton finds this certainty of himself. For the law to sustain the community of members, each and all must know the law to be his own.

At the same time, action, though mine, is also before others. Thus, the "law of the heart, through its very realization, ceases to be a law of the *heart*" (¶371). When the individual acts to set up his own "order," he immediately becomes something for others. To the extent that his act embodies a law, it is thereby something universal, and he has *through his own activity* "purged himself of his particularity" (¶372). "By his act he places himself in, or rather posits himself as, the universal element of existent reality, and his act is supposed to have, even according to his own interpretation, the value of a universal ordinance. But he has thereby *freed* himself from himself; he goes on growing *qua* universality" (¶372). Here in the account of action as inherently universalizing lies the core of Hegel's solution to the problem of the belonging-together of the particular and universal. The law of the heart is not something merely felt but a principle that the virtuous consciousness "*carries out.*" Through action the virtuous consciousness externalizes the law of his heart and demonstrates himself to be a "free reality" (*freie Wirklichkeit*), acknowledging that "reality" (*Wirklichkeit*) is not something to which he is opposed but his own essence (*Wesen*) (¶372). While he is at first all pompous talk and a mere earnestness concerned about his own purity of heart, through his struggle with the way of the world and the *discipline* of action, he proves himself to be a moment of a world of others and that his reality lies in that world, not merely in his heart. Like the unhappy consciousness, who through his good works and rites demonstrated his ability to negotiate the difference between the changeable particulars and the unchangeable universal, so too virtue proves through his action to be something other than what he takes himself to be. The affectivity of his heart finds its realization through his action in a world of others who are engaged by and implicated in his action.

The earnest consciousness of the law of the heart meant to maintain his singularity against any alien order or law, but his actions and efforts to "promote the welfare of humanity" produce a law for each and all: "in what is law, *every* heart must recognize its own self" (¶373). This earnest consciousness seeks to convert others to his order, but in doing so he demonstrates that law cannot be merely "of the heart." The particular heart in unison with other hearts would be no longer merely particular, but through their affective attachment to the *same law* would participate in the universal.

Unfortunately, precisely because the deed is something particular while the particular content of this particular heart is supposed to be universal—a law or order, rather than an immediate affect—"others do not find in this content the fulfillment of the law of *their* hearts" (¶373). While the man of pleasure rebelled against an inherited order, as if it were a "dead necessity," this earnest consciousness finds itself opposed by other orders and laws that are vivacious and animated by the hearts of men. The hearts of other men have their own law to which they "cling," and they resist the impositions of this earnest consciousness. In this experience the singularity of consciousness "really perishes," as the singleton can no longer disentangle himself from these contested orders and exists only as a moment of them.

This experience produces a self-contradictory, "perverted [*verkehrte*]," and even "deranged" consciousness (¶378). This earnest consciousness means to give himself his own law, but as something universal, as if he were the essential moment and the world were his to remake. At the same time, precisely because the law is universal, it remains an abstraction unless realized in the world of others. This "distraught" consciousness constantly contradicts himself by asserting first the identity of singularity and universality—the heart and the law—and then their alienation. Meaning to cling to his singularity, this earnest consciousness nonetheless posits himself as universal in the law. This "heart-throb for the welfare of humanity therefore passes into the ravings of an insane self-conceit" (¶377). Seeking to impose his order immediately, without the mediation of works, discipline, and corporate forms, this earnest consciousness not only exhibits the "madness" of his internally contradictory nature; he also finds himself caught up in a "perverted" order that is "only a universal resistance and struggle of all against one another" (¶379). He has learned by experience that singularity is perverted and perverting and that he "must sacrifice the singularity of consciousness" (¶380).[21] This self-abnegating consciousness appears in the figure of virtue.

---

21. In ¶380 Hegel again invokes the figure of the Bacchanalian revel. The "universal order" appears, on one side, in the "restlessness" of the singleton, who alternates between the two moments of heart and law, taking now one and now the other as the essential moment. On the other, universal order appears as the "tranquil essence" of the law as something "inner" and not yet realized. Just as observing reason repeated the moments of consciousness, so too active reason repeats the self-negation, the sophistical to-ing and fro-ing, and the struggle against the enemy of self-consciousness.

## The Critique of Virtue

Hegel begins his discussion of the actualization of self-consciousness as virtue by reminding the reader that every shape repeats the logic of negation, contradiction, and inversion. In rebelling against custom, the singleton poses his self-certainty against an "empty universality" (¶381). In acting by the law of the heart, he incorporates the contradiction between particularity and universality within himself, at the same time that he sees it reflected in the world of others to which he also opposes himself. The man of virtue sets himself up against the enemy, or the way of the world, but his disciplines and works address its "inner essence" or the "absolute order" implicit in it. Virtue takes as his end the realization of this good that exists only "in principle," an aim to be achieved through the "sacrifice of individuality." The interrogation, however, will effect an inversion: the man of virtue engages in a "sham fight," and his "faith" and "pompous talk" will be "conquered by the way of the world" (¶¶386–89).

The opposition between virtue and the way of the world prefigures the antagonism between faith and the Enlightenment that Hegel takes to be definitive of modern European culture. For virtue the good is only "implicit" in reality and must be realized through its good works and disciplines: thus, at first virtue only "believes" in a good that is contradicted by the actual. The good or the universal exists for virtue as its own inner essence, which much be externalized and realized by transforming the world. For the man of the world, on the other hand, the universal or the good is something alien to his own principle of utility. He opposes the self-certainty of his own actuality and his ability to make his way in the world to this merely abstract good that exists only in principle. Virtue is no less invested in its own singularity than is the man of the world, but the man of virtue employs his talents and capacities to make the implicit good explicit, thereby sacrificing his singularity to it. The man of the world, on the other hand, employs his abilities to enhance his singularity and to realize ends that he takes as his own. He acts according to utility within a world that he takes as real, rather than acting according to a belief in a world that does not yet exist, or that exists only in principle (¶¶385–86).

The self-conception of the man of the world, however, is just as perverted and perverting as that of the virtuous consciousness. Intending to act only for himself and pursuing his own interests and utilities, he nevertheless ineluctably acts with and for others. A businessman sets about to make money, but in doing so he creates an enterprise that engages others, that offers them employment or supplies their needs while depending on their productivity. A tycoon like Henry Clay Frick acted to serve his own ambitions, but in creating the transcontinental railroad he not only provided services and employment; he changed the character of a nation.

For the virtuous consciousness, the good or the universal exists only 'in principle' and must be realized through his own active struggle with the world. For the man of the world, the good or the universal is a matter of indifference in contrast to his own ambitions and interests. In both cases, action demonstrates that neither the one nor the other comprehends his experience. Each "grows in universality" through his actions. The universal appears as the "gifts, capacities, powers" through which the conflict will be carried out, and it is through the conflict itself "that the good is established in both modes" (¶386).

The knight of virtue fights a sham fight, like Don Quixote tilting at windmills, because, while he might oppose the world and express a belief in a good or universal that exists only 'in principle,' "his true strength lies in the fact that the good exists absolutely in its own right" (¶386). The good is *"already realized"* in the conflict itself. Virtue "holds in reserve" the idea of good that exists only in principle, as if through this belief, he would be able to ambush the man of the world, "fall[ing] on the enemy from the rear during the fight" (¶386). Yet, what the virtuous consciousness actually confronts in the struggle against the enemy is "the universal, not merely as an abstract universal [one existing only *in principle*], but as a universal animated by individuality and existing for an other, in other words, the *actual good [das wirkliche Gute]*" (¶386). Action, the externalization of gifts, capacities, and powers in a world of others, transforms the particularity of belief or ambition into something universal: the deed belongs not merely to the doer, but to the real world of the community.

The virtuous consciousness poses as sacrificing himself to the struggle against the enemy, yet it is only in the exercise of his capacities, gifts, and powers in that struggle that his virtue is realized. Thus, he is not only "like the combatant who, in the conflict, is only concerned with keeping his sword bright, but he has even started the fight in order to preserve [*zu bewahren*] the weapons" (¶386). He exists as the virtuous consciousness only through his struggle against the enemy. Virtuous consciousness intended to bring the good into being by sacrificing his own individuality to the universal, but the universal is only realized in the individual. Virtue is conquered by the way of the world because his actions concern distinctions that exist only in words, and not in action (¶389). The good he champions is only an abstraction, opposed to the real world of action and the individual. Virtue rests on the distinction between the in-itself and actuality, but this is a "distinction which has no truth" (¶389). The man of the world supposedly perverted the good because he adhered to the principle of his own individuality, but "individuality is the principle of the *real* world" (¶389). The man of the world demonstrates in his actions, whether he knows it or not, that "what exists *in itself* exists equally *for an other.*" Individuality, "the principle of the *real* world," embodies the belonging-together of the inner and outer, the particular and the universal, the in-itself and what is for another. The man of the world "does pervert the unchangeable," but he does so by transforming it "from the *nothing of abstraction into the being of reality*" (¶389). Whereas virtue remains entangled in the "cloak" that he has thrown round himself—viz., the idea of a good that exists only in principle—the man of the world sets about exercising the principle of individuality in a world shared with others.

Hegel contrasts this virtuous consciousness, all "pompous talk" and fatuous rhetoric, "inflated with his own conceit," with virtue in the ancient world (¶390). The latter did not oppose itself to the actual world, claiming the way of the world to be something "perverted." Rather, the virtuous man among the ancients understood himself as an individual actor contributing to the life of the community, to "the *spiritual substance* of the nation" (¶390). The ancient man concerned with virtue knew his form of consciousness to be real only through actions in this community of others. The nation was his *element*: he lived in it as a bird lives in the air and a fish in water. Through his action the difference between substance and spirit was overcome and realized in the nation.

In "our time," the man of virtue proves to be no more than a kind of fatuous egoism that would claim for himself a goodness that is merely *inward* or that exists only in his professions of faith—that is to say, he has a "virtue in imagination and name only, which lacks that substantial content" (¶390). Its conflict with the way of the world reveals the emptiness of a good that exists only 'in principle,' an idea, Hegel insists, that must be dropped "like a discarded cloak" (¶391).

The conflict teaches that the good cannot be opposed to individuality, because "individuality is precisely the actualizing of what exists only in principle" (¶391). What seemed to virtue to be a "perversion" of the good turns out to be the "conversion" of the good "as empty purpose, into a reality" (¶391). The conflict demonstrates that the man of the world is not as bad as he seemed, for in exercising the principle of individuality through his actions, he ineluctably converts his particular ambitions into something before others, or something universal.

On the other hand, the man of the world "may well imagine that he acts only for *himself* or in his own interest," but he too does not know what he is saying (¶392). When he insists that "everyone acts in his own interest," he merely proves that neither he nor anyone else understands "what action is." Action overcomes the difference between in-itself and for-another, between what exists only in principle and what exists in reality, between particular and universal. The experiences of both the man of the world and virtuous consciousness in their conflict demonstrate that neither of them knows the truth of his experience: "the movement of individuality is the reality of the universal" (¶391). Working through the dichotomies between inner and outer, faith and utility, universal and particular, spirit and substance will require more struggle, further shapes of consciousness, and additional moments of loss, where consciousness is obliged again to abandon what he thinks he knows. But the conflict between virtue and the man of the world has already revealed that it is only in the individual and his action that the universal or the good can be made substantial.

### 3.C. *DIE SACHE SELBST*: ACTION, LAW, AND ANTIGONE ON THE MORAL "INSOLENCE" OF REASON

Now, at last, we come to the "real issue." How do universality and particularity, concept and substance, thought and being intercalate (*durchdringen*) one another in the individual? How is it that, far from being opposed, universality and particularity belong together (*zusammenhangen*) in the individual? How is it that the concept is only realized (*verwirklicht*) in the substance of the individual? How do these distinctions come to be revealed as moments of the unity of individuality?

At the beginning of his analysis of self-consciousness in the shape of reason, Hegel declares that "reason is the certainty of consciousness that it is all reality" (¶233). This certainty, however, has not yet attained the status of truth. Reason demonstrates himself to be all reality through his action; however, reason does not yet comprehend himself as such. The consciousness of reason continues to be afflicted by the difference between what is in-itself, or being, and what is for-another, or known. This distinction fractures both his experience of the perceptual world and his ethical life, or his relation to himself and to the world of others.

### From Singleton to Individual: The Community of Action

Through the critique of virtue, 'we,' philosophical consciousness, have learned the truth of the claim with which the analysis of reason began: action is the "element" of individuality, the substance in which universality and particularity "intercalate" (*durchdringen*). Just as the properties of the object of perception belong together in the thing—while each retains its specificity and its distinctness from the others and from the unity of the thing—so too particularity and universality belong together in the individual and his action.[22] In the observation of nature, the scientist is anything but passive: he orders and categorizes, he designs experiments and tests hypothesis, he speculates and posits explanatory theories. Through his activity, the substance of nature becomes something spiritualized and thought. When he performs an experiment and publishes his conclusions, other scientists try to replicate his results, confirming or disputing his claims. Thus, the action through which the scientist's thought claims to reflect nature is not his as a merely particular being; rather, his action is realized in the community of scientists, without whom his claims would remain a truth "for himself alone" (¶71).[23] Through his action, substance is spiritualized at the same time that his particular intention becomes something universal. The experience of consciousness has demonstrated that "the *singular [einzelne]* consciousness is *in itself* absolute essence." Hegel's use here of the term *einzelne* rather than *individuell* leaves no doubt that

---

22. The belonging-together of the properties with one another and of the properties with the unity of the thing provides the paradigm for understanding *die Durchdringung*, or "intercalation," of the universal and particular in the individual and his action. See section 1.b.

23. Note the analogy between, on the one hand, the publicity of scientific research and the confirmation of its truths through the replication of experiments and, on the other, the confirmation of the truths of philosophy through the technology of the book, as it circulates to create a community of readers.

he means to refer here to no abstraction, but to the concrete living human being in his singularity. This singular being is the site of the realization of the universal, and, thereby, of absolute truth—truth that is no longer afflicted by the opposition between being, or the in-itself, and knowing, or what is for another. The "real issue" proves to be how this singular being *through his own action* can be transformed or converted (*verkehrt*) into a spiritualized substance that embodies the universal and dissolves the distinctions between inner and outer, in-itself and for-another, being and self-consciousness.[24] How, through his own labor, does the singleton convert himself into a member of a community where his individual actions acquire a universal significance? How does the singleton through his own work dissolve the difference between thought and being, so that the concept is fully realized in the sensuous and the sensuous fully embodies the architecture of the concept?[25]

Through his actions, reason exhibits that he *is* all reality, that he can convert substance into thought so that substance is no longer alien or other but reflects his own thinking. Nevertheless, reason does not comprehend this truth. He is certain of it—and this certainty is what makes possible his action of rendering nature intelligible—but he does not yet comprehend the meaning of his own action. Thus, nature remains for him something alien and in-itself, to be distinguished from his own knowing. Similarly, when he takes as his object the laws of his own action rather than the laws of

---

24. The critique of virtue also makes clearer Hegel's phenomenology of the body. In his consideration of psychology and phrenology, Hegel identifies the body with the individual's "originary" or given being in which "he has played no part" (¶310). While this determinate being, the "*body* of the specific individuality," appears immediately as "his own," it proves to be only a point of departure, for the individual is "only what he has done" (¶310). His originary embodiment does not remain "an immediate fact," but something that the individual must eown or make his own. His body "expresses" the reality that "he has himself *produced*," as the hands of a laborer or the body of an athlete signify a history of activity: "the individual only makes known what he really is, when he sets his original nature to work." It is not as a skull or brain fibers that the body reflects the reality of the individual; rather, it does so only as what Merleau-Ponty called the "*je peux du monde*," as the originary moment of self-realizing action. The apparent contradiction between the individual as a given being or body and a "free activity" or self-consciousness dissolves in work or action. See ¶¶309–11.

25. In attempting to think the belonging-together of the concept and the sensuous, Merleau-Ponty describes thought as the "lining of the sensuous," but this image fails to capture the way in which the concept provides the *infrastructure* of the sensuous. Foucault comes nearer to Hegel's truth in his analysis of the way concepts produce "regimes" of truth defining what can be thought, said, and done and by whom. Concepts create cultures of possibility and support specific forms of life, as the concepts of causality, law, and evidence make the culture of natural science possible.

nature, reason will remain bifurcated by an 'as if,' by the distinction between the good 'in-itself' and the good as it is presented 'for another.'

Just as in the critique of reason's action in relation to nature, Kant is Hegel's primary foil in the account of reason's action in relation to himself and others. Whereas, in Hegel's analysis, action converts particularity into the individuality that embodies the universal, Kant maintains a hard and fast distinction between intention and action and cannot think beyond a good that exists only in principle. Reason must act 'as if' he belongs to a kingdom of ends. He can judge only the consistency of his intentions with a formal principle of duty or universalizability. He remains concerned less with right action than with his own moral purity. The in-itself of the real thus remains no less inaccessible in the domain of human action than it does in nature. Kant invests self-knowledge in the thought of intentions, while Hegel insists that "an individual cannot know what he is until he has made himself a reality through action" (¶401).

Action repeats the problem of beginning that, in Hegel's preface, was seen to plague philosophy itself. Hegel refers again to the "originary determinate nature of singularity" analyzed in the discussion of phrenology and psychology. This "immediate being" consists of capacities, talents, character, "and so on." This tincture that is proper to or belongs to spirit (*diese eigentümliche Tinktur des Geistes*) determines the end of action, as it sets the conditions and possibilities for the becoming of the individual. Otherwise, action would be a "nothing working toward nothing" (¶401). I cannot become an opera singer if I am tone deaf, nor can I become a chef if I have no sense of smell. Yet, this given being remains an empty abstraction until it is realized through the individual's action: "consciousness must act merely in order that what it is *in itself* may become explicit *for it*; in other words, action is simply the coming-to-be of spirit as *consciousness*" (¶401). Thus, like the philosopher who cannot offer in advance—in a preface—a mere summary of a thought that has not yet been accomplished, "an individual cannot know what he is until he has made himself a reality through action" (¶401). Just as philosophy has nothing to do with a mere statement of "aims" (¶1), so too an individual "cannot determine the *end* of his action until he has carried it out" (¶401). Yet, he also cannot act without having this end before him. If the deed is to be an action rather than something that merely happens, the actor must "have the action in front of him beforehand as *entirely his own*, i.e. as an *end*" (¶401).²⁶ Thus, the individual, like the philosopher, "seems unable to find a beginning." In order for the action to be an action rather than an accident, he must have his end in hand beforehand and own the action as his own.

Yet, it is only his deed that can realize his "original nature," which sets the limits of what he can do: "the individual who is going to act seems, therefore, to find himself in a circle in which each moment already presupposes the other" (¶401).²⁷ Consciousness cannot resolve in a concept the impossibility of finding a starting point that does not already presuppose the other moments; it is only in action that "all differences intercalate [*sich durchdringen*] and are dissolved [*sich auflösen*]" (¶405). Thus, the individual has no choice, "whatever the circumstances," but to act "without further scruples about beginning" (¶401). The deed is no more external to the purpose or end than is the "original nature" of talents and capacities. Action overcomes the dichotomies between purpose and work done, between inner and outer, between being-in-itself and being-for-another.

"Whatever it is that the individual does, and whatever happens to him, that he has done himself, and he *is* that himself. He can have only the consciousness of the simple transference *of himself* from the night of possibility into the daylight of the present" (¶404). Hegel does not mean to suggest that an individual cannot make mistakes or come to regret his action. Yet, whatever he has done constitutes what the individual has become, and in spite of his mistakes and regrets, he has discovered himself in and as this transition from aim to work. Whatever mistakes and regrets he might suffer, he remains capable of *reworking* the actual. The density of his own history may exert resistance, but the individual in his activity always exceeds it and retains some power of working it otherwise.

---

26. Robert Pippin suggests that this difference between a "genuine action" (*Handlung*) and a mere "thing done by me" (*Tat*) appears late in Hegel's philosophy, certainly after the Jena period of the *Phenomenology*. However, here in ¶401 Hegel operates with just such a distinction. If I accidentally knock a cup off the table, this is not an action but an accident. An action requires the owning of an end, however confused or unconscious it may be. Here Hegel refers both to *das Tun*, "a doing," and *die Handlung*, "a deed." See Robert B. Pippin, "Hegel's Social Theory of Agency," in *Hegel on Action*, ed. A. Laitinen and C. Sandis (Basingstoke, UK: Palgrave Macmillan, 2010), 61.

27. Here, Hegel prefigures the analyses of the "hermeneutical circle" in Heidegger, Gadamer, and others. The hermeneutical circle is not vicious; rather, it names the way in which any act, including an act of interpretation, is delimited by expectation and intention.

This conversion of an abstraction, the implicit "original nature," into the reality of the work constitutes the happiness of reason. The actual world no longer appears, as it did to the virtuous consciousness, to be an alien reality against which the individual must struggle. Further, the actual world is no longer taken to be merely a reality accessible to reason's powers of interpretation and understanding, as it had been for the observing reason of natural science. For reason as the author of action, the world also provides the conditions of possibility for the work through which reason's abstract, merely implicit "original nature" can be realized.[28] "The individual [*das Individuum*], therefore, knowing that in his actual world he can find nothing else but its unity with himself, or only the certainty of himself in the truth of that world, *can experience only joy in himself*" (¶404). In his work or activity, the singleton comes to know himself in the universality of action, not as tied to this or that particular deed or result but as the *movement* that overcomes and dissolves the distinctions between inner and outer, between being and self-consciousness, between self and other, and between particular and universal.

For the consciousness who realizes himself through his own activity, the dichotomy between being and doing with which he began now reappears, but as a *result* (¶406). While action overcomes the dichotomies between

---

28. In "Hegel and the Philosophy of Action," Charles Taylor identifies Hegel's analysis of action with "expressive theories of meaning," and expression with "self-revelation as a special kind of bodily practice" (35). This interpretation, however, is significantly misleading. Action for Hegel is not so much self-expression, as *self-realization*. The action does not merely reveal an existing interiority; rather, it realizes the identity of the singleton in a way that *retroactively* determines that interiority. Whatever my intention may have appeared to be, its truth is constituted only in my action. I may think I offer my friend assistance out of kindness and generosity, but my action may reveal that in truth I wanted to make her dependent and to demonstrate my own superiority. The truth of the intention does not precede the action, so that it is merely expressed in it; rather, the action reproduces the intention in its truth. See Charles Taylor, "Hegel and the Philosophy of Action," in *Hegel on Action*, ed. A. Laitinen and C. Sandis (Basingstoke, UK: Palgrave Macmillan, 2010), 22–41. Hegel remarks that the body is the "expression" of the individual, as the individual is "only what he has done," but it is so as something that "he has himself *produced*." It bears the "signs" of a history of action (¶310). The action realizes, makes real, or produces the interiority of intention and identity no less than the exteriority of the deed or work done.

Pippin also attributes to Hegel an account of actions as "expressive," although he acknowledges that, for Hegel, actions do not "disclose" intentions but retroactively constitute them. This is the meaning of "the famous Hegelian *Nachträglichkeit*, belatedness" (Pippin, "Hegel's Social Theory of Agency," 63). Pippin himself writes, "only as manifested or expressed can one (*even* the subject herself) retrospectively determine what must have been intended" (66). Thus, the act cannot merely *express* an intention; it constitutes it. This is not "backward causation" but self-realization in action (69). Pippin also adheres to a belief in the sincerity of intentions (71) that Hegel rejects: I can certainly be mistaken about my own intentions, however "sincerely" I hold them, and it is my deeds that will prove it so. This "sincerity" is just the object of attack in Hegel's analysis of "honest consciousness" (¶433).

inner and outer, being and self-consciousness, purpose and deed, means and end, willing and achieving, all of these contradictions reappear in the work done, which is, after all, a contingent happening. Through the particular deed or work, the individual, who has demonstrated himself to be in truth the movement of action, again finds himself in an "accidental relationship to reality." "Fortune decides as well in favor of an ill-disposed purpose and an ill-chosen means, as against them" (¶407). It appears that the unity of being and doing achieved in action—the unity between the "originary nature" and its realization—"vanishes" in the work. The "contingency" of the work seems to contradict the "concept of action" (¶408). Yet, the work as an "objective reality," like the objective reality of the "originary nature" or bodily endowment, "is [only] a moment which itself no longer possesses any truth on its own account" (¶409). Active reason knows the contingent work to be his own and to be only a moment of his reality as self-realizing activity, so that his certainty in himself as this self-realizing activity "endures in the face of the experience of the *contingency* of action" (¶409). Active reason knows that reality is only a moment of his own experience, which does not exist "in its own right." Thus, the "true work" is not the particular action or its objective result but the movement of activity in which being and doing belong together. Action happens "because action is in and for itself the essence of actuality," the self-realizing activity through which both active reason and reality are made determinate (¶408). The "true work" cannot be reduced to the particular deed or result; it exists only in the "unity of *being* and *doing*, of willing and achieving," manifest in active reason's self-realizing activity, which "endures" and surpasses any deed and any work done (¶409).[29]

The "real issue" then proves to be the "intercalation" (*durchdringen*) of individuality and objectivity in this self-realizing activity. Reason demonstrates

---

29. The theme of "the work" will reappear in the analysis of spirit proper in the dialectic between the singleton and his culture. The singleton is formed or "molded" by his culture, while at the same time the singleton sets about making the actual world of culture his own. He both produces his culture and is produced by it (¶490). His work participates, on the one hand, in the power of the state, which is his substance insofar as he has reality only as a member of it, and, on the other, in the production of wealth as the fulfillment of his own interests: "in working for himself he is at the same time working for all and all are working for him.... His self-interest is something merely in his mind, something that cannot get as far as making a reality of what it *means* to do, viz. to do something that would not benefit all" (¶494). Like the man of the world, the man of culture thinks he acts only on his own behalf, without realizing how his actions always already implicate others or how his productivity provides a general benefit.

that action is his "substance" and that objective reality acquires significance or is made determinate only through reason's own activity. Yet, as "this particular individual," reason has come on the scene as an "immediacy," for whom activity or the "real issue" remains an abstraction distinct from his own substance (¶410). Here active reason repeats the transition from sense-certainty to perception. The immediate unity of active reason, for whom the "real issue" remains something other and opposed to his own particular being, becomes sundered into constitutive moments: purpose, means, action, deed, or the work. Like perception, to-ing and fro-ing in its sophistical movement within the oppositions between the one and the many and between consciousness and the object, active reason "busies" itself now with one and now with another aspect of its action, where each aspect has validity just because it is a moment of the "real issue." In doing so—again repeating the "ruse" of perception—active reason takes now one and now another aspect to be the truth of the "real issue" and "forgets them one after another" (¶414). When this "honest" consciousness "does not attain the real issue in one of these moments or in one meaning, it for that very reason gets hold of it in another" (¶412). If his action fails to achieve its purpose, then the honest consciousness gives himself credit for willing the action; abstract purpose or mere willing is taken to be the "real issue." Or, if his work does not endure, he figures, this is because he has superseded it; he still finds himself realized in it, "like naughty boys who enjoy *themselves* when they get their ears boxed because *they* are the cause of its being done" (¶413). If, on the other hand, something occurs without any action on his part, he makes it his own merely by taking an interest in it. A stroke of "good fortune" becomes "his own doing," or an "event of historical importance" is made "his own" just because he takes an interest in it. Though his agency has no part in the affair, the event becomes something in which he sees himself realized and for which he can take credit, merely because he has favored or opposed it—as if this amounted to effectively supporting or combating the event. Hegel's analysis proves timely in an era when social media provide a platform for inflated rhetoric without regard for knowledge or expertise, enabling anyone and everyone to make political events his own affair. Pontificating reason puts himself forward as having a hand in the affairs of the day, without the risk of taking action or exerting any real agency; this creates nothing more than a cacophony of talking heads.

This "honest" consciousness, then, is "not as honest as it seems" (¶415). Like perception, he spends himself in a sophistical to-ing and fro-ing among his constitutive moments, taking now one and now the other as essential. He keeps himself busy with empty purposes or actions, which, being merely willed, are no action at all, on the one hand, while concerning himself only with this or that particular deed, on the other. The reality of action as the movement of self-realization that overcomes the dichotomies—of inner and outer, self and other, universal and particular, concept and substance—escapes him.

Moreover, he concerns himself with purposes and deeds as if these were "only his own affair" (¶415). Yet, he finds himself in a world of others who are also actors and for whom his own actions are something public, available to their scrutiny and affecting the matters in which they concern themselves. "A consciousness that opens up an issue soon learns that others hurry along like flies to freshly poured milk" (¶418). This honest consciousness, in opening up an issue, meant to express only his own interest, but precisely to the extent that he is engaged in the issue, it is the issue that is the truth of his action and not merely his own interest; in his action "something has been opened up that is for others as well, or is a real issue on its own account" (¶418). His action, instead of being merely *particular* to him (*ein einzelnes eigentümliches Tun*), turns out to be "for others as well" (¶418). The deed or issue that this honest consciousness regards as his alone nonetheless proves to be an object for all the others, who "all regard themselves as affected and invited to participate" (¶418)—just as anyone and everyone on social media feels at liberty to pontificate once an issue has been opened up. This dishonest consciousness was never merely concerned with the issue as such, but with the issue as *his own*. So too all the others take up the issue as *their own*. Each one "interferes in the action and work of others, and, if he can no longer take the work out of their hands, he at least shows an interest in it by passing judgment on it"—as if, through blaming or praising the work, each one makes it his own (¶417). Like the talking heads of social media, this dishonest consciousness mistakes action or the real issue for something that belongs to the particular consciousness, and, at the same time, he mistakes mere willing, opining, and judging for the reality of action. The community made up of such dishonest consciousnesses is no more than a "spiritual zoo," in which each one exists in his own cage howling at the others. In this world, "individuals, amid confusion and mutual violence, cheat and struggle over the essence of the actual world" (¶537). Because each one adheres to his action and to the issue as something particular and *his own* concern, each one is both deceived and deceiving; being with others in this state can only yield the world of combat that characterizes politics and social media today, a world in which reconciliation and collective agency are impossible.

The dishonesty of this honest consciousness, however, is manifest to him through his experience. By acting or opening up an issue, he necessarily becomes involved with others, as his action is always before others and something with which they can become involved or with which they can concern themselves, a matter for their judgment. Similarly, the others who concern themselves with his action or involve themselves in the issue likewise might "pretend that their action and efforts are something for themselves alone and in which they have only themselves and their own essential nature in mind. However, in doing something, and thus bringing themselves out in the light of day, they directly contradict by their deed their pretense of wanting to exclude the glare of publicity and participation by all and sundry" (¶417). An action always belongs to a singleton (*der Einzelne*); yet, it is also "immediately for others" (¶418). The truth of action lies not in an abstract purpose or mere willing, nor in the particular deed. Action spiritualizes the substance of each singleton, not only by making his embodiment or "original nature" his own, but also by transforming him into a moment of a community of others. "Actualization is . . . a display of what is one's own in the element of universality, whereby it becomes, and should become, the affair of everyone" (¶417). Action transforms substance from the immediacy and separateness of particularity into "substance permeated by individuality" (¶418). The movement of action—the transition from inner to outer, from what is one's own to what is before others, from the substance of embodiment to the subjectivity of purpose and deed—demonstrates that the action of the individual is always already an action "for each and all."

Here then appears the first figure of the absolute. We have arrived at a point where consciousness need no longer go beyond itself, for nothing is other to it, the very criterion invoked at the beginning of the phenomenological analysis (¶80). Consciousness does not "want" to go beyond this object, because he finds himself realized in it, and he "cannot" go beyond it, because he has no reality apart from action: "it is all being and all power" (¶420). As a self-conscious agent, he finds himself already engaged with a world of others, who are equally engaged by his action. Action transforms the singleton into an individual who belongs together with others in such a way that his particular deed has a universal significance, and this belonging-together has proved to be the real issue of the phenomenological analysis.

### Law and the Insolence of Reason

The truth of consciousness has been revealed to be not a mere knowing of objects but a self-realizing doing in a world of others. The real issue is no longer what can be known, but how to act. The real proves to be not merely the immediate substantiality of sense and perception, but an *"ethical substance."* The concept of law, which transformed the particularities of sense and perception into moments of the universal, reappears here. However, here it is not discovered as a law of nature but as the acquired property (*das erworbene Eigentum*) of a self-conscious, self-legislating reason.

Just as with custom or the law of the heart, reason first finds these laws as immediacies. Their validity is guaranteed by the "healthiness" of reason itself: "healthy reason [*die gesunde Vernunft*] knows immediately what is right and good" (¶422). Adhering to the phenomenological rule, 'we,' philosophical consciousness, do not need to add any of our own "bright ideas," for we find reason articulating ethical laws, as if they were transparent and immediately given. What 'we' must do instead, as with every shape or moment of consciousness, is test healthy reason's claim to know the truth of the ethical substance immediately and to be able immediately to pronounce the law.

Hegel considers two examples articulated by healthy reason: "Everyone ought to speak the truth," and "Love thy neighbor as thyself." In both cases, the laws prove self-contradictory. In the first case, speaking the truth depends on whether or not the speaker *knows* the truth. So, what the proposition stipulated as a universal necessity turns out to be completely contingent on what healthy reason does or does not know. Moreover, if healthy reason only *"ought to know"* the truth, it follows that "it does not *immediately* know what is true" (¶424). In the second case, the commandment to love one's neighbor similarly proves contingent on its content: "unintelligent love will perhaps do him more harm than hatred" (¶425). If I do not know what is good or bad for the beloved, then my actions may make him worse off, not better.

The second case proves more interesting than the first, as Hegel takes the occasion to distinguish between the "intelligent universal action of the state" and the individual "sentiment" of beneficence. The individual is capable only of actions that are quite "single and isolated, of help in need which is as contingent as it is transitory" (¶425). The state, on the other hand, exerts "so great a power" that it can offer "intelligent, substantial beneficence . . . in its richest and most important form" (¶425). Not only can the state protect the individual against the harm that might be inflicted by other individuals; it can also develop policies that will provide a culture of possibilities and securities for each and all. Hegel here foresees policies such as universal health care or universal education that "love" each and all intelligently by providing for the welfare and agency of individuals.

Ethical laws stated in the propositional form as given immediacies will always fall prey to the contradiction between their claim to universality and the inevitable contingency of their content. Reason's claim to be "healthy" does nothing to alleviate this problem. The only way of escaping it is to revert to a principle of universalizability by which such laws, afflicted with contingency, are to be tested. In so doing, healthy reason takes up the existent laws not as immediacies, given in their truth, but as propositions in need of reason's own verification.[30]

Hegel distinguishes between the phenomenological analysis, undertaken by philosophical consciousness, which compares what reason claims to be with what its experience demonstrates it to be, and the testing proposed by reason as a condition of truth, a procedure for determining the validity of the ethical proposition. Reason takes up the merely given law in order to determine if it can be willed universally. This procedure, however, proves fruitless. Given that reason's criterion is an empty concept of universality devoid of content, it proves to be a tautology, for which "one content is just as acceptable to it as its opposite" (¶430). To prove this point, Hegel considers the example of the law of property. On the one hand, to negate property within a community appears self-contradictory. In a community with shared ownership of goods, either each receives according to his need, contradicting the principle of equality of individuals that makes a community come into existence, or goods are equally shared, contradicting the principle of need on which the very idea of sharing depends. On the other hand,

---

30. Of course, in this critique Hegel is again taking aim at Kant's moral philosophy.

holding fast to the law of property proves similarly contradictory. By possessing a thing, I contradict its universality, its availability to each and all. To the degree that others recognize my ownership, my ownership only establishes my equality and dependence on the others, not my privilege. Conversely, if I relinquish my property right by giving something away, I can transform the object from my property to another's without contradiction. Similarly, if I retain and claim as my own the property of someone else that has been entrusted to me, I fall into no contradiction—I no longer view it as the property of another.

The principle for testing laws—the test of abstract universalizability—proves to be a tautology that cannot establish the right or make distinctions within the ethical substance.

> The criterion of law which reason possesses within himself fits every case equally well, and is thus in fact no criterion at all. It would be strange, too, if tautology, the maxim of contradiction, which is admitted to be only a formal criterion for the cognition of theoretical truth, i.e., something which is quite indifferent to truth and falsehood, were supposed to be more than this for the cognition of practical truth. (¶431)

Just as in the domain of physics the principle of contradiction establishes only a formal criterion rather than determinate laws, so too in the domain of ethics, a principle of universalizability establishes only the formal criterion that the ethical law must be a law for each and all, without generating any determinate content. In the domain of ethics, the concept of law is afflicted with the same oppositions that arose in the attempt of the understanding to grasp the truth of the real. The formality of law opposes itself to the many determinate laws. The formal unity of the concept of law cannot account for its own application in the multiplicity of actual cases, nor for the many parts of any determinate law.[31]

The activities of giving and testing laws both prove futile in making the ethical substance determinate. Further, they set consciousness on a fundamentally "unethical path" (¶437). To suggest that healthy reason on its own can legislate the right implies both "an invalid establishing and existence of actual laws, and . . . an equally invalid immunity from them" (¶434).

---

31. See my discussion of law and the understanding, section 1.c.

Whether as law-giver or the tester of laws, reason seeks to legislate directly without the mediation of collective forms, as if the singleton himself alone were capable, through some procedure, of establishing the commandments of ethics and moral life. "To legislate immediately in that way is thus the tyrannical insolence which makes caprice into law and ethical behavior into obedience to such caprice" (¶434).[32] By making law in the domain of ethics and moral life dependent upon his own test, reason arrogates to himself the power to establish "the good and the right," as if his own "health" and "intelligent insight" were what give force and validity to ethical commandments (¶434).[33] Yet, this would be to divest the ethical of its power to command, as if it could be expressed in laws that reason might, according to its own procedure, decide to follow or not. By making the law contingent on its own test, reason pretends to have "transcended" the commandment of the right, as if the procedure were truly universal, while the commandments were merely "conditioned and limited" (¶437).

Reason produces only the "'ought to be' of an unreal commandment and a knowledge of formal universality" (¶435). Ethical life is thereby reduced to an empty "willing and knowing" on the part of the singleton. He can judge only whether his own intentions are consistent with the formal principle of universalizability, and he remains concerned not with doing what is right but with ensuring his own moral purity.[34] This honest reason proves dishonest: he displays the cardinal crime of *pleonexia*, arrogating to himself a power that belongs elsewhere.

---

32. Hegel will repeat his critique of this "tyrannical insolence" in his analysis of the "terror" of the French Revolution. The revolutionary government proves to be a form of terror and no government at all precisely because of its immediate identity with the wills of particular singletons, who attempt to legislate directly without the mediation of collective forms. Robespierre, the man of reason, decrees the death of Danton and is in turn put to death himself. The Committee of Public Safety was not so much a collective form as a site for conspiracies and the contestation of power among particular individuals.

33. While Hegel distinguishes rigorously between ethics and morality, the latter, as a self-conscious law, arises organically out of the former, as the social relations in which we find ourselves *claimed by the right*.

34. Again, Kant's moral philosophy is the primary target of Hegel's critique. Kant not only makes the right contingent on reason's own test; he also makes ethical agency merely speculative or hypothetical—to act *as if* you belong to a kingdom of ends. At the same time, Kant's moral philosophy focuses not so much on action in a world of others as on the moral purity of the agent: what reason sets out to ensure through its own willing and knowing is just the consistency of his intentions with a principle of universalizability. Given that the formal principle can accept any content, this consciousness, Hegel argues, is not as "honest" as it purports to be. The procedure for testing laws turns out to be no more than a means of affirming the laws that reason has already found immediately to hand.

## HAPPINESS

At this point in the argument, Hegel introduces the figure of Antigone as an avatar of spirit, who demonstrates that the truth of the moral law does not depend on any procedure of reason but instead arises organically out of our social relations and the claims made on us through them.[35] In Sophocles's eponymous play, Antigone insists that she must bury her brother Polyneices in spite of the objections of Creon, the head of state, both because he is her brother, and because she has herself promised him, not once but twice, that she would do so. This obligation defines her: were she to break her promise and fail to perform her duty to her brother, she would no longer be Antigone. This duty, like her duties to her father, constitutes her *substance*, and to be true to herself and her own life she must bury him.[36] In these relationships, the right commands her immediately.

As a parent, I, too, immediately find myself commanded by the right. As a mother, I have a duty to my children that derives from the relationship itself, rather than from any rational argument or procedure. My duties to my students define me as a teacher, just as a doctor's duties to his patient define him as a doctor. The substance of these identities lies in the commandments laid on them by the relationships themselves.[37] At the moment that reflection begins, the singleton finds that he is always already entangled in relationships that make ethical claims on him. The paradigm of these relationships Hegel locates in the family, the nexus of relationships into which the singleton is thrown by fate and by which he is from the very beginning commanded. The singleton needs no argument for the necessity of taking care of his children or his aged parents; rather the burden would be on him to demonstrate why he should be freed from the command of the right in these relationships. As Antigone insists, there is no identity outside of these relationships. How could the singleton be himself—his mother's son or his son's father—without acting to realize the duties that are the substance of these relationships?

---

35. It is for this reason, as Pippin rightly claims, that Hegel insists on "both the priority and superiority of the standpoint of 'ethical life' to that of either 'abstract right' or 'morality.'" Pippin, "Hegel's Social Theory of Agency," 74.

36. See Sophocles, *Antigone*, lines 450–70.

37. Hegel's critique of Kant does not hinge, as Pippin suggests, on the claim that practical reason depends on "social norms," rather than on a purely formal norm. Rather, for Hegel, practical reason depends on social *relationships*, whose contents always already have ethical commandments embedded in them. The relationship between mother and child embodies universal commandments, not merely historically generated "social norms," however differently these might be articulated across cultures. Cf. Pippin, "Hegel's Social Theory of Agency," 61.

Now, at last, we have come to the *real issue*. Only now are we ready to begin the phenomenology of spirit. All along we have discovered, again and again, that natural consciousness did not know what he thought he knew, that he did not know where the truth of his experience was to be found. All along we have been focused on the wrong objects: the sensuous, the thing of perception, the beyond, nature, abstract law, the singleton's own willing and knowing, the procedures of reason. Only now have we discovered the truth: that the smallest unit of substance is a world (¶441). The substance or truth of spirit lies in action in a world of others, where the singleton is always already caught up in relationships that issue commandments on him. The singleton has learned that his own particularity—his own sense of himself as *this one* standing on his own, his own identity—occurs only as a moment in and of a world of others.

The question of the phenomenology of spirit, the *real issue*, proves to be how the history of human activity produces social forms out of the natural relationships of the family that are capable of sustaining collective agency, while attaching and safeguarding the singularity of each and all. Now we are ready to begin.

# PART II

## THE PHENOMENOLOGY OF SPIRIT

*Chapter Four*

# SPIRIT, OR TRANSUBSTANTIATED LIFE
## Infrastructures of Community

> As *substance*, spirit is unwavering, righteous self-sameness; but as *being-for-self*, it is dissolved [*aufgelöst*], a self-sacrificing benevolent essence, in which each brings forth his own work and takes his own share. This dissolving and singularizing [*Vereinzelung*] of the essence is even so the *moment* of the action and self of all; it is the movement and soul of substance and the resulting universal essence. Just because it is in itself a dissolved being, it is not a dead essence, but *real* and *living*.
>
> —G. W. F. HEGEL, *PHENOMENOLOGY OF SPIRIT*, ¶439

At the beginning of the phenomenological analysis, Hegel enjoined the reader to make himself the site of the "little research." As the point of the analysis has been to demonstrate how philosophical consciousness lies implicit in natural consciousness, it was necessary to start with natural consciousness in his immediate certainty. Now that the analysis has demonstrated the singleton to be himself only as a moment of a community, the phenomenological research must begin again in immediacy, where community has always already been given, with the *family*. In Hegel's analysis, the nation develops out of the family and, through the gender division of labor, becomes the sustaining infrastructure of community life.

The beginning of Hegel's analysis of spirit parallels that of chapters 1 through 5 of the text: the reader has each time mistaken his object, and he must begin his analysis again and again from the beginning with a new object. The reader has mistaken spirit for a thing, an idea, a bone, a psychological law, or a law of reason. Finally, the reader discovers through the figure of Antigone that spirit only fully manifests itself as action in a historical world of others. Like the transition from chapter 3 to chapter 4 of the text, in this transition a transformation takes place not only in how consciousness represents itself or in the objective truth with which it identifies itself, but also in consciousness itself: it becomes self-conscious, aware of its constitutive role in objectivity. In both the earlier case and here, consciousness comes to know itself as a node in a nexus of relationships; it comes to know that its truth is to be a member of community.

Beginning again for the fourth time, the phenomenological analysis takes up the figure of the singleton, produced in the transition from immediacy to reason, as a moment of a whole. The community will take the form of the modern nation-state. Just as we began again after discovering the figure of self-consciousness—by asking how it emerged out of animal life—so too, here at the emergence of spirit, Hegel begins again, asking where community is found in natural life and how the self-governing nation-state emerges out of it. The real issue (*die Sache selbst*) here lies in the elaboration of infrastructures of association adequate to negotiate the difference between the self-standing (*Selbstständigkeit*) of the self-certain self-consciousness and his membership in community. Managing death and sexual difference proves central to this endeavor.

The analysis of spirit, or life-worlds, tracks the evolution or unfolding (*Aufhebung*) of forms of membership or kinds of community out of the natural given of the reproductive family. This formal history will express the whole of spirit from the point of view of a constitutive moment, the singleton.[1] It will embody all the possible shapes of consciousness and all the possible forms of objectivity, as well as their self-conscious appropriation and their articulation in forms of life. The natural consciousness that submits to divine and human law will find his realization in the exercise of his freedom by suspending the law in an act of forgiveness. The end of this history will constitute the end of history. All the possible shapes and forms of consciousness and of objectivity will have been self-consciously appropriated in their genetic systematicity through the interrogative method of phenomenology. Knowledge will need no longer to go beyond itself because there will be nothing other to it.

At every stage of the analysis, the same tripartite logical figure, initially presented in the first three chapters analyzing consciousness, has reappeared: (1) immediacy as determinate negation or the "two-ing" (*Entzweiten*) of what first appeared a simplicity, of which the analysis of the "now"

---

1. This analysis completes the proper phenomenology of spirit. The subsequent analysis in chapter 7 of the forms and institutions of religion retraverses this material development from the perspective of the whole, rather than that of the singleton.

provides a paradigm; (2) the to-ing and fro-ing of various forms of sophistry—from perception to skepticism to the "insincere shuffling" of moral consciousness—among oppositions that turn out to be "distinctions which are no distinctions" because each moment is essential and belongs together with the other; and (3) the appropriation of these oppositions as moments of the whole, an operation that produces self-consciousness, a performance that transforms substance into subject. This conceptual infrastructure operates as the logic both of the parts, however discrete, and of the whole itself.

The chapter on spirit, like the entire text, recapitulates these forms. Repeating the critique of custom, the phenomenological interrogation reveals how the immediacy of ethical life in the family necessarily gives way to an alienated spirit, afflicted by the opposition between reason and faith, the actual and the beyond. From this strife emerges a resolution of the self-certain singleton and the other, who come to know each other as moments of experience or members of community.

Consciousness produces this resolution itself through an act of forgiveness that demonstrates his freedom in transcending the law at the same time that it lets the other go free without denying his indebtedness. The singleton finds himself realized in the general wills of the family and state, which depend on this community of forgiveness. Only through the performance of confession and forgiveness can the intercalation (*Durchdringung*) of the universal and the singleton be achieved. Otherwise, natural consciousness remains caught in the logic of judging and judged that produces and reproduces alienation and terror. At a time when tribalism and the spirit of revenge fuel wars across the globe, Hegel's analysis remains urgent.

The various forms of life that compose human experience and human history live the whole of experience *from the point of view of the moment that determines them*. Just as for Leibniz each monad reflects the whole system of being from its own perspective, so too each determinate shape of spirit reflects the whole of spirit from the perspective of its own experience. It is "real" and "living" only because the abstract 'I' of spirit has always already "dissolved" and made itself determinate:

> As *substance*, spirit is unwavering, righteous self-sameness; but as *being-for-self*, it is dissolved [*aufgelöst*], a self-sacrificing benevolent essence, in which

each brings forth his own work and takes his own share. This dissolution and singularizing [*Vereinzelung*] of the essence is even so the *moment* of the action and self of all; it is the movement and soul of substance and the resulting universal essence. Just because it is in itself a dissolved being, it is not a dead essence, but *real* and *living*. (¶439)

The self-certainty of the singleton belongs to his "dissolution" and "singularizing" in the essence or element of his existence—as this particular being in the genus life, as this particular member of the family, or as the citizen in the state or as this faith or this insight. This dissolution of the essence constitutes the movement and life of spirit. Here again reappears the image of the Bacchanalian revel: spirit is at once absolute rest and absolute motion, always the same with itself as a movement of dissolution in which determinate forms of life, like the singleton, pass in the eternal flux of the species.

> The true is thus the Bacchanalian revel in which no member is not drunk; yet because each member, as he detaches [*sich absondert*], is immediately dissolved [*sich auflöst*], the revel is just as much transparent and simple repose. Judged in the court of this movement, the singular shapes of spirit do not persist any more than determinate thoughts do, but they are as much positive and necessary moments, as they are negative and evanescent. (¶47)

The determinate forms of spirit are necessary but evanescent. Hegel would have us believe that, in their flux, the loss of the singleton leaves no trace on the transparent stillness of the concept, as if the specificity of the singleton can be captured by the logic of the same without remainder. In the movement of self-sundering and return from otherness that composes spirit, the moments are necessary but transcended by the motion itself, and, because each moment incorporates all that has gone before in the genetic phenomenology, nothing is lost. Or, what is lost leaves no trace. Can the singularity of the singleton, the germ from which the whole of the phenomenological analysis unfolds, be thought *in general*, as 'singularity,' as a universal form that bears no singular face?

Not only the fate of the singleton as a mortal being is at stake in the phenomenology of spirit, but also the destiny of sexual difference. Spirit comes on the scene already divided into two. Only the irreducible difference of sexual difference will prove successful in negotiating the dichotomy between the universalities of spirit and the singularities of substance or bodies.

Hegel names woman the "eternal irony of the community," and it may be that she supplies a point of irony in Hegel's own text. Perhaps her ironic status undoes his claims to systematicity, to completeness, to "leaving nothing behind." He would have us believe that he can erase woman from the narrative, leaving her behind in the family as man moves into the universal domains of politics, science, and philosophy, without violating Hegel's own principle. Will the erasure of the feminine voice in the narrative of spirit leave no trace? And, what ironies will result in this analysis of sexual difference from the fact that Hegel has spoken *of* woman and *for* women, but never *as* a woman? Only Antigone is allowed to speak for herself, and she speaks for the family and the fraternal order—as an avatar of the very gender division of labor that Hegel installs as necessary, consigning women to the care of the body and the precinct of the family. Hegel installs sexual difference at the very origin of spirit as absolutely necessary to it. Can it be that in the end this difference makes no more difference than the mortality of the singleton in the articulation of the "life" of the concept and, like mortality, can be erased?

## 4.A. ETHICS OF FAMILY AND NATION: SEXUAL DIFFERENCE IN ACTION, OR LEAVING THE SISTER BEHIND

The shapes that have appeared in the phenomenological analysis up to this point were not "real spirits," but only "abstract forms of it" (¶¶440–41). These thought-positions constitute representations of spirit, rather than actual spirit "that exists and prevails." Hegel has repeatedly criticized natural consciousness for his inability to negotiate the difference between his representations and his experience. Consciousness tends to confuse his representations of himself with his actual existence, substituting the former for the latter as his truth, just as stoicism, skepticism, the unhappy consciousness, and even reason each identify the truth of experience with an abstract 'I' rather than with a form of life.

These "isolated" representations, however, appear only in "spirit which is a concrete existence." They constitute the self-representation of *some form of life* (¶447). At the same time, the shapes of spirit proper are "distinguished from the previous ones by the fact that they are ... actualities in the strict meaning of the word, and instead of being shapes merely of consciousness are shapes of a world" (¶441). The phenomenological interrogator asks, "How does the world of community first come on the scene in life?" The phenomenologist *finds* the world of the family immediately given, as a living, if unconscious, embodiment of the logic of membership that defines community. He no longer confuses the truth of experience with mere representations but finds it instead in the infrastructures and institutions of actual forms of life.

The family, Hegel argues, is the "element" of the nation (¶¶450, 455, 475). As a fish lives in water or a bird in the air, so the nation exists only in and as a community of families. As the "*immediate*" and "*unconscious*" embodiment of the concept, the family "stands over against" the self-conscious order of the self-governing nation-state (¶450). Yet, the family already embodies the logic of parts and wholes that negotiates the opposition between the singleton and "what is truly universal, the community" (¶451). In the ethical infrastructure of the family, each "*singular* member" acts so as to take the "*whole* family" as his end. At the same time, the family as a whole has as its end each singleton or singular member. Thus, the family already articulates, though unconsciously and immediately, the logical figure that defines community: a whole dissolved (*aufgelöst*) into a plurality of singularities that are themselves only passing or "vanishing" moments in the movement or "life" that is the truth of the whole.

Hegel argues that the duties of family members to one another and to the whole family do not arise out of contingencies of "feeling or "love." They arise, rather, from the very sense of what it is to be a member of a family. Whether I like my brother or not, as a member of the family I am responsible for burying him. The family concerns the singleton *in his singularity*, not as citizen, scientist, or thinker—the universalized subjects of politics, science, or philosophy—but as this one, this mortal body. At the same time, "in the ethical household, it is not a question of *this* particular husband, *this* particular child, but simply of husband and children generally" (¶457). While a woman loves *this* husband or *this* child, she does so *as his wife* and *as his mother*, that is, in virtue of what is ethically commanded by these universal figures, not in virtue of some contingency of feeling or attachment. The family embodies both the moment of singularity and that of

## SPIRIT, OR TRANSUBSTANTIATED LIFE

universality, but in an unconscious practice rather than a self-conscious resolution.

The exemplary duty of the family lies not in any particular service or assistance to the living, but in the obligation to respiritualize the dead member. In death, the singleton presents the impossible presence of a "pure being," of a singleton that no longer *becomes*. In death the singleton has become a physical thing like any other, subject to "irrational" forces: left on the battlefield, the dead singleton will be eaten by crows and dogs, and his bones will eventually turn to dust. Mortality affords no "consolation and reconciliation" (¶452). The duty of the family, then, lies in transforming this "*course of nature*" into an "action *consciously done*." Through the burial rite, the family "takes on itself the act of destruction," substituting self-conscious action for unconscious processes: "the family keeps away from the dead this dishonouring of him by unconscious appetites and abstract entities, and puts its own action in their place" (¶452). Thus, the divine law of the family prescribes the rituals and practices that will rescue the dead other and respiritualize him "by making him a member of a community." The burial rite transforms the impossible presence of the dead other, revivifying by remembering and, thereby, reinstalling him as a node in a nexus of living relationships.[2]

On the one hand, Hegel has insisted on the self-conscious singleton as the site of the concept's realization. On the other, here, in his account of the funeral rite, he attempts to further his erasure of the stubbornly irreducible difference of the singleton. The "smashing" and "pulverizing" of the singleton's self-standing (¶364), the insistence on the "purity" of the concept and the need to "purify" natural consciousness by tearing him away from his adherence to the sensuous (¶77)—these gestures depend on the erasure of the particularity of the singleton and on the erasure of his mortality that is the mark of his irreducible singularity. Hegel introduces his

---

2. Whatever beliefs the Greeks may have held about immortality—commentators often cite in defense of her adamantine will Antigone's belief that she would see her brother again in the afterlife, but only if the proper rites were performed—in Hegel's analysis the value of the rite accrues not to the dead but to the living. It serves intergenerational community by teaching each and every one to think of himself as a moment in the tide of generations. Thus, death is no longer irrational but consciously appropriated by the community. Failure on the part of the state to respect the law of the family leads to the fouling of the community's sacred spaces, where dogs and birds of prey regurgitate the remains of the unburied son. See Sophocles, *Antigone*, act 1, lines 1010–32; and Hegel, *Phenomenology of Spirit*, ¶474.

analysis of the ethical world of human and divine law by insisting that the self-consciousness under consideration already takes the form of the 'we.' "In the essence we are considering here, singularity [*Einzelheit*] has the meaning of *self-consciousness* in general, not of a particular, contingent consciousness. The ethical substance is, therefore, in this determination the *realized* [*wirkliche*] substance, absolute spirit realized [*realisiert*] in the plurality of existent consciousnesses" (¶447). Each member finds his truth in the actuality of the community—first in the unconscious substance of the family and then in the nation, where the self-conscious self-legislation and reciprocities of citizenship replace the contingencies of tribal "blood-relationships." The singularity of the singleton will thus always already have been superseded in the 'we.' Here Hegel attempts to tear singularity away from particularity and to invest it in a "plurality of consciousnesses," but the fact that the singleton exists only as a member of community in no way compromises the location of self-consciousness in *his* immediacy, in an immediacy that is always of *this one*. Mortality and death, the universal condition, always has a singular face that cannot be erased.

In Hegel's analysis, however, the mortality of the singleton will always already have been superseded by the species in the becoming of generations: "the family ... weds the blood-relationship to the bosom of Earth, to the elemental imperishable individuality" (¶455). Ruthless in his thinking of mortality, Hegel displays a sad and touching faith in the immortality of Earth. This *terrestrial faith* undergirds his claim that the truth of the singleton is the species or the "plurality of consciousnesses." Yet, now, after Hegel, in *our* time, the idea of the species as immortal cannot be maintained, nor can a belief in the immortality of Earth. Hegel cannot erase the stubborn particularity of the mortal human by rendering him a moment of an immortal species.

Hegel's exorcism of death and of the particularity that mortality stubbornly asserts is inextricably intertwined with an equally vexed effort both to exploit and to erase sexual difference. Hegel assigns to women, as the labor that distinguishes them, the care of the body—and, more particularly, the care of the *dead* body. In Sophocles's *Oedipus at Colonus*, Ismene "runs around" dressed like an Athenian cavalryman, attempting to negotiate among the political and religious powers that threaten her family. Antigone, on the other hand, remains by Oedipus's side, attending to his bodily needs. While Ismene transgresses gender norms, Antigone reaffirms the very gender division of labor that Hegel means to install as necessary. In the play bearing her name, Antigone adheres to her fraternal duties, shunning the future and her little sister in favor of the dead brother. I have argued elsewhere that Antigone is no feminist heroine; she reinforces not only the division of life into public and private—state and family—but also the assignment of women to the care of the body and the management of death.[3]

The "alternation of successive generations" in the family, wherein, wave after wave, parents give way to children, "has its enduring basis in the nation" (¶456). The motif of the Bacchanalian revel reappears here with its logic of rest and motion: the nation as the moment of self-sameness seems to stabilize the generational flux of the family, while it is only the generational flux of the family that gives vivacity and actuality to the nation. While the particular consciousness is swept away in the tides of generations, the figure of the citizen persists; but that generalized figure only has vitality in the family member.

The unconscious divine law under the care of women seems to be superseded by the self-conscious, human law of the state:

> Human law in its universal existence is the community, in its activity in general is the manhood [die Männlichkeit] of the community, in its real and effective activity is the government. It *moves* and *maintains* itself by consuming and absorbing into itself the separatism of the Penates, or the separation into independent families presided over by womankind, and by keeping them dissolved in the fluid continuity of its own nature. (¶475)

As any family matures, its "self-contained life ... breaks up and goes beyond itself" (¶458). Parents age as their children grow up, for example, and Hegel lays out clearly the divergent destinies of brother and sister (¶458). The brother "leaves behind" the family and the sister in order to be free for the universal activities of science, politics, and philosophy. He "passes over" from the family's hidden precincts of divine law to the public and self-conscious community of human law. The sister, on the other hand,

---

3. See Mary C. Rawlinson, "Beyond Antigone: Ismene, Gender, and the Right to Life," in *The Returns of Antigone*, ed. T. Chanter and S. Kirkland (Albany: State University of New York Press, 2014), 101–24. See also Rawlinson, *Just Life: Bioethics and the Future of Sexual Difference* (New York: Columbia University Press, 2016), 83–105.

becomes a wife and as such "remains," as the "housewife" (*Vorstand des Hauses*) and the "guardian of divine law" (¶459).[4]

Contrary to critiques leveled by many feminist commentators, however, Hegel does not advance the hegemony of the state at the expense of the family.[5] In Hegel's reading of *Antigone*, both Antigone and Creon are guilty of the hardheadedness and hardheartedness of sticking to one moment of the law at the expense of the other, when both moments prove essential: "neither of the two [laws] is by itself absolutely valid" (¶460). That "stubbornness" costs both the family and the state its future. Such hardheadedness and hardheartedness prove inimical to the life of the community.[6]

Hegel argues not only against one-sidedness, but also against the *confusion* of state and family, which always produces tribalism. Families fight over property and power, and brothers within families fight over the patriarchal seat. The state stabilizes this violence by drawing the brother into the fraternity of citizenship and by nesting the authority of his patriarchal seat within the lateral relations of mutual recognition within the polis.[7]

While it is crucial to keep the state and the family distinct, however, it is equally essential to give each its due: "neither of the two is by itself absolute" (¶460). While the state might take its revenge against the brother who offended its sovereignty, its failure to respect the divine law of the family only results in the pollution of sacred spaces, fouled by the regurgitations

---

4. The translation of *Vorstand des Hauses* as "housewife," rather than Miller's "head of household," seems more in keeping with the actual position of women and the familial and domestic roles Hegel assigns them. The term *head of household* evokes the rights of the *Hausherr*, "the lord of the house," discussed in Kant's *Metaphysics of Morals*. See Immanuel Kant, *The Metaphysics of Morals*, trans. Mary Gregor (1797; Cambridge: Cambridge University Press, 1991), 100. This term implies control over property, personal mobility, and the disposition of children, none of which inheres in the case of women—neither in Antigone's time, nor in Hegel's, nor, indeed, in many places in our own. "Housewife" conveys more clearly that woman is *bound over* to the body and domestic labor.

5. See, e.g., Judith Butler, *Antigone's Claim* (New York: Columbia University Press, 2000); Seyla Benhabib, "On Hegel, Women, and Irony," in *Situating the Self* (New York: Routledge, 1992); and Patricia Jagentowicz Mills, "Hegel's Antigone," in *Feminist Interpretations of G. W. F. Hegel*, ed. P. J. Mills (University Park: Pennsylvania State University Press, 1994), 59–88. Bonnie Honig provides a critical counter to these conventional readings in *Antigone Interrupted* (New York: Cambridge University Press, 2013). My own reading positions Antigone clearly on Hegel's side, as an agent not of feminism, but of fraternity and the gender division of labor. See note 3 of this chapter.

6. Hegel's critique of this stubbornness of head and heart becomes more explicit in his analysis of morality or judging consciousness. See section 4.c.

7. Insofar as it takes patriarchy as the structure of gender subjection, feminism misses its mark. The power of patriarchy, including its power to subjugate women, depends on fraternity. Each man's dominion in his own family as the father depends upon his recognition by his brothers, each one lord of *his* family.

of the beasts that have feasted on the family member (¶¶473–74). The failure to respect the sphere of the family and divine law proves as disastrous as the confusion of the state and the family.

If, on the one hand, Hegel insists on "purifying" the concept of its adherence to the sensuous and the singleton's singular face, he, on the other, nonetheless rejects yet again the Kantian ideal of moral purity, already vigorously criticized in the analyses of virtue and of reason as law-tester. No deed can do justice to both laws or to all the obligations to which a singleton is subject. Do I live up to my obligations at work or do I fly across the country to tend my aged mother? "By the deed [the singleton] becomes guilt" (¶468). This guilt is nothing "external and accidental" but belongs to action itself. "Innocence, therefore, is merely non-action, like the mere being of a stone, not even that of a child" (¶468). Hegel's radical account of the irreducible duality of ethical agency in being claimed by the right undermines not only the metaphysics of the one, but also any proceduralism, however rational, that claims to be adequate to determine ethical judgment. Proceduralism cannot account for the contradiction built into the claims of the ethical, any more than it can articulate the actual shape of ethical agency as it emerges out of the shapes of family life. The ethical substance "has in the ethical powers, a genuine content that takes the place of the insubstantial commandments which healthy reason wanted to give and to know; and thus it gets an intrinsically determinate standard for testing, not the laws, but what is done" (¶461). To decide—from Latin, *decidere*—means to cut off. No action proves adequate to realize all the ethical claims at play, nor can any agent embody simultaneously all the dimensions of ethical life. Neither man nor woman will be sufficient to the human. Although Hegel might simulate the singleton leaving the sister and mother behind in the phenomenological analysis, the trace of the two cannot be erased. The irreducibility of sexual difference will have always already marked the ethical, limning the incompleteness of the ethical subject and his guilt as structural rather than accidental.

Indeed, not only do *both* laws prove essential, the truth of the nation and human law, which supersedes the family only by unfolding from it, in fact lies in the divine law and death. Twice in this chapter Hegel explains the necessity of war to the nation (¶¶455, 475). The reversion to tribalism that threatens the universal bonds of citizenship arises not only in families but also in other forms of association that develop within the community.

"Systems of personal independence [*Selbständigkeit*] and property [*Eigentum*]" and "special and independent associations" related to various forms of interest, employment, or enjoyment—guilds or unions, trade groups, clubs and cultural associations, ethnic or religious affiliations, or social demographics such as fox hunters, bikers, hikers—tend to devolve into tribes or factions that undermine the universality of citizenship and the ability of the state to undertake collective action. These affiliations "tend to isolate themselves... and to become rooted and set in this isolation, thereby breaking up the whole and letting spirit evaporate" (¶455). As natural consciousness follows its own interests and ends, associations arise to compete among themselves and with the state for the singleton's allegiance. For this reason, "government has from time to time to shake them to their core by war." Through conscription and war, the government destabilizes these other associations and "violates their right to independence" (¶455). War not only threatens the independence of property and civil associations; it also makes "the personality of the singleton himself feel the power of the negative" (¶475). Under conscription, the singleton and his associations find their independence canceled by the government, as it displays its power over life and death. The singletons "are made to feel in the task laid on them their lord and master, death" (¶455). In representing himself to himself, the singleton necessarily passed through a "struggle unto death" in his emergence as a self-consciousness in relation to another like himself. That representational thinking, which yielded the abstract figures of master and slave, here gives way to a phenomenology of actual spirit, an account of how the state installs and sustains the community as a fraternity of citizens by laying on each and every one his mortally serious "task." Death "shows itself to be the real power of the community and the force of its self-preservation" (¶455). Hegel, like Hobbes, places at the heart of community the fear of death.

While the state's denial of burial to the dead warrior violates the integrity of the family and the divine law, the dependence of the state on conscription to prevent a lethal tribalism reveals how human law actually depends on divine law—how the mutual recognition among citizens, divested of their particularizing interests and associations, can only take place by passing through the reality of mortality and the state's command over the life of the singleton. "The community therefore possesses the truth and the confirmation of its power in the essence of divine law and in the realm of the nether world" (¶455). The very "negativity" that threatens property, propriety, and personality also "preserves the whole" (¶475). If family is to be "absorbed" into the nation, it nonetheless remains the "element of the nation," the living substance on which the state depends. If divine law is to be "superseded" by human law, then the latter will remain, nonetheless, dependent on the former as "its power and authentication" (¶460). Similarly, if man "leaves behind" the mother and the sister, he nonetheless remains dependent on women's labor to care for the body and respiritualize the dead.

A man "works off" his particularity or "grows into" the universal through his participation in the discursive realms of science and public life, as a scientist finds his truth confirmed by his peers or a manager finds his own agency confirmed in the success of his company. Women, having no access to these domains, remain tied to particularity and to the repetitive, rather than "formative," labor of caring for the body. The "formed thing" speaks back to the slave/worker of his own thought and agency, but women's labor, the care of the body, offers no such reflective moment in Hegel's analysis.

Hegel insists that "in her vocation for singularity and in her pleasure [woman] is immediately universal and remains alien to the singularity of desire" (¶457). She serves the singletons of the family and the singularity of her family, but her relationships are formal, rather than a reflection of the "singularity of desire." Her relationships are at once absolutely universal and absolutely particular. For this reason, Hegel would deny her the "right of desire" (*das Recht der Begierde*). Through his participation in the public domains of citizenship, man separates the moments of singularity and universality that are fused in woman's experience. As a citizen, man embodies "the *self-conscious* force of *universality*," and thereby "purchases the right of *desire*" at the same time that he "preserves his freedom from it" (¶457). In distinguishing the particularity of his natural attachments in the family from his participation in the universal figures of citizenship, man opens up a zone of agency. Woman, conversely, finds herself immediately given in a *universal* command to serve "husbands and children generally," so that the contingent being of this husband and that child "can be replaced by another" (¶457). Hegel gives so little phenomenological attention to maternal love that he grotesquely assumes that a dead child "can be replaced by another." He assumes that maternal love is homogeneous, that a mother loves all her children in the same way. Thus, he is completely blind to the differentiation and specificity of maternal love, as the mother gives each child what it needs and treats each one as irreplaceable.

Woman constitutes the "eternal irony of the community" because she is excluded from the public realms of the nation-state, and yet she is essential to their installation and sustenance (¶475). In her fierce devotion to the singleton, she represents the "enemy" (*das Feind*) against which the community must struggle. If it is the destiny of the young man to go to war, it is the destiny of woman to be there to bury him—just as it was her destiny to give birth to him and to care for him in his old age, as Antigone cared for Oedipus.[8] If "she" is the enemy of community, it, nonetheless, depends entirely on her labor.

The theme of the "struggle against the enemy" has appeared before, and it connects the figure of woman with the mastery of the body, nature, and the sensuous, actual world. In his "struggle against the enemy," the bifurcated unhappy consciousness undertakes not only prayer and worship, but also fasting and other forms of mortification of the flesh in order to free his true spiritual self from the facticities of the body (¶208). Hegel has also described how in his "struggle against the enemy" the man of virtue pits his own purity of heart against the evil of the sensuous actual world (¶386). In each case, consciousness struggles against a moment that is, nonetheless, essential to his own experience—just as the community struggles against "womankind" as an internal and essential "enemy."

Hegel maps the difference between family and state, human and divine law, onto sexual difference. He installs as necessary to spirit a gender division of labor that defines the two realms, a social appropriation of an irreducible biological difference. "Nature, not the accident of circumstance or choice, assigns one sex to one law, and the other to the other law; or, conversely, the two ethical powers themselves give themselves an individual existence and actualize themselves in the two sexes" (¶465). Taking seriously the necessity of the two to the continuation of the species, of the two as the condition for each one—for each singleton—Hegel forever undermines his own metaphysics of the one, while attributing to women's labor and to the

---

8. A good visual image for Hegel's account of sexual difference can be found in David's *Oath of the Horatii*. The sons swear their allegiance to their father and the *patria* on a sheath of swords, while their mother and sisters weep in the corner. Jacques-Louis David, *Le Serment des Horaces*, 1784, Louvre, Paris.

domains of women's experience a philosophical weight he is himself unprepared to measure.[9]

Hegel displays little interest in taking the family as a serious object of phenomenological analysis. He treats the actual relations of the family—husband–wife, parents–children, brother–sister—in a few cursory paragraphs. While admitting that the heterosexual couple embodies the gender division of labor and life's division into public and private spheres upon which spirit depends, Hegel dismisses its importance as an infrastructure of life. The relationship between a man and a woman, he insists, is "not pure," due to an "admixture of singularity"; the family must be subjected to the same logic of purification that has determined the emergence of the concept almost everywhere (¶457). With remarkable naïveté—reflecting the abstractness of his thinking about sexuality, the influence of the Oedipal plays, and, perhaps, his relation to his own sister—Hegel advances the brother–sister relation as "devoid of desire" (¶457). In this "equilibrium of the blood," Hegel asserts, a "recognizing and being recognized" occurs—even for the sister, who is excluded from the mutual recognition of citizenship. Yet, the sister sees herself in the brother only insofar as he is a member of the family, not in his excursion into public space and his participation in the practices of the universal. This "recognition" amounts to no more for the sister than that her duty to her brother is "the highest." Neither women's labor, nor maternal thinking, nor the complex dramas of family life are afforded any serious phenomenological analysis.

Similarly, Hegel offers only a caricature of women's sexuality: on the one hand, the utilities of the wife for whom sexuality and reproduction are a defining duty, and, on the other, the mother's incestuous attachment to her son. In anticipation of psychoanalysis—which will prove no less clueless than Hegel on female sexuality—the Oedipal plays are central in Hegel's

---

9. Luce Irigaray and Elizabeth Grosz have gone further than any other thinkers in thinking through the irreducibility of the two. See, e.g., Luce Irigaray, "The Eternal Irony of the Community," in *Speculum of the Other Woman*, trans. Gillian C. Gill (1974; Ithaca, NY: Cornell University Press, 1985); and Irigaray, *Democracy Begins Between Two*, trans. Kirsteen Anderson (1994; London: Athlone, 2000). On life as becoming and the "proliferation of differences," see Elizabeth Grosz, "Darwin and the Ontology of Life," in *Time Travels* (Durham, NC: Duke University Press, 2005); and Grosz, "Irigaray and Darwin on Sexual Difference: Some Reflections," in *Engaging the World: Thinking After Irigaray*, ed. Mary C. Rawlinson (Albany: State University of New York Press, 2016), 157–72.

account, as if they supplied templates of identity.[10] Once "the youth" crosses the border between family and nation to serve the nation in war, the family, including the sister, is "left behind." At this point, the arena of domestic life goes silent, as if Hegel's paltry paragraphs might be adequate to the history of the family and maternal labor. After all the precise analyses of the various forms of labor through which reason develops itself and discovers its freedom, Hegel can spare barely a few sentences for women's work. Indeed, he offers little more than the mean caricature of virtually incestuous mothers who are angry and disdainful of wisdom. (Perhaps Hegel has in mind the myth of Phaedra's treachery, set in a time and place where the common practice of marrying young women to old men often meant that the man's sons from his previous marriage were nearer her age than he was himself.) However dismissive Hegel might deign to be, he has nevertheless opened up the *two* as the condition of the one, and he has thereby made his metaphysics of the one untenable. There will always already have been two, and one not reducible to the other without remainder.

In spite of himself, Hegel opens up sexual difference and the untilled terrain of women's experience as an essential field of inquiry for metaphysics, epistemology, politics, and ethics. His work calls for a robust phenomenology of women's labor and of maternal love.[11] The failure to think through

---

10. Cf. Sigmund Freud, "Femininity," in *New Introductory Lectures on Psychoanalysis*, vol. 22 of *The Complete Psychological Works of Sigmund Freud* (1933; London: Hogarth, 1964), 112–35. Freud notes at the beginning of his lecture that "throughout history people have knocked their heads against the riddle of the nature of femininity.... Nor will *you* have escaped worrying over this problem—those of you who are men; to those of you who are women this will not apply—you are yourselves the problem" (113). After basing his analysis on what a woman lacks—the penis—and insisting that a girl's ardent attachment to her mother must "end in hate" to make way for her attachment to her father, Freud concludes by noting that while his analysis may generate hostility, he has addressed "women in so far as their nature is determined by their sexual function" (135). He reminds us that "an individual woman may be a human being in other respects as well," and invites the reader to consult the poets, until "science can give you deeper and more coherent information" (135).

11. Although they think through the irreducibility of sexual difference, neither Irigaray nor Grosz develops these phenomenologies further. Carol Gilligan's work on moral development displays the necessity of taking gender into account and indicates what we can learn about human experience from women's experience. See, e.g., Gilligan, *In a Different Voice* (Cambridge, MA: Harvard University Press, 1982). Sara Ruddick's work on maternal thinking demonstrates the difference made by taking women's labor and agency into account in developing concepts in politics and social justice. See, e.g., Ruddick, *Maternal Thinking* (Boston: Beacon, 1989). Fictions of equality distract philosophical attention from sexual difference and obscure the necessary task of articulating the universal forms implicit in women's labor and women's experience. There is a tendency to think that this work has been done or that it precludes attention to race and sexuality or that it stereotypes women. Quite the contrary, only philosophical reflection on the history of women and women's labor as a narrative of human experience can treat the erasure of the two, of difference, in the one.

the formative activities to which women have for millennia been assigned assumes either that these essential and necessary human activities contribute nothing to the universal life of spirit—something that Hegel explicitly denies—or that they are already summarized in man's labor, which Hegel adamantly rejects. It will take time to work through the differences and distances that constitute a woman's labor and her relations with others.[12] In spite of himself, Hegel proves an essential ally in that endeavor. In spite of himself, he has already undermined in advance the hegemony of the one to which, after the *Phenomenology*, he will devote the rest of his philosophical career.

---

The "oppressive stance" against woman and the singularity of which she is the figure produces a new shape of consciousness (¶475). Against the specificity of the family and the nation, there appears the formal figure of the "legal person." "Personality" detaches itself from the "life of the ethical substance," so that the person counts merely as a "unit" (¶480). Once again, the "universal" appears only by "dissolving" itself (*sich auflösen*) into a multiplicity. Here the multiplicity comprises not merely a "plurality of consciousnesses," but a multiplicity of *individuals* (*Individuen*) in which "all count the same, as *persons*," insofar as each one is no more than an instance of the universal (¶477).

This figure of consciousness—a formal 'I' that knows itself as a moment of the universal only by "purifying" itself of the sensuous—repeats the logic of stoicism, skepticism, and the unhappy consciousness (¶¶479–83). "What was for stoicism only the *abstraction* of an *intrinsic* reality is now an *actual world*" (¶479). For the "person," his "self-standing" is no longer merely a thought, the thought of the sensuous as negated; rather, the man of the "state of right" experiences his self-standing concretely by leaving behind the singularity of the family and the nation for the universality of abstract right and the "equality" of persons.[13]

---

12. See, e.g., Mary C. Rawlinson, "Women's Work: Ethics, Home Cooking, and the Sexual Politics of Food," in *The Routledge Handbook of Food Ethics*, ed. Mary C. Rawlinson and Caleb Ward (London: Routledge, 2017), 61–71.

13. The universal domains of science and philosophy do not respect the boundaries of nations any more than those of the family.

The man of the "state of right," however, just because he counts only as the formal unit of a "person," also experiences a "loss of reality" (¶480). Just as skeptical thought appeared only as a negating power, so too here the universality of "person" and "right" depends on purifying the concepts of any content. The "legal person" learns that he is "without any substance" (¶482). Each one is substitutable for the other without a trace, as each one counts only as a bearer of universal rights that are the same for each and all.[14] Yet, to the extent that "person" and "right" are purified of specificity, the emergence of these concepts unleashes "the chaos of spiritual powers which, in their unfettered freedom, become elemental beings raging madly against one another in a frenzy of destructive activity" (¶481). The abstractions of "person" and "right" call for the emergence of a sovereign power, a "lord and master of the world," capable of reining in the powers no longer mastered by tradition and blood. As in the frontispiece to Hobbes's *Leviathan*, the sovereign power comprises a "universal multiplicity of singletons."[15] Yet, to the extent that his embodiment of the will of each and all is merely *formal*, a mere representation of the general will rather than an actual embodiment of it, the sovereign's "power is not the *union* and *harmony* of spirit in which persons would recognize their own self-consciousness" (¶482). Instead, he comes to know himself "in the destructive power he exercises against the self of his subjects, which stands over against him," while his "activities and self-enjoyment" are "monstrous excesses" (¶¶481–82). Confusing the state with a person is just as bad as confusing it with the family.

Like the unhappy consciousness, the man of the "state of right" exists as a bifurcated consciousness. The formality of the legal person, the figure of

---

14. Women have already been explicitly excluded from this logic of the same, and other exclusions of race and class are implicit here too.

15. The British Museum describes the frontispiece, an etching from 1651, as follows:

An allegory of governance and the nature of civil and ecclesiastical authority. A crowned man whose body is made of numerous human bodies, emerges from a mountain at the foot of which is a city, holding a sword in his left hand and a crozier in in [sic] right hand; below is the title inscribed on a tapestry and surrounded by ten framed allegories: castle, crown, cannon, military trophies, battle on the left, church, bishop mitre, thunder, inscribed trident and forks, and assembly of magistrates [on the right].

Image and description at the British Museum Collection Online, www.britishmuseum.org/research/collection_online/collection_object_details/collection_image_gallery.aspx?partid=1&assetid=82477001&objectid=1345512.

universality in which each and all are the same, extrudes from itself all the content of life and is thus lifeless. From here on out, the phenomenological analysis tracks the emergence of infrastructures of life adequate to negotiate this difference between the abstract legal person and the man of flesh and blood.

## 4.B. CULTURE OR ALIENATION: REALIZING THE WE IN THE I

### 4.b.I. The World of Culture: Transforming the Mortal Singleton Into Language, or Leaving the Singleton Behind

> The self knows itself as actual only as a *transcended* self.
> —G. W. F. HEGEL, PHENOMENOLOGY OF SPIRIT, ¶491

> What is not grasped conceptually, *is not*.
> —G. W. F. HEGEL, PHENOMENOLOGY OF SPIRIT, ¶548

In the chapter on culture, Hegel, writing with both hands, means to drive home the truth that, while the universal is only actual in the singleton (¶589), the singleton exists only as a member of the whole. Spirit, the whole, is itself articulated into a plurality of "spiritual masses"—not only the family and the nation, but also religion, commerce, science in the broadest sense of critical thinking and debate, and other forms of civic association. While the analysis of family membership and membership in the nation has already initiated a demonstration that the truth of the singleton is to be a member, the analysis of culture drives the point home through an interrogation of those public institutions through which the differences among the singletons are actually negotiated. Hegel continues to emphasize the violence of this working-through. In the market and government, men struggle over wealth and power, just as they vie with one another in debate in order to claim authority over truth.

Moreover, Hegel's analysis of culture explicitly takes up the question of language, both as the site of the singleton's actualization and as an institution that transcends him so as to complete his transubstantiation. Hegel insists that the singleton "comes into existence as such" only through the "force [*Kraft*] of speech" (¶508). The singleton's truth turns out to be what he has said and done, not what he *is*.¹⁶ Thus is substance "humiliated" (*erniedrigt*) (¶532) and the immediacy of experience rendered a "vanishing moment."

The phenomenological analysis began with just that self-certainty of immediacy, which, under the interrogation, can no longer sustain itself or 'say what it means.' From the beginning, Hegel has identified truth with the adequacy of the singleton's narrative of his experience to that experience. Thus, from the beginning, the truth of experience lay not in immediacy but in its transubstantiation, in the transformation of substance into subject, experience into language. The analysis has revealed not only that the singleton's truth and reality lie not in himself but in his membership in various communities, but also that his actuality within his own life history is not in his immediate being, but in his words and deeds.

Though earlier chapters of Hegel's text contain historical referents, no other chapter so directly tracks a specific historical period as the line of conceptual development. In the transition from the monarchy of Louis XIV, through the Enlightenment, to the French Revolution, Hegel finds the working-through of the difference between the singleton and the universal and the emergence of an adequate concept of freedom or self-standing (*Selbständigkeit*). What self-consciousness has attained up to the starting point of this movement—both in history and in the analysis—remains fragile. The world of culture "still contains the aspect of being a spiritual animal kingdom in which [singletons], amid confusion and mutual violence, cheat and struggle over the essence of the actual world" (¶537). The historical unfolding of self-consciousness seems poised to "relapse," so that the singleton would be condemned to repeat the same struggles he has already endured. Only another passage through the figure of mastery and slavery and another experience of the terror of death will

---

16. As the analysis of reason demonstrated, "action is the category of the 'I.'" The deed, though, as the analysis of moral consciousness will demonstrate, is itself a "vanishing moment." Language, however, endures as the institutional site of membership. Recall Derrida's claim that 'my-death' is structurally necessary to saying 'I am': that is, for my utterance to make sense, it must be possible for another to displace me from the speaking position and to adopt the utterance as his own. Language, from the very beginning, embodies the phenomenon of displacement that initiated the struggle from which self-consciousness and the forms of mastery and slavery emerged. Speaking or writing, putting experience into language, is, thus, the paradigmatic deed. See Jacques Derrida, *Speech and Phenomena*, trans. David B. Allison (1967; Evanston, IL: Northwestern University Press, 1973), 96. Derrida's essay is on Husserl, but he cites his plan to take up this theme in relation to Hegel (77), as he does the next year in the essay "Différance."

SPIRIT, OR TRANSUBSTANTIATED LIFE

prove adequate to keep the unfolding (*Aufhebung*) of both concept and self-consciousness driving forward.

### ALIENATION: THE PRODUCTION OF THE WORLD OF CULTURE AND THE MAN OF CULTURE

In the state of right or law (*Rechtszustand*), the singleton has been alienated from himself absolutely in the purely formal figure of the "person of right," a figure in which his determinate identity is not reflected. The tyrant knows himself only in the absolute power that he exerts over his subjects, and he makes no place for them to find themselves reflected in him. This "absolute person" "stands over against all the rest," in his legitimate violence and power over life and death.[17] While the "lord and master" knows himself only in his "complete supremacy" over his subjects and his power of "laying waste of everything," in fact he is an empty, merely formal universal that does not provide any infrastructures of experience through which his subjects might find themselves as members of a whole: "his power is not the unanimity of spirit [*die Einigkeit des Geistes*] in which persons would recognize their own self-consciousness" (¶482). His subjects exist only as objects of his will and are not reflected in him as self-conscious, willing beings in their own right. The power of the lord of the world produces not the one-mindedness of spirit, in which each knows himself to be a member of the whole, but an "atomicity" of discrete persons, which in its "rigidity" impairs the fluidity of spirit and the continuity of each with the

---

17. Hegel criticizes this "lord and master of the world" for misunderstanding his personhood, which can be "true only as a universal multiplicity of single individuals" (¶481). Hegel's implicit reference here to the Hobbesian sovereign, who is represented in the frontispiece to Leviathan as comprising a multiplicity of individuals, indicates that he is not criticizing Hobbes's idea of sovereignty or monarchy but the tyranny of ancient empires. In an earlier essay, "The Positivity of the Christian Religion," Hegel remarks, "the despotism of the Roman emperors had chased the human spirit from the face of the earth." Quoted in Michael N. Forster, *Hegel's Idea of a Phenomenology of Spirit* (Chicago: University of Chicago Press, 1989), 59–60. The volume also includes the text of Hegel's early essay as an appendix. Neither Forster nor Pinkard—in the latter's discussion of the "form of Roman life" (Terry Pinkard, *Hegel's Phenomenology: The Sociality of Reason* [Cambridge: Cambridge University Press, 1994], 146–50)—pays sufficient attention to the theme of violence in Hegel's analysis of the state of right, although Pinkard does note that the world of abstract right is held together by force (Pinkard, *Hegel's Phenomenology*, 334). The extremity of Hegel's language in this passage emphasizes the extremity of the violence in this formation of life, where "ruin and devastation" prevail. This is the world of the stoic, who, like the slave, negates existence in favor of pure thought in an effort to escape his misery, or of the skeptic, for whom nothing exists except the negative power of thought. These passages confirm the extreme violence that has proven essential throughout to the unfolding of self-consciousness and the concept.

others. "The personality of the state of right [*die rechtliche Persönlichkeit*] thus learns rather that it is without any substance, since the alien content makes itself authoritative in it, and does so because that content is the reality of such personality" (¶482). The state of right provides no adequate concept of membership, of the belonging of each to the whole, nor any material infrastructure or institutions to sustain it.

The work of culture negotiates this difference between the specificity of the singleton and a universal will in which each one would find himself reflected. The institutions and practices of culture achieve the appropriation of nature and the transformation of substance into subject. This is the first sense in which culture is a world of alienation: "through culture . . . the individual [*das Individuum*] acquires standing and reality. His true *original nature* and substance is the alienation of himself as spirit from his *natural* being" (¶489).[18] Through his cultural productions and his participation in the institutions of culture, the singleton metamorphoses into an individuality, no longer an atom but existing in continuity with others in the community of spirit, as manifest in government, the market, and language. "This individuality [*diese Individualität*] cultures itself [*bildet sich*] into what it *in itself* [*an sich*] is, and only thereby *is* it *in itself* and a real existence" (¶489).[19] Through the work of culture (*Bildung*), the immediacy that the singleton first appeared to be reappears, no longer as a natural being or an element of nature, but as result or product, artificial or man-made.

Thus, the world of culture, unlike sensuous immediacy, is already a "spiritual essence [*geistiges Wesen*]. It is in itself the intercalation [*die Durchdringung*] of being and individuality, and its existence is the *work* of self-consciousness" (¶484). Just as the "formed thing" reflected back to the slave his own freedom of thought, culture too embodies a history of agency.[20] In

---

18. Note that the "original" nature of the individual, the transubstantiated singleton, lies in the work of culture, not in his natural existence. The individual comes into being as a fabricated being.

19. Miller translates *bildet sich* as "moulds itself by culture." The English verb *to culture*, however, exactly captures Hegel's sense. Culture "maintains [the singleton in] conditions suitable for growth." See entry for "Culture," Oxford English Dictionary.

20. The etymology of *agency* proves pertinent here: in Middle English it means "force capable of acting on matter," from the Latin *agens*, "something capable of producing an effect," from the present participle of *agere*, "to drive (cattle), ride (a horse), be in motion, do, perform, transact." *Agere* stems from an Indo-European root meaning "to drive," and it is related to the Greek *ágein*, "to lead or carry off." Agency reflects not only the power of thought to fabricate a world, transforming substance into spirit, but also Hegel's identification of spirit with motion, as over against the fixity of determinate thought-positions. ("Agency," Merriam-Webster's Dictionary.)

this way, culture first appears to self-consciousness as a world *already given*, into which he is thrown. This is the second sense of alienation. "Although this world has come into being through individuality [*Individualität*], it is for self-consciousness an alienated world which has the form of a fixed and solid reality over against it" (¶489). The man of culture finds himself situated in an alien world made by others.

"At the same time," however, "he sets about making it his own" (¶490). On the one hand, culture cultures him; it educates him and shapes who he is, integrating him into the very practices and institutions of the world that at first seemed alien to him. On the other hand, through his own cultural productions, he appropriates the world of culture and "makes it his own." Precisely because the world appears alien to him, he "must now take possession" of it (¶488). This "externalizing" of himself constitutes the third sense of alienation. His labor, and above all his speech, brings the world of culture into being, even as it realizes his own essence or what he is in truth.

The individual finds himself competing with others in the domains of wealth and power. This activity produces the modern free market economy, as well as modern forms of state power. Wealth itself is "ensouled"; it is "only for itself, develops an *intrinsic being of its own*, . . . [and] receives within itself a spirit of its own" (¶515). As Terry Pinkard argues, the productivity of the market "creates a kind of common capital on which individuals may draw in order to satisfy their own desires and needs; it requires only of the individual that he cultivate his talents and acquire traits that can be useful in such a society. Each may satisfy himself only by making himself useful to others; each thus is socialized into the form of life that constitutes modern life."[21] Hegel recognizes the market as the primary nongovernmental, nonreligious institution through which singletons become individuals or through which the differences among them are negotiated and community produced. Just as the "man of the world" thought he was acting only to serve

---

21. Pinkard, *Hegel's Phenomenology*, 310. Pinkard gives an excellent analysis of the influence of Adam Smith on Hegel's thinking. As Pinkard notes, what the debates between Smith and the other Scottish economists "turned out to be about was the historical development of a new set of modern social institutions—the free market foremost among them—that both expressed and supported [the] emerging idea of independent individualism itself" (111). Hegel "is not arguing for international commerce as a pragmatic solution to achieve some fixed end. His argument is that the creation of a system of international commerce is necessary in order to maintain civil society as a genuine ethical end—that is to maintain a form of life in which freedom can be realized and in which modern life's self-understandings are made rationally sustainable" (320).

his own self-interest but instead produced works and institutions that benefited the community, so too, by participating in the market, each through his actions serves all the others as well. In his enjoyment of his wealth, the man of culture comes to know himself in his own particularity, but "wealth produces universal labor and enjoyment for all" (¶494). As usual, self-consciousness exhibits an inversion of his own intentions. Each one means to work just for himself, but he "is at the same time working for all and all are working for him" (¶494). His participation in the market converts his particular action into something universal.

The participation of the man of culture in the institutions of state power also converts his particular will into a moment of the universal. Unlike the "lord of the world," the sovereign of the modern nation-state understands himself as the embodiment of a general will. The famous dictum of Louis XIV, "*L'ètat, c'est moi*," depends not merely on the power of tyranny but on the recognition of the governed. Thus, as Hobbes argues in the *Leviathan*, each subject rightly finds himself alienated from the particularity of his own will in submitting to the universal will of the sovereign.[22] Under sovereignty, the "person" can no longer be rendered in the mere formality of abstract right; rather, the nobleman who serves his king undertakes "sacrifices" and "renunciations" and has a determinate content. His nobility consists in "the heroism of *service*, the *virtue* which sacrifices the singleton [*das einzelne Sein*] to the universal, thereby bringing into existence the *person*, one who voluntarily renounces possessions and enjoyment, who acts and is effective in the interests of the ruling power" (¶503). This renunciation or alienation from the particularity of the subject's will repeats the logic of the "struggle unto death" that produced self-consciousness and the relation of master and slavery. Yet again, Hegel insists that the development of self-consciousness depends on a moment in which life is risked absolutely, but in such a way that life is spared, so that everything that was lost in the risk can be recovered and made his own—an "acquired property" (*erworbene Eigentum*).[23] "The sacrifice of existence which happens in the service of the state is indeed

---

22. Hegel, however, is hardly as sanguine as Hobbes about the capacity of sovereignty to secure peace. Hegel's analysis follows the evolution of sovereignty to revolution, from Louis XIV to the Terror.

23. Cf. ¶28: "This history of the cultural development of the world. . . . This past existence is the already acquired property of universal spirit which constitutes the substance of the individual, and hence appears externally to him as his inorganic nature." This history of agency, strictly speaking, exists only in the institutions and artifacts of the world of culture.

## SPIRIT, OR TRANSUBSTANTIATED LIFE

complete when it has gone as far as death"; however, the dead vassal can no longer recognize his king (¶506). Just as in the "struggle unto death" that yielded master and slave, it is here necessary that the renunciation not have "gone as far as death" (¶506). The "true sacrifice" proves to be one "in which he surrenders himself as completely as in death, yet in this renunciation he no less preserves himself" (¶507). Life is put at risk so that it can be transubstantiated, transformed into spirit.

Through the vassal's renunciation or alienation of his own will, "the state power is at the same time raised to the position of having a self of its own" (¶507). Both the elevation of the monarch and the subjection of the vassal take place in language. The monarch represents the extremity of singularity; he is the absolute singleton. Thus, "his own proper *name*" expresses his power, for "it is in the *name* alone that the *difference* of the singleton from all the others is not merely *meant*, but instead is made actual by all. In the name, the singleton *counts* as a pure singleton, not only in his own consciousness, but in the consciousness of everyone else" (¶511). The proper name reflects the monarch's existence as a "unique atom" and a "universal power."

The power of the name, the monarch's power, however, derives from the language of flattery. The power of the "unlimited monarch" depends on his courtiers constantly "telling" him who he is. Unlike the lord of the world, whose subjects were mere atoms at his mercy, the absolute monarch is only established as the absolute singleton through the self-alienation of his nobles, who, through flattery, divest themselves of their own "intrinsic being," their own "thinking," their own 'I.' The nobles, far from being discrete atoms, participate together in the language of flattery and form a community around the king that sustains him. The king, "this particular singleton, thereby knows himself, *this* singleton, to be the universal power, knows that the nobles not only are ready to serve state power [*Staatsmacht*], but that they position themselves around the throne as ornaments, and that they are always *telling* him who sits on it what he is" (¶511). The nobles recognize the king and, thereby, establish his absolute power, but they do so only at the expense of their own agency.

This self-alienation produces a "disrupted consciousness," whose language of flattery is "the fulfilled language and the true existent spirit of the entire world of culture" (¶520). In his self-alienation and alienation from the natural world, this dirempted consciousness produces a world of "pure culture," in which each moment is subject to the logic of "absolute and universal inversion [*absolute und allgemeine Verkehrung*]" (¶521). In sacrificing himself to establish the absolute power of the king, the nobleman demonstrates, rather, his own independence and the dependence of the king on him. "Looked at formally, everything is *outwardly* the inversion of what it is *for itself*" (¶521). All the constitutive moments "exercise a universal justice [*allgemeine Gerechtigkeit*] on one another." "True spirit" exists as the complex of independent moments in this "universal justice," as the "universal *talk* and disrupting *judgment*" that would undermine the independence of each moment (¶521). This "nihilistic game" of "judging and talking" is, therefore, what is "true and invincible" (¶521). While the "honest singleton" of law-making reason thoughtlessly took one moment and now another to be the essential moment, ignorant and unconscious of his contradictions, the disrupted consciousness of flattery is, rather, the "consciousness of inversion, indeed, of absolute inversion." In him, the moments are brought together by thought through his judging and talking, and he exists, then, in his "witty [*geistreich*] speech." This "vain" consciousness "knows, not only how to pass judgment on and chatter about everything, but how to give witty expression to the essential moments of reality, as to the determinations set by judgment, in their *contradiction*; and this contradiction is their truth" (¶526). For this vain self, power and wealth are the "highest purposes of his exertions." State power and wealth are the "real acknowledged powers," but by exercising power and acquiring wealth, this vain self effects another inversion. In so doing, he demonstrates that he knows power and wealth to be "selfless" and that "*he* is the power over them" (¶526). In fact, not power and wealth, but his "witty talk" proves to be his "highest interest, and the truth of the whole." His "witty talk" negotiates the contradictions among the moments, and through it he "develops into a spiritual self that is of truly universal worth." This wit, "determined neither by reality nor by thought," exists only as language (¶526).

### LANGUAGE: LEAVING LIFE BEHIND ONCE AND FOR ALL

From the beginning, language has been the main theme of the *Phenomenology*. "The force [*Kraft*] of spirit is only as great as its expression

## SPIRIT, OR TRANSUBSTANTIATED LIFE

[*Äusserung*], its depth only as deep as it dares to spread out and lose itself in its exposition" (¶10). The method of phenomenology consists just in testing self-consciousness, the site of the "little research," to see if he can say what he means. Can he give voice to who he is in truth? Is the narrative of his experience adequate to that experience? Over and over again, self-consciousness fails the test, but each failure produces a new and more adequate shape, which in turn will be found wanting, and so on. The analysis can terminate only in a narrative that proves "absolute," insofar as there is "nothing other to it," nothing that remains unarticulated in it, nothing that is *left behind*.

The analysis has revealed that self-conscious exists only in language, only as a *transcended* self.[24] Only language can embody the identity of the pure universal 'I,' which persists and transcends all determinate content, with the particularity of the singleton in the flux of becoming. Self-consciousness exists only "for others," as in being "*perceived* or *heard*," but this being heard or perceived passes away. So, the "real existence [of self-consciousness] is just this: as a self-conscious now, as a real existence, it is *not* a real existence, and through this vanishing it *is* a real existence. This vanishing is thus itself at once its abiding" (¶508). The same logic of determinate negation that first appeared in the analysis of sensuous certainty and the 'now' is recapitulated here in the 'I.' Just as the 'now' preserved itself as the form of experience through the negations of each determinate 'now,' so too the pure 'I' of language and the concept maintains itself through the negation of the determinate contents that make the singleton this one and not the others. The opposition between the universal and particular that first appears in sensuous certainty reappears here, not as a mere opposition but as a belonging-together (*Zusammenhang*) effectively negotiated by language.

In every other "externalization" (*Entäusserung*), self-consciousness remains "sunk in some actual existence," as if the 'I' could be identified with some determinate, passing moment (¶508). Self-consciousness is "reflected back into itself from its actions, as well as from its physiognomic

---

24. In the ethical world—the first formation of spirit—the linguistic being of the singleton is already apparent. Action depends on the articulation of a law or the utterance of a command (¶508).

expression, and *leaves behind* unsouled [*lässt . . . entseelt liegen*] this incomplete [*unvollständige*] existence, in which there is always at once too much as too little" (¶508, my emphasis). Too much content, but too little concept. Too much content, because any determinate moment makes available an infinity of content. And too little concept, because no determinate moment on its own can reflect the mobility and generativity of the concept or the mobile logic of the whole system of moments. The 'I' of self-consciousness constantly transcends its own determinate contents, *leaving them behind* in the flux of becoming as moments that are no longer animate.

Indeed, Hegel here demonstrates that spirit *is* language, insofar as language supplies a *"middle term"* that mediates the opposition of the "two rigid, unyielding sides" of the pure 'I' and the determinate singleton (¶509). This mediation realizes the logic of recognition that first appeared as a mere form or was merely represented in the struggle unto death and the slave ideologies: each side knows itself only in its opposition to or alienation from the other, both in being heard by the other and in being each one a divided self. "Through this mediation spirit comes to exist *qua* spirit as a reality" (¶509). Hegel continues to emphasize the theme of purification here. This mediation yields a "pure self," and the opposing moments are *concepts*, not beings. The transubstantiation of the singleton has already occurred.

The logic of appearance, the "arising and passing away that never arises or passes away," turns out to be the truth of self-consciousness, who exists only as this "vanishing" (¶47). Hegel means, once and for all, to *leave behind* the substance of the singleton by transforming him into a linguistic being, who exists only as something *conceptual* or as thought.[25] Hegel's terrestrial faith, his belief in the immortality of Earth, sustains his belief in the immortality of appearance and of the genus life. The mortality of the singleton does not trouble this faith, for if the universal is only actual in the singleton (¶589), the eternal tide of generations will always assure its realization despite the death of the singleton. The truth of the singleton is to be the site of this complex process of mediation or alienation through language; thus, the universal is actualized, but in such a way as to transcend the specificity and mortality of each and all. What persists is the logic of mediation, and the death of the singleton leaves no trace.

25. Hearing is thinking as much as speech. To hear is to think and to be heard is to be thought.

## SPIRIT, OR TRANSUBSTANTIATED LIFE

But perhaps the singleton and his mortality can no more be *left behind* than the sister can.[26] Hegel's own method stipulates that nothing can be left behind unarticulated in the 'I' that produces the conceptual narrative. Perhaps the irreducible specificity of mortal life—for the reality of death is always *my* death and never an abstraction—resists and always exceeds the grasp of the concept.[27] Perhaps, in the end, Hegel will be able to represent the closure of the phenomenological project—"that point at which knowledge need no longer go beyond itself because nothing is other to it," nothing still unarticulated in the concept—only through violent acts of erasure. Woman and the mortal singleton have already been erased. Hegel will complete this erasure of specificity through the erasure of the irreducibility of the signature in art. These erasures not only violate the method; they leave a trace and give to the universal a singular face.

Hegel cannot have it both ways: he cannot insist on the determinate, as a necessary and ineffaceable moment, while at the same time installing a purified 'I' that exists only conceptually in language. Indeed, his own logic requires that he maintain the incommensurate difference as irreducible, rather than resolve it in a purified 'I.' Over and over again he employs the most violent language in his attempt to "pulverize" the singleton and to "humiliate" and "betray" substance. He attempts to tear the concept and language away from their adherence to the sensuous, but this would produce only the sort of empty abstraction that he himself decries.

---

26. In these passages, Hegel uses very similar language to that he employed to describe the brother's departure from the family, leaving the sister behind. Here he uses the formulation *liegen lassen* and there *verlassen*, which both convey the sense of a departure that leaves something behind.

27. Death may be universal, but it always wears a singular face, as Ivan Ilych so painfully learns:

> The syllogism... "Caius is a man, men are mortal, therefore Caius is mortal," had always seemed to him correct as applied to Caius, but certainly not as applied to himself. That Caius—man in the abstract—was mortal, was perfectly correct, but he was not Caius, not an abstract man, but a creature quite, quite separate from all others.... Had Caius kissed his mother's hand like that, and did the silk of her dress rustle for Caius? Had he rioted like that when the pastry at school was bad?... "Caius really was mortal, and it was right for him to die; but for me, little Vanya, Ivan Ilych, with all my thoughts and emotions, it's altogether a different matter. It cannot be that I ought to die. That would be too terrible."

Leo Tolstoy, *The Death of Ivan Ilych*, trans. Rosemary Edmonds (1886; New York: Signet Classics, 1960), 131–32.

Death effaces the singularity of the singleton, just as Hegel argued in his meditation on the dead brother. After death, after a "long succession of disparate experiences, [the singleton] brings himself together in a single fulfilled shape, and has unfolded himself out of the unrest of the accidents of life into the calm of simple universality" (¶452).

Hegel himself demonstrates that the essence of being is "two-ing" (*Entzweiten*). Any unity immediately sunders itself into its constituent moments. Hegel's own attempt to install absolute knowing, a logic of the one, a master narrative, will always already have been undone by the sister and the irreducible two of sexual difference. It will always already have been forestalled by the reality of the mortal singleton, by the ineradicable difference between his determinate being and the pure 'I' of language. And, as we will see, it will always already have been deferred indefinitely by the ineffaceable difference of the artist's style, which cannot be subsumed by a cultural form or erased in an abstract concept.

### 4.b.II. Enlightenment: The Struggle of Reason with Faith Over Truth

Just as men vie with one another over wealth and power, so too they struggle violently against one another over truth. The historical period of the Enlightenment consists in just such a contestation, in which reason or "pure insight" attacks religious faith as a form of superstition. Pure insight demands of religious consciousness, indeed of *"every consciousness: be for yourselves* what you all are *in yourselves—reasonable"* (¶537). Just as skepticism subjected every certainty to the shattering effects of the negative power of thought, so reason assaults faith in order to destroy the confidence of its belief and to force the man of faith to yield those beliefs to the command to "be reasonable." Faith and pure insight appear to exclude each other and to exist in a ferocious and irresolvable antagonism. At this point in the phenomenological analysis, however, dear reader, you should know better than to accept that either the man of faith or the man of reason is saying what he means. Indeed, you should already be anticipating how the logic of inversion will demonstrate that each one exists as himself only in and through a relation to the other. Moreover, faith will have its own reason, just as reason will turn out to be a kind of faith.

Hegel introduces both faith and reason as forms of language. Faith appears as a form of consciousness whose object is the *"absolute being"* of the "beyond" or "supersensible world." The man of faith finds himself alienated from this "beyond," at the same time that it appears to him as his truth. In the language of prayer and praise, he articulates both his submission to this beyond and his exile from it, while also renouncing his attachment

## SPIRIT, OR TRANSUBSTANTIATED LIFE

to the actual world. He *professes* his faith and *confesses* himself before the absolute being. Only through these professions and confessions do his actions of penance, ritual, obedience, and service become spiritualized and his own. Like the unhappy consciousness, however, the man of faith does not own this spiritualization as his own, nor does he recognize in the community of the church a genuinely universal self-consciousness; rather, "the realm of pure thought necessarily remains a beyond of his actual world" (¶534). The man of faith knows his truth to be thought, but that thought is not taken up as his own self-conscious concept—he only adopts it as a content or object of his faith.

Reason or pure insight also comes on the scene as language. Alluding to the culture of the French *salons*, Hegel identifies pure insight with "blather" (*Faselei*), "witty chatter" (*geistreiche Geschwätze*), and "the vanity of witty judgments" (*die Eitelkeit des geistreichen Beurteilens*). The man of reason or pure insight "has his substance and support solely in the spirit which exists *qua* judging and discussing" (¶540). Thus, the man of reason exists only insofar as there is something before him to be judged: "pure insight only manifests its own peculiar activity so far as it opposes itself to faith" (¶540). While faith is a form of consciousness, reason or pure insight appears as self-consciousness and has no content other than its own conceptual activity (¶548). "Pure insight is not only the certainty of self-conscious reason that it is all truth: it *knows* that it is" (¶536). Skepticism, as well as theoretical and practical idealism, "are inferior shapes compared with that of *pure insight* and its diffusion, of the *Enlightenment*," insofar as pure insight has no object, for nothing is alien to it (¶541). Reason or pure insight knows itself to be absolute, and it knows that any object is only a moment of its own movement.

The man of reason opposes himself to the man of faith, condemning faith as a "tissue of superstitions, prejudices, and errors" (¶542). Through the deceptions of the priesthood, which would preserve all insight as its own, "the general mass of people is befooled." "Naïve" and "unreflective," the multitude falls prey not only to the priesthood but also to the despotism with which the priestly caste conspires. "From the stupidity and confusion of the people brought about by the trickery of priestcraft, despotism, which despises both, draws for itself the advantage of undisturbed domination and the fulfillment of its desires and caprices, but is itself at the same time this dullness of insight, the same superstition and error" (¶542). Thus, the man of reason's opposition to the man of faith is not the same as his attack on the priesthood or despotism; rather, he opposes the man of faith only in order to rescue him from his naïve superstition, through which he is subjugated and alienated from his own rationality, self-consciousness, and identity with all reality. The man of reason recognizes himself in the man of faith, who is like himself pure self-conscious activity, but his recognition is only implicit and as yet unrealized.

By the time the man of faith realizes he is under assault, it is already too late. Hegel likens the "diffusion" of the Enlightenment to a "perfume" or a "penetrating infection, which does not make itself noticeable beforehand" (¶544). The general mass of naïve consciousness cannot resist the spread of the "disease," and the consciousness of faith realizes only too late that he has already been "infected." Faith's "struggle" against the Enlightenment only "betrays that the infection has occurred. The struggle is too late, and every remedy adopted only aggravates the disease" (¶545). Just as nothing could withstand skepticism or the negative power of thought, so too faith finds itself powerless against the diffusion of the Enlightenment through all the members of its body.

But the man of reason does the man of faith an injustice. The man of faith, in his very struggle with reason, demonstrates that he is himself like the man of reason, also capable of pure insight and, thus, a *reasonable* being even if only implicitly. Yet, the man of reason trivializes faith, and he fails to appreciate its truth. While the man of reason takes himself in the movement of his thought to be absolute, the man of faith already knows, if only implicitly, that his own truth does not lie in his existence as a singleton, but in his membership in the whole—a whole represented by the absolute being of the beyond toward which his faith orients him. Moreover, in his prayers and professions as well as his obedience, good works, and acts of contrition, celebration, or penance, the man of faith in fact produces the universal community that transcends him and in which the absolute is realized (¶550). The man of reason acts as if the absolute being that is the object of faith were a material thing, as if the man of faith identified the absolute being with a piece of wood or a bit of dough. However, for the man of faith the crucifix that he venerates or the wafer that he consumes *have already been spiritualized* and do not exist as mere sensuous things (¶553). Similarly, when the man of reason accuses the man of faith of basing his faith on historical events and the "fortuitous" preservation of "particular historical evidences," he misunderstands religious narratives as texts to be compared to the accuracy of newspapers, as if they related actual events in the ordinary, sensible world (¶554). Faith may be guilty of representational thinking in that it attempts to represent the spirituality of pure thought to itself in an image, but its only object is that pure thought or spirit of which it knows itself to be *in truth* a member. The man of faith has already transcended his attachment to "perishable things" and to his own mortal being as a singleton. In the man of faith "it is spirit itself which bears witness to itself, both in the *inwardness* of the *singular [einzelne]* consciousness and through the *universal presence* of everyone of faith in it" (¶554).[28] Thus, the truth of the singleton as a member of the community of spirit is already realized in the man of faith, even though he is not yet self-conscious of it.

At the same time, by accusing the man of faith of believing in a reality that is merely his own creation, a figment of his imagination, the man of reason condemns himself; his own truth is precisely that everything that can be said to *be* is produced in the movement of thought. The pure insight of the man of reason "therefore seeks to overcome [*geht also darauf... aufzuheben*] every kind of independence other than that of self-consciousness, whether it be the independence of what is actual or being-*in-itself*, and to make it a concept" (¶536). Worked over by reason, everything becomes a moment of thought: "what is not rational has no *truth*, or, what is not grasped conceptually, *is not*" (¶548). Like the man of faith, the man of reason gives himself his own object.

The diffusion of the Enlightenment merely replaces the adored absolute being of the man of faith with nothing other than the pure insight of reason itself. Having taken it upon himself to smash the idols of religion, the man of pure insight produces "the new serpent of wisdom raised on high for adoration" (¶545). Pure insight erects a vacuous *Être suprême*, the void

---

28. As Jean Hyppolite points out, Hegel "subtly distinguishes" faith from both religion and the unhappy consciousness. The man of religion knows the absolute to be manifest in his community, while, for the man of faith, the absolute "stands contraposed to actuality—and therefore it is only a faith." On the other hand, the man of faith knows himself to be a moment of the absolute, while belief for the unhappy consciousness exists only as a "pious fervor." Jean Hyppolite, *Genesis and Structure of Hegel's* Phenomenology of Spirit, trans. Samuel Cherniak and John Heckman (1946; Evanston, IL: Northwestern University Press, 1974), 420. As Hegel remarks of the unhappy consciousness, "his thinking as such is no more than the chaotic jingling of bells, or a mist of warm incense, a musical thinking that does not get as far as the concept" (¶217).

or thought thinking itself as pure and without content.[29] Reason grasps the ontological difference between beings and absolute being, and it attributes all determination to the side of the actual world, while the absolute remains empty. The man of reason "puts himself and his finite riches in their proper place" (¶557). He is not empty like the absolute but "rich only in singularity [*Einzelheit*] and limits" (¶557).

Indeed, the man of reason knows the "singularity [*Einzelheit*] in general of consciousness and all being, a singularity excluded from absolute being" (¶558). He embraces as a positive truth "that every consciousness is *absolutely certain* that it *is*, and that there are other real things outside it" (¶558). In this way, the man of reason has returned to the certainty of sense-certainty, but not as an immediacy; rather, he takes it to be a result of his own experience and rational activity. The sensuous, actual world is related to the beyond of the absolute both positively and negatively. The man of reason works over the sensuous according to the distinction between being-in-itself and being-for-another, so that the actual world has become the absolute as it appears and a result of his own operation.

Everything for the man of reason exists both in itself and for another. "Everything is at the mercy of everything else, now lets itself be used by others and is *for them*, and now, so to speak, stands again on its hind legs, is stand-offish towards the other, is for itself, and uses the other in its turn" (¶560). Thus, the man of reason installs *utility* as the essence or truth of being; everything exists for him, "for his pleasure and delight." This utility, for the man of reason, becomes the essence of man in general:

> Just as everything is useful to man, so man is useful too, and his vocation is to make himself a member of the group, of use for the common good and serviceable to all. The extent to which he looks after his own interests

---

29. In commenting on this "wonderfully vacuous title that the Enlightenment gave to [God]," Pinkard notes Hegel's sarcasm in criticizing "pure insight" for holding to "the idea that what counts as authoritative is only that which a detached individual (detached ironically or by listening to the voice of reason) can come to hold," and its attempts to "reassure itself that it is not an empty practice as it accuses 'faith' of being." Pinkard, *Hegel's Phenomenology*, 393n81. Though the critique of "pure insight" focuses, as Pinkard argues, on the deists of the Enlightenment, Hegel alludes directly to the French Revolution both here and in the analysis of absolute freedom and terror that follows. Thanks to Hébert, the leader of the Enragés, "the Commune extoled the cult of reason and the Supreme Being; in the Cathedral of Notre Dame it held a ceremony wherein a Goddess of Reason, all too present in the flesh, was worshipped." André Maurois, *A History of France*, trans. Henry L. Binsse (1949; London: Methuen, 1960), 315.

must also be matched by the extent to which he serves others, and so far as he serves others, so far is he taking care of himself; one hand washes the other. (§560)

Like the man of the world opposed to virtue, who seemed to be pursuing his own interests, so too the man of reason believes he relies on the singularity of his own reason. And, just as the actions of the man of the world turned out to actually advance the welfare of others, the truth of the man of reason is that, by *being reasonable*, he necessarily demonstrates himself to be a moment of a community of others, where each is bound up with the others in relations of mutual utility.

In his opposition to faith, the man of reason renders the actions of the man of faith *inutile*. The man of faith's acts of renunciation and sacrifice prove "purposeless" (*unzweckmässig*). He does not give away all his possessions nor renounce all his pleasures; he only relinquishes "a small portion" of them, so that his action is only a "*sign*" (*Zeichen*) and merely "represents" (*vorstellt*) true sacrifice and renunciation (§§569–70). These actions, though "single performances," have for the man of faith a universal significance and realize his belonging to and obedience to the universal being of the beyond. The man of reason, however, will not let the man of faith enjoy his unconscious contradiction between the overall retention of his property and his pleasures, on the one hand, and his particular sacrifices and self-abnegations, on the other.

In the end, the man of reason "holds an irresistible authority over faith" (§572). Reason makes explicit the moments that are constitutive of faith in an unconscious or nonconceptual way. What for faith are oppositions—between the beyond and the actual sensuous world, between a man's own singularity and the universality of the absolute being, between consciousness and being—self-conscious reason knows to be moments of one unitary self-consciousness and the movement of the concept. Faith "has two sorts of eyes, two sorts of ears, speaks with two voices, has duplicated all ideas without comparing the twofold meanings" (§572). The Enlightenment upsets the "*beautiful*," nonconceptual security, trust, and certainty of faith in its acts of submission, acts that enabled it to hold the two worlds apart.

Faith and Enlightenment now appear as the same: "the consciousness of the relation of what is in itself finite to an absolute without predicates, an absolute unknown and unknowable" (§573). The man of reason, who operates according to the distinction between being-in-itself and being-for-another, represents "*satisfied* Enlightenment," while the man of faith embodies "*unsatisfied* Enlightenment," or "*sheer yearning.*" Nevertheless, it remains to be seen "whether Enlightenment can remain satisfied; that yearning of the troubled spirit which mourns over the loss of its spiritual world lurks in the background" (¶573). The man of reason failed to do justice to the man of faith by discounting the meaning of the latter's acts of submission, contrition, sacrifice, and abnegation. These acts display his conviction of membership in a community of faith, even if they only *represent* the man of faith as a moment of the universal.

Moreover, reason is "caught up in the same internal conflict that it formerly experienced in connection with faith, and it divides itself into two parties" (¶575).[30] One party begins from the sensuous and abstracts to pure matter; however, pure matter is not a material thing like a stone, but a thought. Pure matter presents pure or undifferentiated thought as the absolute.

The other party begins with pure thinking as the opposite of finite consciousness, but this beyond of pure thinking, insofar as it exists "*externally*" to consciousness, also stands in relation to consciousness, and it "is thus the same as what is called *pure matter*" (¶578). For both parties, both consciousness and being are split into a being-in-itself and a being-for-another—thus, thought and being are "the same": thought as thinghood and thinghood as thought.

While the pure insight of the man of reason keeps the moments distinct as oppositions, 'we,' philosophical consciousness, recognize here the "revolutionary movement" first encountered in the concept of life. In thinking life as the genus, Hegel distinguished between the flux of becoming and the singular living beings that arise and pass away. The truth of life is precisely that "pure revolutionary movement" (*reine achsendrehende Bewegung*) in which all distinctions are superseded. Yet, the movement cannot abide in its "self-repose" unless the distinctions are "independent": "it cannot unfold [*aufheben*] the different moments if they do not have abiding existence [*Bestehen*]" (¶169). The flux abides in its restless repose only insofar as the different moments are present in it as "differentiated members [*Gliede*] and

---

30. For a discussion of the particular historical figures associated with each moment in this analysis, see Pinkard, *Hegel's Phenomenology*, 177–79.

parts with their own being-for-self" (¶169). Thus, philosophical consciousness must think "distinctions which are no distinctions."[31]

Both parties of the Enlightenment exhibit the same logic in holding the constitutive oppositions as oppositions. "This simple revolutionary movement [*diese einfache achsendrehende Bewegung*] must pull itself apart because it is only motion by differentiating its moments. This differentiating of its moments leaves the unmoved behind as the empty husk of pure being, which is no longer realized, nor has any life within it, for the differentiating is all the content" (¶579). In differentiating the moments outside the unity of this movement, pure insight—the exchange of the moments of the in-itself, for-another, and for-itself—"*does not return* [*zurückkehren*] *into itself*," and reality appears to it as object, as utility (¶579). This object is no longer alien, but its own, "one which it no longer repudiates and which, too, no longer has for it the value of the void or the pure beyond" (¶580). Grasping the object as useful, self-consciousness "penetrates" the object and finds his "certainty" and "enjoyment" in it (¶581). By being reasonable, self-consciousness has not only set himself up as the locus of thought and judgment; he has also rendered the world of objects his own and existing only with reference to his own ends. In its mastery of faith and the actual world, reason exhibits itself as *absolute freedom*.

Nevertheless, "that yearning of the troubled spirit which mourns the loss of its spiritual world [still] lurks in the background" (¶573). Though Hegel insists that this "blemish" has been removed in the constellation of the two parties of the Enlightenment, this has occurred only "in principle" (¶573). The man of reason remains "afflicted with oppositions": between being-in-itself and being-for-another, between the singular consciousness and the beyond, between sense-certainty and pure thinking. Enlightenment appears only as the "still *unconscious* activity of the pure concept," and it does not yet find its truth in the movement of the whole (¶565).

Moreover, though the man of the Enlightenment belongs to the "*world*" of the useful and realizes himself there, he still distinguishes himself from it.[32] When the two "come into collision . . . the Enlightenment will taste the

---

31. Here again appears the Bacchanalian revel: the belonging-together of rest and violent motion in the logic of appearance (¶47).

32. Both Michael Forster and Robert Pippin note rightly that this section is essentially a rewriting of the earlier chapter on reason, but each draws mistaken conclusions from this fact. See Forster, *Hegel's Idea of a Phenomenology of Spirit*; and Pippin, "You Can't Get There From Here:

fruit of its deeds" (¶580). And the man of reason will find his results far more bitter than expected.

### 4.b.III. Absolute Freedom and Terror

> The time has come, which was foretold, when the people would ask for bread and they would be given corpses.
>
> —MADAME ROLAND, *MEMOIRS* (1793)

While the man of reason has found his "concept"—his "self-certainty" and "enjoyment" in "utility"—utility remains a "predicate of the object" (¶582). Yet, his activity cancels the otherness of the object and demonstrates that utility really belongs to the subject, and "from this inner revolution there

---

Transition Problems in Hegel's *Phenomenology of Spirit*," in *The Cambridge Companion to Hegel*, ed. Frederick C. Beiser (Cambridge: Cambridge University Press, 1993), 52–85. Forster, in seeking to establish his dubious main point—that "Hegel did not when he began writing the *Phenomenology of Spirit* plan to include a Spirit chapter at all" and that it was "conceived at the last moment"—cites two merely contingent reasons: that the analyses of the chapter on reason were "chronologically cramped and artificial," so Hegel had an "incentive" to rework them; and that the earlier chapter with its German focus was "dubiously parochial," so Hegel needed to develop a "more French-oriented" revision (Forster, *Hegel's Idea*, 454–55). Forster seems not to understand, as Hegel himself clearly states in comparing the chapter on reason with that on the Enlightenment, that the earlier chapter focused on the theoretical development of reason, particularly in Kant's philosophy, while the chapter on the Enlightenment focuses on the practical political and social world in which the concepts of reason are realized, hence its focus on the salons and the French Revolution. Moreover, the claim that Hegel's transition to his critique of moral consciousness, away from explicitly historical events, is motivated by a lack of confidence in how to interpret those events displays both a thorough misunderstanding of Hegel's critique of reason in the *Phenomenology* and a failure to grasp his main point: the utilities, calculations, and legislations of reason prove inadequate as a foundation for community. Only an act that has no reasons or cannot be produced by a rational calculus, viz., forgiveness, will prove sufficient to sustain the reciprocity of community.

Similarly, Pippin gives credence to the view that Hegel's "individual chapters do not appear to have been well planned or thought out in advance" (Pippin, "You Can't Get There," 54). He offers two reasons. First, the structure of the book is "puzzling," because superimposed over the I–VII enumeration of the chapters is another designation: A. Consciousness, B. Self-Consciousness, C. AA. Reason, and so on. Contra Pippin, however, this clearly indicates the way in which reason is both the result of the dialectic of consciousness and self-conscious—the third term of resolution, in which the dichotomy is unfolded—and the first term of the next triad, reason–spirit–religion. These two interlocking triadic forms produce the result: DD. Absolute Knowing. Pippin also suggests that the more historically oriented analyses in the chapter on spirit are "difficult to integrate" with the more "idealized presentation[s]" of the earlier chapters; but Hegel makes quite clear that the earlier chapters deal only with representations of spirit, while the subject matter of the chapter on spirit is the actual worlds in which spirit realizes itself. To be fair to Pippin, however, he rejects the idea that the *Phenomenology* is a "hopeless gallimaufry of insights, suggestions, and stories," and he argues quite rightly that it is organized by a single line of argument and a single question: how does the 'I' become a 'we'—how does the singleton come to know himself as a member of community ("You Can't Get There," 78–79).

## SPIRIT, OR TRANSUBSTANTIATED LIFE

emerges the actual revolution of the actual world, the new shape of consciousness, *absolute freedom*" (¶582). In working over the difference between the singleton and the universal, Hegel has constantly reminded us that the truth of the singleton will turn out to be membership in community. This truth has been on the scene at least since the emergence of self-consciousness from the struggle unto death.[33] Yet again, violence and death will be required as a precondition for the actual emergence of a community of members who find their self-certainty and enjoyment in that membership. The violence and death of the French Revolution will prove to be not only the bitter fruit of Enlightenment reason, but also a transformative moment that gives rise to a community of self-conscious and self-constituting subjects.

By making the useful his own, the man of reason divests it of its objectivity as something "distinct from the 'I,'" and he revealed it to be a reflection of his own subjectivity—his own certainty and enjoyment. Thus, he has discovered that "all reality is solely spiritual," or that the truth of the object is his own will: "the world is for him simply his own will, and this is a general will" (¶584). This will differs from the general will of the Hobbesian sovereign or the will of the monarch in that it is not produced by "silent assent" nor in "assent by a representative." It is not based in the myth of a social contract, in which each one is self-alienated by having always already transferred his particular will to the sovereign. It is, Hegel insists, a "true [*reell*] general will, the will of all singletons [*Einzelnen*] as such" (¶584).[34] In the moment of absolute freedom, the singleton attempts to "ascend the throne of the world" immediately, without the intervention of mediating infrastructures and institutions. He asserts himself as a general or universal will "without any power being able to resist him" (¶585). For this reason, the truth of the man of absolute freedom will turn out to be terror and death.

Hegel emphasizes both the singularity of this will and its universality. On the one hand, will consists in the "consciousness of personality" (¶584). Each man knows himself in willing in his self-certainty and independence as a singleton. On the other hand, this general will "can only realize itself in a work which is a work of the whole" (¶585). The deed of this general will

---

33. It first appeared in perception, where the object was determined as a community of properties, and it was elaborated in the discussion of the reciprocity of the play of forces.

34. The use of the adjective *reell* conveys a sense of reliability and trustworthiness, in contrast to the alienated will of the singleton under a sovereign ruler.

is the deed of each and every one, so that each and every one is responsible for its work. The various "spheres" into which spirit has articulated itself and in which the singleton is made determinate—the family, communities of faith, economic and political associations, science, and communities of discourse—are transcended in absolute freedom so that the singleton no longer finds his identity in them.

> In this absolute freedom, therefore, all social groups or classes which are the spiritual spheres into which the whole is articulated are abolished; the singular consciousness [*das einzelne Bewußtsein*] that belonged to any such sphere, and willed and fulfilled himself in it, has put aside his limitations; his purpose is the general purpose, his language universal law, his work the universal work. (¶585)

The man of absolute freedom no longer defines himself in relation to a world of alien objects or utilities; rather, the opposition or antithesis with which he is afflicted consists "solely in the difference between the *singleton* and the *universal* consciousness" (¶586). Just as the Kantian moral subject would realize himself by transcending himself in giving himself a universal law, so too the man of absolute freedom must *leave behind* his singularity in order to realize himself as universal. And, just like the Kantian moral subject concerned only with thoughts and intentions, the man of absolute freedom "can produce neither a positive work nor a deed" (¶589).[35] As the antithesis to the singleton, this universal will cannot act, for action always results in some specific determination—deeds and words that belong to some specific sphere of action. The man of absolute freedom, however, insists that his action embodies nothing but the "universal work" and the "universal law." Absolute freedom cancels the "independence" (*Selbstständigkeit*) of the singleton or the "real," over whose "corpse" hovers "the exhalation of a stale gas, of the vacuous *Être suprême*" (¶587).[36]

---

35. The difference between the Kantian moral subject, to be analyzed in the next section, and the man of absolute freedom is that the Kantian moralist knows himself to be a pure form of knowing and willing, while the man of absolute freedom attempts to exercise his will through actual deeds. By exercising his will, the man of absolute freedom seeks to make it determinate, while at the same time maintaining its absolute universality. This difference will emerge from the analysis of absolute freedom.

36. Robespierre instituted the Cult of the Supreme Being (Culte de l'Être suprême) on 18 Floréal, Year II (May 7, 1794).

Hegel contrasts absolute freedom with a "conscious freedom" that can act, that is capable of "universal works of language," that can produce "laws and general institutions," only by "divid[ing] itself into stable spiritual 'masses' or spheres and into the members of various powers" (¶588). It would make itself determinate only through articulating itself in determinate powers and "particular spheres of labour which would be further distinguished as more specific 'estates' or classes" (¶588). Rather than holding fast to itself as absolute, this freedom or "violence" (*Gewalt*) lets itself be articulated into distinct agencies, "legislative, judicial, and executive powers."[37] This "universal freedom" makes itself actual by separating itself into its "members" (*Glieder*), thereby freeing itself from any antithesis to the singular individual and "apportioning the *plurality* of individuals [*Individuen*] to its various constituent parts" (¶588).[38] Thus, any singleton, "the being of personality," can belong only to a part of the whole.

The man of absolute freedom, however, will not let himself be "cheated" in this way: neither by participation in a self-legislation that accords to him only a share of the work, nor through being "*represented* in law-making and universal action." He insists on arrogating to himself immediately the universal will, "*himself* making the law and accomplishing not a particular work, but the universal work itself" (¶588).

Hegel's point is that an abstraction like absolute freedom cannot produce words or deeds, institutions or associations. Only the singleton can act, and he does so either on his own or as a member of community. For the universal to be realized, it must "concentrate itself into the one of

---

37. In his lectures on the philosophy of history, Hegel famously remarked, "America is ... the land of the future, where, in the times that lie before us, a world historical significance will reveal itself" (quoted in Pinkard, *Hegel's Phenomenology*, 437n111). From the context, he is clearly talking about the Americas—North and South—but, though it plays no role in the argument of the *Phenomenology*, the American Revolution certainly had caught his attention. In the same text, Hegel describes the United States as "the permanent example of a republican constitution" (Hegel, *The Philosophy of History*, trans. J. Sibree [1837; New York: Dover, 1956], 85). In his comments on the letters of the French lawyer and Girondist Cart, Hegel observes, "the tax imposed by the English parliament upon tea imported into America was minimal, but the belief of the Americans that by accepting payment of that sum, however insignificant, they would be yielding at the same time their most precious right, made the American Revolution." Quoted in Jean Hyppolite, *Studies on Marx and Hegel*, trans. J. O'Neil (1955; New York: Harper Torchbooks, 1969), 40. In *Phenomenology of Spirit*, Hegel's description of a universal freedom realized by dividing itself into powers suggests the American constitution (see ¶588).

38. Hegel uses here the plural of the term *Individuum* rather than *Einzelne* precisely because he is now referring not to the singleton on his own but to the singleton who knows himself to be in truth a member of community.

individuality and put at the head a singular [*einzelnes*] self-consciousness" (¶589). The other singletons, then, would be excluded from this deed, and they would share in it only insofar as the deed was mediated by the "spiritual spheres" of the community and was done in and for the community of which they are members. The man of absolute freedom, however, is incapable of such action, for he claims to make universal law and to accomplish the universal work without need of these forms of mediation. Thus, he "can produce neither a positive work nor a deed" (¶589). The man of absolute freedom produces "merely the *fury* of destruction" (¶589).

The universality of absolute freedom proves to be an "abstraction" that does not allow itself to be realized in an "organic membership" (*organische Gliederung*). It maintains its own unity and does not let itself be expressed in a *plurality* of individuals, powers, and spiritual communities or masses. "And, moreover, by virtue of its own abstraction, it divides itself into extremes equally abstract—into a simple, unyielding, cold universality, and into the discrete, absolute, hard rigidity and self-willed atomism of actual self-consciousness" (¶590). Having destroyed the spiritual formations that composed the world of culture, the man of absolute freedom has only his freedom as his object, and he exists only for that freedom. The two extremes of abstract universality and abstract singularity each exist here "indivisibly and absolutely" in an "*unmediated* pure negation" (¶590). As absolute, this universal will can allow no powers, institutions, or spiritual formations to arise that would divide it into a plurality of agencies. As pure, unmediated negation, it constitutes "a negation, moreover, of the singleton as a being *existing* in the universal" (¶590). It is just such a participation in the universal that the man of absolute freedom cannot allow. The "whole expanse of existence" has been "concentrated into his simple self," so that there can be no "reciprocal action" between an actual consciousness, "immersed in the complexities of existence," and the actual, "*external* world" (¶594). As a pure negation of the singleton, the man of absolute freedom has as his "sole work and deed" nothing but *death*, and he realizes himself by invoking the "*terror* of death" (¶591, ¶593). Thus, through him, "the fear of the lord and master . . . has again entered men's hearts" (¶594).

As André Maurois remarks in his *History of France*, "Robespierre admired only Robespierre."[39] One by one his rivals—monarchists,

---

39. Maurois, *A History of France*, 315.

Girondists, *Enragés*, Cordeliers, Dantonists—each meet their doom. By August 1793, "the party of legality was beaten; the party of violence was prevailing."[40] In September of that year, in what Maurois describes as an "act of collective sadism," massacres were carried out that emptied the prisons: "Who judged? Whoever called himself a judge. Who carried out the sentences? Whoever liked blood."[41] On September 5, 1793, the nominally governing National Convention made the Terror the "order of the day."[42] Robespierre's chief lieutenant, Saint-Just, announced that "the government of the Republic owes only death to the enemies of the people." As Maurois notes, "this was mere rhetoric, but it killed all the same."[43] Thus, as Hegel argues, the "wisdom of the government" is summarized in the "flatness of the syllable" *death* (¶590).

By the time Robespierre was himself executed, alongside Saint-Just, on 10 Thermidor, Year II (July 27, 1794), it was clear that it was "absolutely impossible for [the universal will of absolute freedom] to exhibit itself as anything other than a *faction*. What is called government is merely the *victorious* faction" (¶591). As the man of absolute freedom, Robespierre attempted to rule from a "single point," his own will. He excluded all others and thereby set himself in opposition to any genuinely universal will. At the same time, his actions and orders were *determinate* orders and actions; it was therefore impossible for him not to betray his claim to the absolute and to become objectified in them as a determinate self. It is impossible for him to sustain that abstract universality from which he drew his authority and power. Thus, a faction, precisely because it is a faction, will necessarily be overthrown (¶591).

On September 17, 1793, the Convention passed the Law of Suspects, further empowering the Committee of Public Safety controlled by Robespierre.

> Soon the search was not merely for the guilty but for suspects and those considered suspect were various: nobles and their relatives, unless they had publicly displayed their loyalty to the Revolution; all suspended officials; all

---

40. Maurois, 303.
41. Maurois, 303.
42. Albert Soboul, *A Short History of the French Revolution*, trans. Geoffrey Symcox (1965; Berkeley: University of California Press, 1977), xxii.
43. Maurois, *History of France*, 313.

those who had emigrated, even when they had returned to the country within the set time limit; all those who had spoken a hostile word about the Revolution; all those who had done nothing in its behalf. Such a range allowed the condemnation of anyone who was displeasing or a nuisance.[44]

As Maurois notes, the guillotine, in its efficiency and simplicity, accelerated the slaughter. The Terror creates an environment in which "*being suspected . . . takes the place, or has the significance and effect, of being guilty*" (¶591). Having expelled the others from the universal and arrogated it to himself, the man of absolute freedom does not shrink from the "cold extermination" of these others, who have nothing left but "mere being" (¶591).[45] Death under the Terror proves meaningless, without any "inner scope or fulfillment," as it consists in nothing more than the "negation of the unfulfilled point of the absolutely free self" (¶590). "It is, thus, the coldest and most trivial death, with no more meaning than lopping off a head of cabbage or taking a gulp of water" (¶591). Eventually the Terror exhausted itself: "the nation seems as exhausted as some frenzied person who has been bled, and undergone a strict diet."[46] Ten months after Robespierre's death, his most rabid followers, the sansculottes of the poorer classes, staged a last revolutionary action, but on the evening of 4 Prairial, Year III (May 24, 1795), "the people of the Faubourg Saint-Antoine, mainstay of the Revolution since 'Eighty-Nine, surrendered without a fight."[47]

The meaningless death of the Terror produced a people "weary of utter poverty and hatred."[48] By November 1799, the revolution was over: Napoleon had been installed as First Consul and was firmly in charge.[49]

---

44. Maurois, 303.

45. There is a striking similarity between Hegel's analysis of the role of suspicion in the French Revolution, which "allowed for the condemnation of anyone who was displeasing or a nuisance," and Foucault's analysis of the practice of informing under the Nazi regime: "Ultimately, everyone in the Nazi State had the power of life and death over his neighbors, if only because of the practice of informing, which effectively meant doing away with the people next door, or having them done away with." Michel Foucault, *"Society Must Be Defended": Lectures at the Collège de France, 1975-76*, trans. David Macey (1997; London: Penguin, 2003), 259.

46. Jacques Mallet du Pan, Genevan-French journalist and Royalist, quoted in Maurois, *History of France*, 324.

47. Soboul, *Short History of the French Revolution*, 119.

48. Maurois, *History of France*, 325.

49. Initially, Hegel was enamored with the French Revolution, like many of his contemporaries. Only when it gave way to the Terror did it become an object of critique for him. His criticisms in no way suggest a nostalgia for the Ancien Régime; instead, he looks forward to the establishment of a genuine republic of independent, self-governing citizens.

## SPIRIT, OR TRANSUBSTANTIATED LIFE

Thus, in the unfolding of the French Revolution, absolute freedom became determinate as the "terror of death" (¶592). Robespierre and his allies sought to smash all the forms of culture that they had inherited and to erase the "spiritual masses" that had sustained human life prior to the revolution. They created a new calendar to mark this new beginning of time and history. The injustices of prerevolutionary France had become unsustainable, but the revolution effected by the man of absolute freedom proved not to be sustainable either. His absolute will made itself determinate without the mediation of universalizing forms, in which the plurality of singletons could participate. Like the skeptic, whose negative power of thought leaves nothing standing, so too the man of absolute freedom produces only a "fury of destruction." According to the logic of inversion, his positive universal will "changes round into its negative nature and shows itself to be equally that which *puts an end to the thinking of oneself*, or to self-consciousness" (¶592). Just as life had to be risked absolutely in the "struggle unto death" from which self-consciousness first emerged, the man of absolute freedom had to destroy all previous spiritual forms in order to realize his universal will.

The man of reason or pure insight, for whom the indeterminate absolute comprised the opposition between pure thought and pure matter, "is [now] confronted with the absolute *transition* of the one into the other as his reality" (¶592). He has learned that the universal will can only be realized in a plurality of individuals through mediating cultural forms. Thus, the spheres or "masses" into which spirit was organized "take shape once more": "These individuals who have felt the fear of death, of their absolute master, again submit to negation and distinctions, arrange themselves in the various spheres, and return to a shared and limited work [*kehren zu einem geteilten und beschränkten Werke . . . zurück*], but thereby to their substantial reality" (¶593). The fury of destruction and the terror of death, in which all seemed to be lost, have returned the man of reason to himself and to the shared work through which the plurality of singletons share in the universal will.[50]

---

50. As Rebecca Comay argues, "the subject seeks to overcome the terror of its own transience through a sacrifice of particularity, compensated by the thought of eventual redemption." Rebecca Comay, *Mourning Sickness: Hegel and the French Revolution* (Stanford, CA: Stanford University Press, 2011), 90.

Thus, spirit appears to be "thrown back to its starting point, to the ethical and real world of culture, which would have been merely refreshed and rejuvenated by the fear of the lord and master which has again entered men's hearts" (¶594). It would seem that spirit "would have to traverse anew and continually repeat this cycle of necessity" (¶594). What self-consciousness has learned, however, through the experience of absolute freedom is not only the impossibility of realizing the universal will without mediating forms and shared work. Self-consciousness has also learned that he is in truth the universal will only as a "*pure knowing and willing,*" as over against any "immediate existence." The universal will cannot be realized as "revolutionary government," nor in any "faction." As over against the "atomic point of consciousness," self-consciousness finds himself the "*form*" of pure knowing and willing. In this "unreal world," freedom has the value not of power but of truth (¶595). The experience of absolute freedom has "removed the antithesis between the universal and the singular will" by transforming the singleton into a form and *leaving behind* his immediate existence. Having passed through the terror, the man of reason has learned that his truth consists in the formal identity of his will with the universal will, or *morality*.[51]

### 4.C. FROM DISSEMBLANCE TO FORGIVENESS IN HEGEL'S CRITIQUE OF MORALITY: FREEDOM BEYOND TERROR AND THE LAW

Just as Hegel's introduction to the *Phenomenology of Spirit* began with a critique of Kant's epistemology—in which the philosopher seeking truth would be left empty-handed by the subtraction of cognition as an instrument or medium for grasping it—so too he ends the analysis of spirit with a critique of Kant's moral philosophy as similarly self-defeating. The critique of Kantian morality has already been initiated in the critique of lawgiving reason and in the critique of law that courses throughout the text.

As usual, like the other figures, moral consciousness turns out to be something other than what he takes himself to be. His is a fundamentally *deceptive* consciousness that both takes the pure duty of morality to be his

---

51. In Comay's pithy formulation, "I killed off the world but thereby encountered my own infinite capacity for moral freedom." Comay, 125.

## SPIRIT, OR TRANSUBSTANTIATED LIFE

essence and locates that essence in a beyond, rendering it merely hypothetical in the realm of actuality. Moral consciousness turns out to be on the one hand a form of *envy*—a judging consciousness that calls into question the worthiness of those who have been blessed, the lucky souls—and on the other a kind of *hypocrisy*, in which moral consciousness opposes pure duty to actuality in such a way as to render moral action impossible (¶¶625, 631). The judging consciousness exists in the language of his pronouncements and the declaration of his intentions. Thus, this morality concerns himself only with *intending* the good, rather than actually *doing* it.[52]

Like perceptual consciousness or the skeptic, for whom thought and nature or actuality stood opposed to each other as a mere contradiction, moral consciousness engages in a "shiftiness," an "insincere shuffling," between the moments of thought and actuality, between pure duty and determinate duties, between existence and the beyond. Indeed, moral consciousness proves to be nothing other than the elaboration of "a 'whole nest' of thoughtless contradictions" (¶617).[53] In perception, the differences to be worked through were relatively simple: either the thing in itself is a unity (the essential moment) and it only appears to be multiple because of the multiplicity of our senses (the inessential moment), or the thing in itself is multiple (the inessential moment) and it only appears to be a unity due to the synthetic, conceptual activity of consciousness (the essential moment). The sophistical to-ing and fro-ing of the man of the moral worldview proves infinitely more complex, as he encompasses all the distinctions that have been made, all the moments that have been "tarried with" since the phenomenology of *spirit proper* began with an actual self-consciousness and the two of sexual difference.[54] He is a *person* in his own right and *recognized as such*, with all that entails for his participation in various forms of community. He is a *man of culture*, who finds himself in an alien world made by others, but he knows himself in his own words and deeds and sets

---

52. "An action done from duty has its moral worth, not in the purpose to be attained by it, but in the maxim in accordance with which it is decided upon; it depends therefore, not on the realization of the object of the action, but solely on the principle of volition in accordance with which, irrespective of all objects of the faculty of desire, the action has been performed." Immanuel Kant, *Groundwork of the Metaphysic of Morals*, trans. H. J. Paton (1785; New York: Harper Torchbooks, 1964), 67–68 (13).

53. Here Hegel quotes Kant against Kant himself.

54. The sister, who has been left behind in the family, both to care for the living body and to bury the dead, and with her the two of sexual difference continue to haunt this text and its claim to be absolute knowing, a master narrative in which all is to be thought at one go.

about making the world his own. A reader might feel quite dizzy amid the unfolding distinctions, as the man of morality performs his dissemblances.

Working through the distinctions comprising the self-consciousness of morality produces the third "spiritual self," the figure of *conscience*. Unlike the earlier forms of morality, the man of conscience no longer opposes pure duty to actual existence, nor does he locate it in an unattainable beyond. He knows himself to be a "self-actualizing being" and his "action is something *concretely* moral" (¶634). Conscience unfolds (*aufhebt*) the distinctions that were for moral consciousness mere oppositions by realizing pure duty in his own deed, a deed *before others* that has a "stable existence" (¶640). The deed, however, consists just in the declaration that what he does is done from pure duty. Pure duty is empty, like the principle of universalizability in Hegel's analysis of the "moral insolence" of reason, and it can accept any content. Any determinate action, other than the speech act of declaring that what is done is done from duty, exhibits the "*blemish of determinateness*" (¶645). Thus, the man of conscience would be open to conflicts among duties, and his actions would be subject to the judgments of others. Insofar as each one acts only according to *his own law* and his own conscience, while declaring that what he does is done from pure duty, no one has any way of knowing if the actions of others are good or evil—thus, conscience necessarily gives rise to "judging and explaining" (¶649). To the extent that the man of conscience insists that he acts on his own law and from his own conviction of duty, he sets himself over against others and "admits in fact to being evil" (¶662). Only the breaking of the "hard heart" of judging consciousness in the reciprocity of mutual forgiveness will be sufficient to transform the singleton into a member of a self-realizing community, where, like the properties in the perceptual thing, each retains his own independence in his belonging-together with others.[55]

### MORALITY AS A WORLDVIEW

Hegel's first critique of self-legislating reason (discussed here in section 3.c) established the immediacy with which the singleton is claimed by the right

---

55. Recall that, in his phenomenology of perception, Hegel writes of a "community" of properties (¶117, see my discussion in 1.b). The red of the dress coexists inseparably with the dress's silky texture, while each one retains its independence or distinctness from the other.

by virtue of his position as a node in a network of relations, as in the case of Antigone. Hegel returns to this theme here to display the untenable contradictions by which moral consciousness is afflicted and which make the moral view of the world fundamentally deceptive and hypocritical. Moral consciousness takes his truth to be "pure duty," but he is at the same time a sensuous being, whose "instincts and inclinations" appear to be opposed to "pure will" and "pure purpose" (¶603). Thus, it might appear that the actualization of the self-consciousness of morality or pure duty can be achieved only by "getting rid of sensuousness" (¶603). Such an alienation from sensuous existence, however, would render the moral consciousness of pure duty wholly hypothetical, abstract, and impossible to actualize. The pure thought of pure duty, on the one hand, and sensuous existence, on the other, "are *in themselves a single consciousness*" (¶603). Thus, in order to secure pure duty against the infection of sensuous motives, their unity must be thought differently, as "a unity that is not the former *original* unity of both in the single individual, but a unity which proceeds from the *known* antithesis of both" (¶603). Reason exists as pure duty only in this opposition to the sensuous, but the sensuous must be worked over in some way in order that moral consciousness might realize himself and become actual.

In this view, nature first appears to stand over against the world of morality—natural law against the moral law. Nature appears as "indifferent" to moral self-consciousness, as morality would be to it. In order to realize the unity of sensuous existence and pure duty, on the other side of their opposition, moral consciousness "postulates," on the one hand, a conformity of nature and morality as the "final purpose of the world," and, on the other, a conformity of morality and sensuous experience as the "final purpose of self-consciousness" (¶604). This conformity, unlike the "*original* unity" of pure duty and sensuous existence, is, however, not immediately given: it must be brought about by reason's own activity.[56] Indeed, moral consciousness consists just in this activity, and he must "continually be making progress in morality" (¶603). Yet, the actual achievement of this aim would result in the "vanishing" of moral consciousness, which exists only in the distinction between pure duty and sensuous existence, in the setting-aside of the latter in favor of the former. Thus, the achievement of the

---

56. "All maxims as proceeding from our own making of law ought to harmonize with a possible kingdom of ends as a kingdom of nature." Kant, *Groundwork*, 104 (81).

conformity of nature and morality "is to be thought of merely as an *absolute* task, i.e., one that simply remains a task" (¶603). Moral consciousness must constantly be working toward this aim, while in principle never arriving. This view leads only to "the contradiction of a task which is to remain a task and yet ought to be fulfilled, and the contradiction of a morality which is no longer to be consciousness, i.e., not actual" (¶603). Hegel cautions the reader not to seek a "definite idea" here, lest duty be rendered "something unreal," i.e., a dissemblance.

Only "the movement of actual doing itself" could mediate between the two extremes of pure duty and sensuous existence. There reappears here the same logical problem encountered in the first critique of law in the chapter on force and understanding (see my discussion, section 1.c). Just as law was afflicted with a nest of contradictions—between the concept of law and the plurality of laws, between the unity of law and its constituent parts, between the conceptuality of law and its multiple material expressions in the sensuous—so too the consciousness of pure duty finds himself situated in a nest of contradictions. "Moral consciousness as the *simple knowing* and *willing* of pure duty is, in the doing of it, related to an object that opposes its simplicity, related to the actuality of manifold cases, and thereby has a manifold moral *relationship* to that actuality. With regard to the content, what emerges here is the *plurality* of laws, and with regard to the form, what emerges are the contradictory powers of the knowing consciousness and of the unconscious" (¶605). Moral consciousness adheres only to the thought of pure duty, but in doing so he remains abstract and hypothetical.[57] In order to realize himself and the conformity of duty and the sensuous, he must act. In acting, however, he can realize only specific, determinate duties, and these may or may not embody pure duty.

Moreover, in acting, consciousness can only be this specific singleton, "directed toward actuality as such,... for [he] wants to accomplish something" (¶607).[58] Pure duty, then, belongs to another consciousness in whom

---

57. "An absolutely good will, whose principles must be a categorical imperative, will therefore, being undetermined in respect of all objects, contain only the form of willing, and that as autonomy." Kant, *Groundwork*, 112 (95).

58. Quotations from Hegel's *Phenomenology* in this section are based on Terry Pinkard's translation. Georg Wilhelm Friedrich Hegel, *The Phenomenology of Spirit*, trans. and ed. Terry Pinkard (1807; Cambridge: Cambridge University Press, 2018).

## SPIRIT, OR TRANSUBSTANTIATED LIFE

"universal and particular are simply one" (¶606). Having postulated the conformity of morality and nature as well as the conformity of pure duty and the sensuous—both projected into the beyond as infinite tasks—moral consciousness now postulates *another consciousness* in which the contradictions would be overcome. This "lord and ruler of the world" guarantees that the harmony of morality and the sensuous is implicit and is being realized, and his presence guarantees as well that the plurality of duties are, indeed, an expression of pure duty. Thus, in contrast to the divine perfection of a moral consciousness beyond the sensuous, the actual moral consciousness now appears to be an "*imperfect*" moral consciousness (¶608).[59] Yet, insofar as this moral consciousness clings to his thought of pure duty as what is essential in him, he is no more than this thought, and his truth is postulated "*beyond* reality," so that his moral imperfection is "held to be perfect" (¶609).

Given that his perfection exists only in principle or as a postulate, this moral consciousness cannot count on the "harmony of morality and happiness" (*Glückseligkeit*) as something necessary, but only as a "gift of grace" (¶608). The "lord's" beneficence, however, takes into account the moral imperfection of his subjects; he "bestows happiness according to worthiness, namely, according the *merit ascribed* to the imperfect consciousness" (¶609). Thus, morality consists in earning and deserving, on the one hand, and judging and apportioning happiness, on the other, and these activities belong to two different consciousnesses: the former to the actual moral consciousness and the latter to the "lord" in whom pure duty is realized.

Moral consciousness finds his truth not in his actual existence, but in a *representation* (*Vorstellung*).[60] Thinking "only in abstractions," he holds his actuality to be "inessential," while the being that is essential exists only in

---

59. "For human beings and all created rational beings moral necessity is necessitation, that is, obligation, and every action based on it is to be represented as duty . . . as if we could ever bring it about that without respect for the law, which is connected with fear or at least apprehension of transgressing it, we of ourselves, like the Deity raised beyond all dependence, could come into possession of holiness of will by an accord of will with the pure moral law becoming, as it were, our nature, an accord never to be disturbed (in which case the law would finally cease to be a command for us, since we could never be tempted to be unfaithful to it)." Immanuel Kant, *Critique of Practical Reason*, trans. Mary Gregor (1788; Cambridge: Cambridge University Press, 2015), 67–68 (5:81–82).

60. "But where do we get the concept of God as the highest good? Solely from the idea of moral perfection, which reason traces a priori and conjoins inseparably with the concept of a free will." Kant, *Groundwork*, 76 (29).

thought, as a representation.[61] The reality of moral consciousness consists in the "lack of harmony" between the consciousness of pure duty and sensuous existence, and, thus, he must confess that "there is no moral existence in reality" (¶613). At the same time, he takes this harmony to be his truth, so that the unity of duty and reality is for him implicit, as a "beyond of his reality, yet a beyond that ought to be actual" (¶614). Actually, there is no moral consciousness, but there is one, if only in thought or as a representation (¶615). This moral consciousness resides in the hypothetical domain of the 'as if': act *as if* you belong to a kingdom of ends.[62] "In other words, it is true that there is none, yet, all the same, he is allowed by another consciousness to pass for one" (¶615). The postulation of the "lord" in whom pure duty is realized provides the sleight of hand that substitutes the thought of doing your duty for actually doing it.

## DISSEMBLANCE

The man of morality gives himself his own law and knows himself to be the author of it. The moral law appears neither as "something alien" nor in an "unconscious manner" (¶616). It would appear, then, that the knowing subject has finally reached what was installed from the very beginning as the terminus of the phenomenological analysis: that point where "knowledge need no longer go beyond itself" because nothing is other to it (¶80). It appears that the man of morality "no longer needs to go beyond the object, because this no longer goes beyond *him*" (¶616). Yet, moral consciousness still places the realization of duty and his actual conformity with the moral law "*outside* himself as a beyond of himself." At one and the same time, moral consciousness both produces the idea of duty and the representation of God as the "idea of moral perfection," and he accords to God a "holiness," which is denied to himself. Unlike God's, his will can only hypothetically accord with the pure moral law. "The moral worldview is, therefore, in fact nothing other than the elaboration of this

---

61. "The [inward peace of the honorable man] is the effect of a respect for something quite different from life, something in comparison and contrast with which life with all its agreeableness has no worth at all. He still lives only from duty, not because he has the least taste for living." Kant, *Critique of Practical Reason*, 72 (5:88).

62. "Act as if the maxim of your action were to become through your will a universal law of nature." Kant, *Groundwork*, 89 (52).

fundamental contradiction in its various aspects" (¶617). Thus, moral consciousness exists as "shiftiness" and "insincere shuffling," just like perceptual consciousness, who took first the thing and then his own knowing to be the essential moment, shifting back and forth between the unity of the thing and its multiple properties—just as he shifted back and forth between the unity of his own knowing and the multiplicity of his senses (¶617). On the one hand, "in the present, morality is assumed as *given or extant [vorhanden]*, and actuality is so placed that it is not in harmony with it" (¶618). On the other, this duplicitous consciousness knows himself through his deeds, in which he is actualized as this particular singleton and in which his "moral purpose" is made actual. Action "directly fulfills what was asserted could not take place, what was supposed to be merely a postulate" (¶618). The harmony of the actual and the moral purpose in a "beyond" was postulated in the first place in order to a make moral action possible: act *as if* you belong to a kingdom of ends. Action can only realize what is already implicitly given as a possibility. Thus, "the connection between acting and the postulate is so constituted that, for the sake of action, i.e., for the sake of the *actual* harmony of purpose and actuality, this harmony is postulated as *not actual*, as a *beyond*" (¶618). Consciousness shifts back and forth between these two contradictory moments, asserting now one and now the other as the truth, dissembling about each as it makes the other the truth or "being-in-itself" (¶617).

Similarly, this duplicitous moral consciousness shifts back and forth between the abstraction of pure duty and actually doing his duty in some specific deed. On the one hand, the man of morality cares only about pure duty, which is something universal. His concern is not with particular actions but with the moral view of the "whole world." On the other hand, any "actual deed is only a deed of the singleton," something specific and determinate—not a formal purpose or abstract universal (¶619). If this duplicitous consciousness were really concerned about the fulfillment of duty, then he would be concerned with the particular action in which he realizes it. He would be concerned "not [with] pure duty, but with what is opposed to it, actuality" (¶619). In giving himself his own laws, moral consciousness demonstrates himself to be a consciousness that *acts*. At the same time, he divests that action of its moral content, making its moral value purely hypothetical by projecting the actual realization of duty beyond his own experience. The man of morality insists that the moral law *ought* to be actual, while at the same time positioning the realm of nature and actuality to be antithetical to it.[63]

This consciousness thus produces two absurd propositions. First, "because the universal *best* ought to be carried out, nothing *good* is done" (¶619). Any singular action would always be insufficient to realize pure duty, while the acting consciousness would always be afflicted by the difference between what the action is in-itself, in truth, and what it is for him, or what he intended in it. For this reason, this moral consciousness wants to concern himself only with his intentions and not with his actions; he wants to be only a pure willing and not an actual doing.

Second, "because moral action is the absolute purpose, the absolute purpose is, that there should be no such thing as moral action" (¶620). Where the harmony of morality and actuality or nature has been realized, moral action is "superfluous." By embracing as the "highest good" this conformity of morality and nature, this shifty consciousness projects himself into a beyond where moral action proves no longer necessary. In his worldview, the truth of this world lies in an "absolute" where "there should be no such thing as moral action."

First, moral consciousness produces a whole thoughtless nest of contradictions by opposing moral purpose and pure duty to moral action and actuality. Then, moral consciousness dissembles again and produces more contradictions by opposing his own knowing and willing to sensuous experience. On the one hand, moral consciousness would eliminate everything sensuous from his moral purpose, which, as pure rational will, should have nothing to do with "inclinations and impulses." On the other hand, he acts. His worldview consists in giving himself his own law, and this is a law of *action*. His whole purpose is to *realize* or *make actual* the moral purpose of doing one's duty. His thought of pure duty, however, can be made actual only through the mediation of the sensuous; otherwise, it remains only an abstract thought, something for him alone and not universal or before others. "Inclinations and impulses" thus constitute the

---

63. Recall Hegel's critique of reason for making the right contingent on reason's own test. This yields only an "obedience to laws which are merely laws and not at the same time commandments" (¶434) or "the 'ought to be' of an unreal commandment and a knowledge of formal universality" (¶435). Cf. my discussion in section 3.c, of the critique of the moral insolence of reason and Hegel's phenomenological analysis of being commanded by the right in virtue of the social relations in which we are situated.

## SPIRIT, OR TRANSUBSTANTIATED LIFE

condition of possibility for *"self-realizing self-consciousness"* (¶622). What the moral self-consciousness meant to say, then, was not that moral action has nothing to do with inclination and impulse; without these forces setting the self in motion, no action would occur. What he meant to say instead was that inclination and impulse ought to conform to the moral purpose. Inclination and impulse are not mere empty forms but always embody a determinate content. Once again, the harmony between duty and inclination can only be *postulated* and projected into the *beyond*.

The harmony of morality and sensibility in the moral worldview constitutes yet another dissemblance. "The harmony is an other-worldly beyond of consciousness, lying somewhere off in a foggy distance in which there is no longer anything which can be accurately differentiated or comprehended, since the comprehension of this unity, which we just attempted to provide, itself failed" (¶622). The moral worldview would oppose pure duty and moral purpose to all other purposes. This shifty consciousness would act while at the same time opposing himself to the sensible conditions of action. He is "just as aware of the *activity* of this pure purpose as he is aware of his elevation above sensibility, aware of the intrusion of sensibility, and aware of the opposition and struggle with sensibility" (¶622). As this struggle, his own completion "is put off into *infinity*."[64] We are left again with the antinomy that "there is a moral consciousness, and that there is none" (¶632).

Moral consciousness, then, finds himself in the "intermediate state of incompletion" in which this shifty self is supposed to make *progress* toward moral perfection. Such a thought of degrees of imperfection, however, undermines the thought of pure duty: an "incomplete morality is thus impure, or is immorality" (¶626). This consciousness can no more demand happiness or blessedness (*Glückseligkeit*) on the basis of its own "worthiness" (¶624) than it can make judgments about others. While this shifty self claims to have learned from experience that "the moral person often fares badly, whereas in contrast the immoral person is often happy," his own moral incompleteness makes any judgment of others "arbitrary" (¶625). "As

---

64. Note the continuation here of the theme of the "struggle" (*Kampf*) of self-consciousness. It first appears in the "struggle unto death" that gives rise to mastery and slavery, and reappears in the unhappy consciousness's "struggle with the enemy." It returns once more in the "struggle" between virtue and the man of the world and then again in the "struggle" between faith and reason over truth. Indeed, every moment of the phenomenological analysis can be understood as the struggle of self-consciousness to reconcile the contradictions by which it appears to be afflicted: thought and sensibility, reason and nature, in-itself and for others, and so on.

a result, the sense and content of the judgment of experience is only that happiness in and for itself should not have been granted to some people, which is to say, the judgment is *envy* which helps itself to the cloak of morality" (¶625).⁶⁵ His own happiness or unhappiness does not reflect the moral value of his actions, nor does the happiness of others reflect their moral worthiness; rather, happiness is always "bestowed," not earned—a matter of "grace," not moral progress.

Only in the postulated being of the "holy moral legislator" can the contradictions of moral consciousness be represented as resolved, but this too proves to be a dissemblance. In incompletely realizing pure duty, moral consciousness finds himself beset by a multiplicity of *determinate* duties and "falls into dilemmas in concrete cases of actual action" (¶631). These specific duties cannot be holy in themselves, as they contradict not only each other, but also the oneness of pure duty. Moral consciousness projects the resolution of this conflict beyond himself: the multiplicity of determinate duties is to be "made holy through a holy law-giver" (¶626). Yet, the very essence of moral consciousness was to be self-determining, that he give himself his own law. Thus, here he dissembles again, for "the utterly holy is only that which is made holy *through himself* and is holy [not in another consciousness but only] in *moral consciousness*" (¶626). Moral consciousness took pure duty to be *his own truth*, not that of another alien consciousness, and the conflict between pure duty and the many determinate duties cannot be resolved therein.

The conflict between sensibility and thought that afflicts moral consciousness also remains unresolved in the holy law-giver. Moral consciousness, as an *actual* natural consciousness, "is affected and conditioned by sensibility" (¶627), while the holy or purely moral being beyond experience "stands sublimely above the *struggle* with nature and sensibility" (¶628). If morality, however, is to be something actual rather than merely hypothetical, it requires action in the sensuous world: "the *reality* of pure duty is its realization in nature and sense" (¶628). By opposing morality to actuality, moral consciousness would actually make morality impossible: "*pure morality*, as entirely separated from actuality and without any positive relation to it, would be an unconscious, non-actual abstraction in which the

---

65. Hegel previously employed this cloak metaphor in his critique of virtue's commitment to a good that exists only 'in principle.' See my analysis, section 3.b.

concept of morality and the thinking of pure duty—along with both willing it and then acting on that duty—would be unfolded [*aufgehoben*]" (¶628). While the incomplete or impure morality found it impossible to realize pure duty, the pure morality of the holy law-giver beyond experience renders moral action superfluous.

Once again, moral consciousness exhibits the same sophistical to-ing and fro-ing that first appeared in perception. First, he takes the purity of duty to be the essential moment, as if sensibility were inessential, but he finds that this renders moral action impossible. Then, he takes moral progress to be essential, as if pure duty were a lifeless abstraction. First, he finds his truth in himself, in giving himself his own law, but this infects the purity of duty with a multiplicity of determinate duties. Then, he invests his truth in a being beyond experience, but this renders his own moral consciousness unrealized and incapable of being actualized. By taking duty and actuality to be contradictory, this moral consciousness constantly shifts back and forth among these essential moments. The dissemblance and hypocrisy that define this shape of consciousness arise from this contradiction and from the error of clinging to one moment and now the other as if each were the whole truth:

> I act morally while I am *conscious* to myself of accomplishing only the pure duty and of *nothing else*, and this means, in effect, *while I do not* act. But while I actually do act, I am conscious to myself of an *other*, of an *actuality*, which is there before me, and of an actuality that I want to bring about, so I have a *determinate* end, and I fulfill a *determinate* duty in which there is something *other* than the pure duty which alone should be intended. (¶637)

Moral consciousness spends himself in this shillyshallying, which cannot be resolved either by his own thought of pure duty or by his postulation of a perfected moral being beyond experience. Out of this movement, through the unfolding of the difference between pure duty and actuality, a new shape emerges.

## CONSCIENCE

While moral consciousness constitutes himself as a "thought-thing" (*Gedankending*) by thinking himself as pure duty over against sensibility and actuality, the man of conscience knows himself to be a "determinate actuality," as this specific self-certain singleton, and he knows himself to be the particular site of morality. Hegel presents the man of conscience as the "third self" that has appeared in the unfolding of spirit (¶633). The first spiritual self, who emerged from the ethical world, is the *person* under the law, whose existence consists in "being recognized." In the person, universality and particularity belong together immediately, as a motionless and undifferentiated abstraction, merely given, rather than achieved.[66] In the world of culture the second spiritual self is produced through self-consciousness's own experience of alienation and his work of self-exteriorization. Here the difference between universality and particularity is mediated by the institutions of the state and the market, as well as religious community, and, above all, by language.[67] From this alienation, the self returns to itself in the shape of absolute freedom—the singleton that takes himself to embody the universal immediately, not as an empty form but as a license to act and to legislate directly for each and all. Thus, the consciousness of absolute freedom cannot sustain a world and gives rise only to a "fury of destruction."

Moral consciousness again distinguishes the universal from his own self-consciousness, as this singleton, but he only identifies the universal as an empty duty opposed to actuality. He spends himself in an "insincere play of alternating these two determinations" (¶633). Conscience, the third form of the spiritual self, arises out of the incorporation of these two moments within the self, as "*concrete* moral spirit" or "*moral essence actualizing* itself" (¶634). Conscience takes action to be "the pure form of willing" and knows "*actuality* as something brought forth by consciousness" (¶635). In the "unwavering certainty of conscience," there can be no conflict between pure duty and the multiple determinate duties, nor can there be conflict among the different determinate duties, because the man of conscience knows his truth to be just his own conviction of doing his duty. The "content of moral action" is just his existence as *this singleton*, and the "*form* of moral doing is this very self as pure movement, namely, as *knowing*, or as *one's own conviction*" (¶637). The man of conscience no longer stands over against pure duty as something merely postulated in a beyond or an alien being; rather,

---

66. See my discussion of legal personhood in section 4.a.
67. See section 4.b.I.

he exists just as this difference between pure knowing and the specificity of the singleton.

In knowing himself as the site of pure duty in the certainty of his conviction, the man of conscience conducts himself as a "*universality* towards others" (¶640). The man of morality concerned himself with mere intentions, which might or might not be realized, and he lacked this "moment of being recognized." Conscience knows himself as self-actualizing in his doing, and his doing is nothing other than the "translation" of his conviction or knowing that he acts from duty into "the *objective* element wherein it is universal and recognized" (¶640). As birds live in air or fish in water, conscience is the "common element" of self-consciousnesses, in which each one knows himself as a being before others and takes duty to be what is "universal for all self-consciousnesses" (¶640). The self-realization of the man of conscience consists just in his conviction that in his doing—through his action—duty is made actual and that in so acting he participates in what is universal for each and all.

Like moral consciousness, the man of conscience who acts only from duty finds that in action he is beset by a multiplicity of determinate duties and a complexity of moral relationships. Hegel here refers the reader to his critique of reason as tester of laws. Just as the formal principle of universalizability proved "compatible with any content," so too the "pure conviction of duty" can be made determinate in conflicting ways. A man acts to increase and maintain his property so as to serve the welfare of himself and his family and, perhaps, to be useful to his neighbors. Others might see this interest in "self-sufficiency" as the very opposite of doing one's duty. What one calls courage, the other calls cowardice (¶644). The man of conscience, however, frees himself from the "blemish of determinateness" and the conflict of determinate duties just by adhering to his self-certain conviction of acting only from duty. He does not indulge in the "*balancing* and *comparing*" of duties, nor in "calculating the advantage which would accrue to the universal from an action" (¶645). He "*cuts himself off*" from all such calculation and rests only on his own convictions and his own decisions. His conviction overcomes any determinate duty, and he exists in the "majesty of absolute *autarky*" (¶646). In his self-sufficiency, he embodies all the moments of self-consciousness—not as contradictions, but as moments of the whole: the immediacy and substantiality of ethical life in which self-consciousness is commanded by the right, the self-externalization of the man of culture discovering himself in his words and deeds, and the thinking of morality in which a self-consciousness knows himself as a pure 'I' distinct from the determinations of actual consciousness. The man of conscience knows himself as the site of these moments or distinctions, which in him are no longer distinctions but resolved in the immediacy of his conviction (¶621).

Moreover, as the man of conscience, the singleton does not oppose his actuality to the universal or to the common good, any more than he takes his action to be opposed to pure duty. "Instead what the singleton does for himself benefits the universal as well" (¶645). Just as the man of the world thinks he acts only for himself when his labor in fact benefits the whole community, so too the man of conscience, in seeing to his own concerns, actually addresses the welfare of others.[68] "The more he looks after himself, the more there is not only the greater *possibility* that he can be useful to *others* but his actuality consists just in his living and existing in a belonging-together [*Zusammenhang*] with others" (¶645). The man of conscience acts for himself but in an active relation to others, and his own welfare is bound up with theirs.

This self-consciousness proves no less divided than the earlier shapes, but this division is entirely internal to him and takes place in language. If the man of conscience acts on his conviction, he makes himself determinate through a determinate duty that inevitably conflicts with other determinate duties. He would fall into a calculation of duties and inevitably into conflicts with others, who might calculate differently. The man of conscience stands above all this through the self-sufficiency of his conviction, which stands on its own.

Indeed, the man of conscience cannot even be found "where the others think he is supposed to be" (¶648). He is not to be found in the action done, which is subject to the judgment of others, and which gives rise to a plethora of "judging and explaining" with them; rather, he exists in *declaring* his conviction that he acts from duty. Thus, the purity of duty is preserved, as the declaration that the deed was done from duty replaces the deed and purifies action of determination. In "giving voice to himself," this "individuality" realizes or actualizes himself as *a being* that exists only in *language* (¶650).

---

68. See section 3.b for my discussion of the man of the world.

## SPIRIT, OR TRANSUBSTANTIATED LIFE

On the one hand, this individuality knows himself and is certain of himself in the declaration of his conviction. On the other, he exists only with and through others, who cannot know whether, in fact, he acts from duty or not—at least they cannot know with certainty whether his declaration is genuine, for all certainty is *self*-certainty. Moreover, they too distinguish themselves from the determinate duty and find themselves in the declaration of their convictions. Each one acts, knows himself as acting from duty, and declares before others that he does so, but the others, "for the sake of sustaining their own selves," subject the determinateness of duty and action to the "judging and explaining" that would "nullify" it (¶649). Each one is divided by the difference between the declaration that one is doing one's duty and the determinate duty of the determinate action, and the others engage in the same dissembling. Thus, the man of conscience proves not to be where he was supposed to be: in his deed.

At the same time, all this declaring, judging, and explaining makes actual both self-consciousness—the singleton, who knows himself with certainty—and the recognition of this self-consciousness by others. Self-consciousness unfolds out of determinate action so as to realize himself as distinct from it, as a linguistic being that persists across the determinate content. The action has no "stable existence," which belongs to "universal self-consciousness," to the 'I' of each and all. "While he calls himself conscience, he calls himself pure self-knowing and pure abstract will, i.e., he calls himself the universal knowing and willing which bestows recognition on others and which is equal to them, for they too are just this pure self-knowing and willing and for that reason, he is also recognized by them" (¶654). This mutual recognition occurs in the language of declarations, judgments, and explanations, even as it sustains the self-certainty of each and every one.

Each man of conscience thus "conducts a worship service within himself" (¶655). The man of conscience interrogates himself, just as he interrogates others. He is always declaring himself to himself, judging himself, and explaining himself to himself. He is "the moral genius who knows the inner voice of his immediate knowing to be the divine voice, and as he is in this knowing, he just as immediately knows existence, he is the divine creative power who has the vitality of life within its concept" (¶655). He *wrestles* with his conscience, in order to be able to declare it and defend it.

This "solitary worship-service," however, takes place within a "religious community" (¶656). In the rituals and public prayers of a religious community, each one makes his declaration in public before all the others: "others allow the action to count as valid on account of this speech within which the self is expressed and is recognized as the essence" (¶656). Each one extends to the other "the reciprocal assurance of both their mutual conscientiousness and their good intentions," as they participate together in the rituals and public prayers (¶656). "Our father in heaven... forgive us our sins as we forgive those who have sinned against us." This religious speech comprises all the distinctions that have been made in the unfolding of self-conscious spirit, as distinctions that are no distinctions. All the oppositions and contradictions that have arisen are here comprehended and belong together as moments in each singleton's singular experience. Each one realizes himself in the "speaking of the religious community about its spirit" (¶656). The faith of the singleton, his belief, has unfolded into the *shared profession* of faith.

In his "purity," however, the man of conscience gives rise to the "poorest shape of consciousness," and in this "poverty" exists as a "disappearing" (¶657). Hegel likens the man of conscience to the flux of the unhappy consciousness. The difference is that the unhappy consciousness was unhappy because, though his rituals and good works indeed built a community to embody the universal, he credited their efficacy to an alien beyond. The man of conscience, in contrast, *knows* himself in his words and deeds, as he participates in various communities. He is unhappy, however, because, having purified his action of every determination, he is left only with the abstract declaration of his conviction that he acts from duty. Consciousness has here been "swallowed up" in the purity of self-consciousness (¶657). His declarations prove to be "echoes" or "fading tones." This unhappy "beautiful soul" "lacks the force to exteriorize himself [*Kraft der Entäußerung*], to make himself a thing and sustain existence [*sich zum Dinge zu machen und das Sein zu ertragen*]" (¶658). The beautiful soul is not so much a sustainable form of life as a "shapeless vapor dissolving into thin air" (¶658).

The beautiful soul is afflicted by a double dichotomy or two unequal values. First, this singleton is conscious of the difference between what he is in and for himself and what he is for others. He cannot know the others in the certainty of the first person, nor can he be presented to them as anything other than an object—albeit an object that appears to be not a thing but a living self-consciousness like the others themselves. At the same time, he opposes pure duty to the determinateness of action, and he suffers the "anxiety that he will stain the splendor of his interiority [*Herrlichkeit seines Innern*] through action and existence" (¶658). He exists in the difference between his self-certainty as this singleton, for whom the universal is a moment of his experience, and the thought of the universal or the universal consciousness, of which the singleton is only a member.

Acting on the self-certainty of his conviction and taking that self-certainty to be the essential moment, the beautiful soul appears to be *evil*. He acts "on his own law" and according to "*his own* conscience." In doing so, he renders the universal law, which would exist and be valid for each and all, a moment of his own experience. Acting toward others out of "his own law," he would be imposing on them an alien law and thus "mistreating them" (¶662). In acting, he "arrives at a feeling of himself in his own existence [*Sebstgefühl seiner in seinem Dasein*] and thus obtains gratification" (¶665). He knows himself as this singleton in the "motive" and "intention" that his act embodies. His moral ends are "*self-interested ends*," and he presents yet another demonstration of morality as dissemblance. The beautiful soul means to be good, but he instead commits evil.

By proclaiming universality to be the essential moment while reducing the singleton's life and action to the inessential, the beautiful soul presents the most developed form of *hypocrisy*. He adheres to pure duty and declares his conviction that it is the source of his actions, yet he thereby evacuates self-consciousness of all consciousness. Only the empty form of the declaration remains. Instead of proving himself in action, this soul "proves [his uprightness] by means of speaking about his splendid dispositions" (¶664). He busies himself making judgments about the actions of others, which in their determinateness will always fail to realize pure duty. "No action can escape being judged in such a way, for duty for duty's sake, this pure purpose, is the non-actual" (¶665). The judging consciousness plays the part of a "moral valet" to the acting consciousness, opposing the singularity of the singleton and his action to the action's universal aspect, measuring the limitations and imperfections of the action with respect to pure duty. The hypocrisy of this soul is two-fold. On the one hand, he would avoid becoming subject to the judgment of others through a "*lack of action*" on his own part, but "duty without deeds has no meaning at all" (¶664). On the other hand, this hypocrite would have his judgment count as his own action, but his judgment *as an action* will be subject to all the same antinomies and aporias that have arisen from the difference between pure duty and determinate action. Here too the beautiful soul figures morality as a dissembling.

The analysis has worked this complex of distinctions and differences to its point of exhaustion. The phenomenological progression appears stalled and poised to merely repeat this dissembling, without being able to actually resolve the contradictions it displays. The judging consciousness tries to place himself above any action, while making all actions susceptible to his judgment, and "he wants to know that his speech, which is utterly devoid of any deeds, is to be taken as a superior *actuality*" (¶666). The acting consciousness knows that no action, precisely because it is determinate, can be adequate to realize pure duty. This is true for the action of the judging consciousness too, whose judgment is a deed like any other. The acting consciousness thus experiences himself as equal to the judging consciousness in this exposure to the problem of determinates, and he "*gives voice*" to this equality and "*confesses* this to the other," viz., that both are guilty of ineluctably imperfect deeds that do not, on their own, make pure duty actual (¶666).

The judging consciousness adheres to his universal law, to pure duty, and to the declaration of his convictions only insofar as he has a "hard heart" and refuses to reciprocate the other's confession. He contrasts the "beauty of his own soul" with the evil, who act and soil the purity of duty. Here he repeats the mistake of both Creon and Antigone, whose "hard hearts" lead each to stick to one law without recognizing the validity of the other, thus rendering the future impossible. In this way, the "hard heart" of the beautiful soul seems to arrest the progress of spirit and to condemn self-consciousness to a repetitive life of dissemblance, where the contradictions are never actually resolved. "Lacking all actuality," the beautiful soul is "shattered into madness and melts into a yearning, tubercular consumption" (¶668). This lifeless figure reflects the exhaustion in the phenomenological analysis of the complex of distinctions that comprise the singleton.

Only the "breaking of the hard heart" releases self-consciousness from merely repeating the forms of dissemblance (¶669). Each heart confesses his "one-sidedness"—one sticking to the form of pure duty and the law of judgment, and the other to the certainty of the singleton and the law of

## SPIRIT, OR TRANSUBSTANTIATED LIFE

conviction. The self-realization of spirit turns out to consist neither in testing laws nor in following laws, but in *suspending the law*. Each becomes judging and judged, as each recognizes the other as guilty *like himself*. No duty can actualize pure duty, and duties will always conflict. Agents will always be in need of forgiveness from one another as a result. The asymmetrical reciprocity of forgiveness negotiates the contradictions and renders them "distinctions which are no distinctions." The "mutual recognition" that was projected as the end of the history of mastery and slavery turns out to be not a relation of equality, but one of asymmetry and inequality, as each finds himself now in the position of needing to confess and then in the position of needing to forgive. Self-consciousness knows himself as this singleton only as a member in a universal community of forgiveness, in which each is both forgiving and forgiven, in which each lets the other go free (cf. ¶181). Thus, the figure of forgiveness resolves the dichotomy between universal and particular with which the phenomenological analysis began, as well as the long history of dichotomies and contradictions that emerged from it. The asymmetrical reconciliations of forgiveness make possible both community, as the locus of the universal or what is for each and all, and the singularity of the singleton, or the certainty of self-consciousness. Freedom requires not only legislation and the conviction of doing one's duty but also the generous suspension of the law in a reciprocal act of forgiveness.[69]

The community, Hegel argues, is "just as much a pure self-knowing" as is the singleton (¶671). Though the analysis has left sexual difference behind, each singleton, each 'I,' is "extended into two-ness" in the reconciliation of forgiveness, not only by the confession of the difference between his deed and pure duty, but also by his dependence on the recognition of the other (¶671). Only the confession and the recognition of forgiveness prove sufficient to negotiate the opposition of particularity and universality.

Here ends the phenomenology of spirit. As a *phenomenological* project, the analysis up to this point has focused on the whole *from the point of view*

---

69. As Comay notes, "forgiveness has the exorbitance of the gift." Is it true, as she insists, that forgiveness "only arrives too late to make a difference"? Is Hegel not right that forgiveness proves a necessary form of reparation in all personal relationships of any length or depth? Would not Nelson Mandela's choice of truth and reconciliation over judgment and punishment provide an example of a forgiveness that arrived just in time? Have the German government's efforts to commemorate and own up to the horror of the Shoah made no difference? Comay, *Mourning Sickness*, 128.

*of the singleton and his experience.* The real issue (*die Sache selbst*) has been the unfolding (*Aufhebung*) of the singleton so that he comes to know himself as a member of the universal community. Hegel's analysis shifts now to look at the whole from the side of community and the institutions of which the singleton is only a member and by which he is sustained as a singleton. So far, Hegel has analyzed religion "from the *standpoint of consciousness.*" In his penultimate chapter, Hegel will begin again, for the fifth time, to consider the institutions of religion as attempts to think the whole or to give a complete and totalized account of experience and *what is*. The representations found in religion will prefigure philosophy and the *thought* of the whole.

Hegel clearly locates the breaking of the hard heart, the suspension of the law, and the reconciliation of forgiveness, in which each "lets the other go free," in religious community. In contrast, in his own analysis of the state in *The Philosophy of Right*, he repeats the founding tropes of modern political theory: the social contract, the law of property, sovereignty, and the separation of powers in state bureaucracy. In that text, freedom and community seem to have less to do with forgiveness and more to do with the mutual recognition of rights among equals and with subscribing to the universal law of each and all.

Perhaps his analysis of forgiveness proves more politically revolutionary than Hegel expects. First, although he asserts that the reconciliation of forgiveness undoes the inequality that afflicted the acting consciousness, in fact the relationships remain unequal. A self-consciousness cannot be judging and judged at once but constantly exchanges positions with the others—now he acts, now he judges. The inequality of the forgiving and forgiven captures the essential inequality of ethical relationships, which are rarely among equals or rational subjects who recognize the other as the same. Ethical claims and moral dilemmas arise for the most part in relations of unequal power and agency: parent–child, teacher–student, doctor–patient, boss–worker. These relationships require a generosity not unlike that called for in forgiveness, in which the power of the one is not deployed to master the other, but for his sake: to promote his flourishing and to let him "go free."

Might it be possible to imagine not only an ethics but also a politics of forgiveness? In South Africa, after the fall of the apartheid government, Nelson Mandela invoked ancient rituals to put judgment and punishment to the side, favoring processes of truth and reconciliation. Confession and reconciliation value the restoration of the community over holding others accountable and punishable by law. When the hard heart sticks to the law and demands judgment and punishment, it produces a culture of mass incarceration. The singleton remains stuck to his deed, contrary to Hegel's insistence that the deed must vanish so that self-consciousness may remain free. Take a man who arrives in the United States without papers, works for several decades, marries, has children, and makes a life for himself and his family, all while contributing to the community through his labor and his tax payments. The law of the state decrees that he must be deported, and, indeed, because he broke the law while others did not, the hard heart sees that it is unfair to let him remain. But this stinginess undermines and tears apart his community, rather than sustaining it. Some members come to resent the law of the state and fear the police that carry it out, while others regress into patriotic, beautiful souls who only judge the actions of others and report infractions; the community slips backward toward terror, suspicion, and betrayal. Hegel's phenomenology of community calls for a new political imagination, operating beyond judgment and punishment, beyond the ideas of contract, property, and the proper. It poses the question of what a politics might look like that takes seriously the necessity to community of forgiveness and suspending the law.

# PART III
## ABSOLUTE KNOWING

*The Betrayal of Substance*

*Chapter Five*

## LEAVING LITERATURE BEHIND

The Return to Immediacy in the Life of the Concept

> [Philosophers] are like children who imagine that when they come to the end of a plain, they shall be able to touch the sky with their hand.
>
> —ÉTIENNE BONNOT DE CONDILLAC, *AN ESSAY ON THE ORIGIN OF HUMAN KNOWLEDGE* (1746)

The phenomenological analysis has interrogated the institutions, professions, and practices of religion at least since the appearance of unhappy consciousness, but only from the "standpoint of consciousness." In the seventh chapter, Hegel begins again, for the fifth and penultimate time, with a new object. He reconsiders religion on its own as a supra-individual formation, a community of members bound together by language and deed. Religions attempt to offer complete and totalized accounts of existence. Everything that could be or could be said would be anticipated by and implicit within the religion's account of the real and its account of the destiny of humanity and nature.

The shapes of religion break with the previous series of shapes insofar as they represent the truth of spirit *as a whole*, with all of its members or moments articulated. The essential moments of spirit have proved along the way to be "*consciousness, self-consciousness, reason,* and *spirit*" (¶679). Each of these moments has dissolved into a finer analysis, as sense-certainty has distinguished itself from perception, or the giving of laws from the testing of them. These moments had to "run their full course." Each had to be explored in "its own depths" and allowed to form "itself into a totality by its own singular principle" (¶681). Since the preface, Hegel has insisted on the need to "tarry with the negative": to think and live through every thought-position until there was nothing left in it to think. Conceptual labor "creates inwardness" or temporal depth.

These moments—consciousness, self-consciousness, reason, and spirit—cannot be understood as succeeding one another in time. "Only the totality of spirit is in time," and the moments "have no existence in separation from one another" (¶679). The shapes of spirit—the person, the man of culture, and the "beautiful soul" of the "religion of morality"—each embody the totality of the constitutive moments of spirit, but from the depth of a particular moment. The depth of religion provides a horizon for all the other depths. It does not let "the singular principle isolate itself and make itself into a whole within itself"; rather, it puts each shape in its proper perspective and depth (¶681).

When the narrative lines of the different shapes are "gathered up into a single bundle," as in the phenomenological analysis of religion, they "combine symmetrically so that the similar differences in which each particular moment took shape within itself meet together" (¶681). Bundled together in this way, the series of shapes reveals reappearing figures and recurring themes. The sophistical to-ing and fro-ing of perception kept reappearing, as did the beyond of the understanding and the negative power of thought in determinate negation. A nest of recurring oppositions accrued: one/many, inner/outer, self/other, subject/object, in-itself/for-others. The ruse of the essential–inessential distinction kept reappearing in the effort to master these contradictions. The theme of the struggle against the enemy kept reappearing, as did the hard heart. The Bacchanalian revel kept reappearing, as Hegel's figure of appearance, rest and violent motion, the arising and passing away that does not arise and pass away. Philosophical consciousness kept interrogating natural consciousness, putting it on the spot to say what it means, and every utterance seemed unable to sustain itself under the test. Only the breaking of the hard heart and the suspension of law in reciprocal forgiveness proved to unfold (*aufheben*) in each singleton the certainty of existing as a member of an organic whole.[1] Only now can the singleton bring the absolute into being by thinking it, articulating it in his own language and experience.

---

1. The man of forgiveness, unlike the legal person of the state of right, counts for more than a unit in a population or a number; rather, he knows himself as and is recognized as a member of an organic community wherein members are differentiated organs, not mere units or parts to be counted.

## RELIGION

Various forms of community have appeared since the emergence in the object of the figure or logic of membership, as the community of properties of the thing of perception. In this community, each member or property belongs together with the others, but in such a way as to leave each one standing in its independence. Similarly, communities of faith and reason—family and nation—sustain the singleton in his independence, as a member of the community.

In religion the singleton distinguishes the moments, members, or shapes from the generative power that sustains them all. 'We,' philosophical consciousness, can see from the very beginning that religious consciousness, in its rites and rituals, already realizes that the truth of the 'I' lies in the 'we.' Still, religious consciousness remains unhappy because he continues to posit the realization of this reconciliation into a beyond. He does not yet see that the concept itself is the generative power that produces and surpasses every moment, every member.

The religious self represents himself to himself as a moment of the whole and, thus, anticipates the completion of the phenomenological progression in absolute knowing. The difference between religion and absolute knowing lies in the distinction between *picturing* or *representing* the whole system of moments or shapes, on the one hand, and *thinking* it, on the other. Religion, as a form of *consciousness*, knows the whole system of shapes or moments only as an object, albeit, in revealed religion, as a self-conscious one.[2] The absolute remains alien to the man of religion as something beyond his experience and only represented in it. Absolute knowing, however, consists just in this self-consciousness who thinks of himself as a moment in a complete and closed system of moments, thinking the whole as an immanently given system of concepts that provides the infrastructure of the real.

Both Hegel's chapter on religion and his chapter on absolute knowing begin with a summary of previous shapes and thought positions, as well as

---

2. This chapter will not offer a detailed reading of Hegel's schematic summary of the history of world religions, from the worship of nature to the "revealed religion" of the Christian incarnation. His analysis not only smells sharply of superficiality and chauvinism, particularly in his remarks on "the Orient," but it is unnecessary to the philosophical point at stake: the difference between the picturing of the whole in religion and the thinking of it in absolute knowing.

a meditation on time. The summary in the chapter on religion follows the unfolding of the unhappy consciousness, in the divinely given laws of ethical life, in the struggle between faith and reason or the Enlightenment, in the "religion of morality," and finally, in the figure of conscience—the self that knows himself to be the site of the universal in thought, word, and deed. Unlike the "moments" of the text as a whole—consciousness, self-consciousness, reason, and spirit—which are essential to any possible experience, and, thus, cannot be said to be in time, the shapes of religion come to be and pass away. The unhappy consciousness is a localized moment within the history of stoicism and medieval Christianity, just as the monarch and the man of the Enlightenment exist likewise as historical figures. "Only the totality of spirit is in time, and the shapes, which are shapes of the totality of *spirit*, display themselves in a temporal succession; for only the whole has true actuality and therefore the form of pure freedom in [the] face of an 'other,' a form which expresses itself as time" (¶679). The four constitutive moments—consciousness, self-consciousness, reason, and spirit—persist as the eternal form of human experience, even as the shapes of spirit in which this form is embodied unfold in time. Spirit exhibits an organic or genetic logic in which each shape emerges from the one before, and time is just this organic logic unfolding itself. Religious consciousness knows himself as a moment of this unfolding, but he remains unhappy: he pictures this unfolding as something alien and beyond, not yet realized in him. Recall the figure of the messiah: either he is yet to come, or he has already left the tomb.

## ABSOLUTE KNOWING: THE LAST BEGINNING

Instead of locating the truth of the whole in an alien self-consciousness beyond experience, as religious consciousness does, the self-consciousness of absolute knowing knows himself as the site of the thinking of the whole. The object of absolute knowing, the last and unique object of the phenomenological progression, is not something other than consciousness, but "immediate being" or "immediate consciousness" itself. Absolute knowing thus returns to sense-certainty, to immediacy, thinking it now as the germ from which absolute knowing has unfolded. As the unfolding of the moments and shapes in their necessary genetic or organic logic, from sensuous immediacy to absolute knowing, the phenomenological interrogation has "created inwardness" where before there was only appearance. This creation takes time—both the time of history, through which the shapes of spirit appear across millennia in actual collective forms, and the time of the singleton, whose production of the narrative of spirit through his own self-interrogation requires that he "tarry" with each shape to digest the richness of its determinations. Only these traversals of time, this "creation of inwardness," make possible the emergence of absolute knowing as the self-conscious reflection or articulation of the shapes not merely as historical forms, but as "*specific concepts* and as their organic self-grounded movement" (¶805). The man of absolute knowing is not "hardheaded" any more than he is "hardhearted"; he does not repeat the usual error of natural consciousness in "remaining stuck to a moment." He thinks himself as the movement of the unfolding or the *life of the concept*.

The "reconciliation of consciousness with self-consciousness . . . closes the series of the shapes of spirit" (¶794). Hegel again makes clear that he has religious community in mind. From one side, the collaborative practices of religion—rituals, good works, public professions and confessions—actually do create community, as we first saw with the acts of the unhappy consciousness, in which the singleton finds his truth as a member of the whole. From the other side, religion requires a profession and confession from the singleton himself that makes him conscious of himself as the site of "not only the intuition of the divine, but the divine's intuition of itself" (¶795). This "beautiful soul" exists as the difference between the determinate content of the unfolding of spirit, or spirit in the singleton, and the movement or pure form of the unfolding of spirit and of self-consciousness, or spirit in history. After the long passage through the dissemblances of morality, the suspension of the law and the unequal reciprocities of forgiveness release the singleton from the conflicts of determinateness, but only with respect to duty. The difference between the determinateness of the singleton and the indeterminacy of the narrative voice of philosophical science has not yet been mastered. Absolute knowing appears when consciousness comes to know itself as the pure movement of self-consciousness, in which all the determinate shapes are generated and unfolded, but also surpassed as mere moments of the one movement.

A series of renunciations will be required (¶796). Hegel explicitly refers to the figure of determinate negation put forward at the beginning in the analysis of sensuous certainty. Just as the consciousness awash in the flux of becoming is forced to let go of the determinate 'now' to preserve the 'now' as the form of experience, so too the man of absolute knowing thinks himself in thinking the movement of the concept as his truth, and he detaches himself from any particular content—though, in another philosophical sleight of hand, not from determinateness *as a concept*. Each shape "exhibits the life of spirit in its entirety" (¶796). The phenomenological philosopher of absolute thinking identifies himself with what appears over and over in each one as the essence or truth of spirit: the movement of self-consciousness, the self-sundering and return from otherness, that generates and manifests itself in the whole series of shapes but surpasses them all.

Hegel reminds the reader again that this truth could only come at a time "ripe to receive it" (¶710). In order to produce itself as self-knowledge, spirit must have expressed itself in historical forms of life that are now available for reflection and narration. "As spirit that knows what it is, it does not exist before, and nowhere at all, till after the completion of its work of compelling its imperfect 'shape' to procure for its consciousness the shape of its essence, and in this way to equate its *self-consciousness* with its *consciousness*" (¶800). Only this coincidence of knowing or narrating and being would justify Hegel's claim to closure and to the necessity of the logic of unfolding exhibited in the series of shapes. Self-consciousness "wrests" from consciousness its "entire substance" and "has absorbed into itself the entire structure of the essentialities of substance" (801). What has been is given again in thought as an unfolding system of concepts.

As he "sets aside" determinateness, so too this absolute thinking "sets aside his time-form," identifying himself with the movement that persists and traverses time, rather than with any determinate shape caught up in time's flux. Time, Hegel insists, is "the concept itself," unfolding in time and as time in the shapes of spirit. Spirit "necessarily appears in time, and it appears in time as long as it does not *grasp* its pure concept, which is to say, as long as it does not erase time" (¶801, trans. Pinkard). Actual spirit comes on the scene as the belonging-together of determination or substance and motion, on the one hand, and subject, or the negative power of thought, on the other. In absolute knowing, all the determinate shapes have been articulated as concepts made determinate in the movement of their unfolding as a unique system of shapes. This movement, unlike the shapes themselves, does not appear in time, as it is the unmoving form of becoming. By

## LEAVING LITERATURE BEHIND

identifying himself with this motion that has no time, the man of absolute knowing would free himself both from determinateness and from mortality or being in time.

This "erasure" of time also brings history to an end. In declaring the end of history, Hegel does not foretell a cessation of events; rather, he means that history is no longer philosophically interesting, insofar as all possible shapes and forms of self-consciousness and of objectivity have already been articulated in history and have now, through his phenomenological analysis, been thought as a necessary system of concepts. History no longer has anything to teach philosophy. Whatever happens will have been anticipated, as the thinking subject has arrived at "that point at which knowledge need no longer go beyond itself because nothing is other to it" (¶80). The genetic logic has ensured the necessity of the path and outcome. Absolute knowing has come forth from sensuous certainty with the same necessity as the oak emerges from the acorn or the man from the boy. When the complete system of shapes has been externalized as consciousness and in history, it can be thought *as such*, as a complete and totalized complex of concepts, and its determinate history of emergence can be *left behind*.

History is at the end of its interest for philosophy because there is no longer any possibility of novelty in it, only of repetition of the moments and shapes already articulated. Art arrives at a similar end in the "erasure of time." All the possible shapes and forms of the practices of self-representation in art will have been articulated in the conceptual system that constitutes the possibilities of history and thought. In art, as in history, there can be no more novelty. "The circle of the creations of art embraces the forms in which absolute substance has externalized itself" (¶754). The completion of that externalization completes the history of art, as a history of forms.

Moreover, Hegel takes an approach to art that reduces the work to a symptom of culture, or the "embodiment" of the spirit of "a free people" (¶700). The concept of a work of art consists in its being a conscious production "made by human hands"; however, in creating his work, the artist will have "depersonalized" himself: "to himself as a particular singleton he gave in his work no actual existence" (¶708). The work represents a worldview or form of life more than the specific style of the artist.[3] Art ceases to

---

3. Many contemporary philosophers follow Hegel's approach. See note 17 to "On Reading Hegel's *Phenomenology of Spirit*."

be philosophically interesting, according to Hegel, when it no longer exerts the cohesive force on a people that the Greek dramas did on the Greek city-state or the cathedrals and paintings of Christianity did in medieval and Renaissance Europe. Art, treated in the *Phenomenology* as a form of religion, proves its truth in binding a people together.

Here, and in his *Aesthetics* as well, Hegel reduces the work to an instance of a general form. Works are subsumed under the general categories of the symbolic, the classical, and the romantic. They are grouped according to media—painting, music, architecture, literature—and divided into a variety of subgenres. A hierarchy of arts is established, with the self-conscious arts of language and literature surpassing the unconscious or inarticulate spirit of the plastic arts, such as sculpture and painting. Despite a few references to the genius of Homer, Sophocles, Shakespeare, and Raphael, Hegel's phenomenological interrogation does not take up the experience of style or the specificity of the work of art as anything more than a symptom of a cultural form.

Given his reliance on *Antigone* in the course of his argument in the *Phenomenology*, the lack of any detailed discussion of the play might seem surprising. But Hegel appropriates the play for his own ends, before it has a chance to speak for itself. In his discussion of art as religion, Hegel again quotes a fragment of the lines from *Antigone* that he quoted in his critique of the moral insolence of reason and his account of how the singleton is commanded by the right. The ethical commandments that arise out of our relationships with one another represent "a law that is 'everlasting and no one knows whence it came'" (¶712). Antigone represents this emergence of ethical obligation out of human relationships, but she is also "the stubborn daughter of a stubborn sire." Like Creon, she exhibits the "hardheadedness" of sticking to one moment of the right at the expense of the other, and in her stubbornness, she contributes to the erasure of the future.

Had Hegel read more carefully and in particular paid attention to the second play, written last, he might have noticed Ismene's agency and the priority she gives to human relationships over abstract principles. She is the only Cadmean who, in her efforts to negotiate with powers both political and divine, exhibits the fluidity that Hegel associates with spirit and thought. She eschews the usual Cadmean stubbornness or hardheadedness as the very trait that has brought on the family's troubles and downfall. Nothing matters more to her than her relation to her sister. Even when the righteous Antigone sneers at her in public, Ismene continues to reach out to her sister: "what would my life be without you?" Not only does she recognize the claim of the right, but Ismene also practices the suspension of the law through forgiveness. She would preserve relationships over adhering relentlessly to one aspect of the right at the expense of the other. So powerful is the heroic Antigone who emerges from Hegel's reading of the play that even feminist rereadings rarely pay attention to Ismene's agency and the question of sisterly solidarity.[4]

Perhaps Hegel fails to pay attention to the specificity of the work because that very specificity undermines his attempt to protect philosophy from the problem of style. In the preface to the *Phenomenology*, Hegel acknowledges the reliance of philosophy on the technology of the book, but he makes no mention of it here. As the book circulates, it creates for itself a community of readers, transforming what was first the thought of the author alone into something universal. In claiming for philosophy an absolute knowing, Hegel would erase or set aside the specificity of its conditions of emergence and the specificity of its narrative. Hegel writes as if he were style-less or the zero degree of style, as if he could erase his own authorship and leave a book that was nothing but the anonymous self-articulation of spirit.

Hegel attempts to install a narrator, who, through the negative power of thought, has "purified" himself of every determination and knows himself as this movement rather than as a determinate shape. Positioned at the "outside of heaven" or "on the horizon," the philosopher of Hegelian phenomenology would always already have anticipated what arrives with experience. He would give voice to spirit thinking itself in its totality as the life-sustaining concept that traverses all the shapes. Thinking himself as determinate negation, he would return to the certainty of immediacy after traversing all the possible forms of consciousness and objectivity. As this motion, he would surpass any determinate moment, while retaining determination as a conceptual moment—determination without determination. On the one hand, the self-conscious singleton is the site of the realization of the concept; on the other, he is effaced in it.

---

4. For an exception, see Bonnie Honig's *Antigone Interrupted* (Cambridge: Cambridge University Press, 2013). See also Mary C. Rawlinson, "Beyond Antigone: Ismene, Gender, and the Right to Life," in *The Returns of Antigone: Interdisciplinary Essays*, ed. T. Chanter and S. D. Kirkland (Albany: State University of New York Press, 2014), 101–24.

## ART/LITERATURE

> Only the impression . . . is a guarantor of truth.
> Thanks to art, instead of seeing one world only, our own, we see that world multiply itself and we have at our disposal as many worlds as there are original artists, worlds more different one from the other than those which revolve in infinite space, worlds which, centuries after the extinction of the fire from which their light first emanated, whether it is called Rembrandt or Vermeer, send us still each one its special radiance.
> —MARCEL PROUST, À LA RECHERCHE DU TEMPS PERDU, VOL. 6

A work of art is "made by human hands" (¶708). The artist transforms substance into subject. From the stone he produces the statue of the god or hero that embodies the cultural ideals of a particular people and epoch. These works endure and prove their universality by traversing times and cultures. In "our time" the works no longer evoke fear and passion, as these gods are no longer worshiped; however, they prompt an "*inwardizing* in us of the spirit which in them was still *outwardly* manifest" (¶753). These works unfold profound temporal and historical depths "in us," inscribing the horizon of their own time at some distance from ours.

The phenomenological interrogator finds in the work of art not a mere thing of perception, but an embodiment of a shape of consciousness or form of life. What self-consciousness takes as truth in the work is another self-consciousness. Spirit makes itself its own object in the work, both through the artist and through the spectator (¶708). Thus, the activity of the artist/spectator constitutes "the night in which substance was betrayed and made itself into subject" (¶703). Art reveals the truth of substance to be subject.

The hierarchy of the arts tracks the degree of this spiritualization, from sculpture to literature—from the formed thing to tragedy and comedy. The artist finds in the statue that "he did not create a being *like himself*" (¶709). The sensuous thing remains alien to self-consciousness, whose element of existence is language. Only in language can self-consciousness "have its very concept for its shape, so that the concept and the work of art produced know each other as one and the same" (¶702). Here too Hegel works to erase the singularity of the singleton and the determinateness of sensuous life. "Just as the singular self-consciousness [*einzelne Selbstbewußtsein*] is *immediately* present in language, so it is also immediately present as a *universal* infection; the complete separation of being-for-itself [*Fürsichsein*] is at the same time the fluidity and the universally communicated unity of the many selves; language is the soul existing as soul" (¶710). The singleton has "worked off every unconscious existence and fixed determination in the same way that substance itself has become this fluid essence" (¶703). In participating in the language of tragedy and comedy—whether as actor, spectator, or chorus—the singleton appears, but *not as himself*; rather, he appears only as an effect of a "universal infection," or contagion. After all the "purifications" and "pulverizing" of the singleton, after all the "struggles against the enemy," Hegel has reduced the singleton to saying 'I' so that it marks a distinction without a difference. This self-consciousness knows himself as a member of a whole in which each one can substitute for the other. In the end, there can be only one narrative of spirit, a master narrative for the mastery of difference. Religion absorbed art: the absolute one erased the indelible multiplicities of style.

Mortality, too, Hegel would have us believe, has been exorcised. In the closing passages of the *Phenomenology*, Hegel echoes the admonition with which he closed the preface: at a time when the universal gathers such strength, less must be expected of the singleton, and he must expect less for himself (¶72). The "self-knowing spirit" of absolute knowing knows "its limit: to know one's limit is to know how to sacrifice yourself" (¶807). Hegel hews to his terrestrial faith, his belief in Earth as the "eternal individual." If nature and history are eternal, the singleton should "sacrifice" himself to the tide of generations, of which he is, in truth, only a moment. The mortality of the singleton leaves no trace because someone will always come to replace him, just as the Bacchanalian revel appeared to be calm repose because each member was replaced as soon as he dropped out.[5] The singleton sacrifices his singularity and detaches himself from every determination in order to know himself in the truth of the concept. In so doing, he makes his mortality a thing of no consequence in the flux of becoming. The immortal "life" of the concept erases the mortality of the singleton and his singularity, his determinateness. All very well for man in the abstract, but not so convincing for Ivan Ilych, little Vanya.

---

5. As Comay notes, these sacrifices make "no claim to redeem the lives squandered on the slaughter bench of history." Rebecca Comay, *Mourning Sickness: Hegel and the French Revolution* (Stanford, CA: Stanford University Press, 2011), 125.

Like death, sexual difference haunts these passages in its images and metaphors. Hegel reinforces the invisibility and silence assigned to woman by articulating her role in the "metamorphosis of the Earth-spirit" as a "feminine principle of nourishment," in contrast to the "spiritual fermentation" under "the masculine principle, the self-impelling force of self-conscious existence" (¶721). Hegel continues to rely on the gender division of labor, even as he attempts to arrest the unfolding of woman in order to assign her forever to the care of the body, thereby solving the problem of the integration of private and public labor, family and public life. She lingers over the religious rituals of bread and wine as a "silent maternal yearning."[6] She supplies the nourishment, while man supplies the form and direction of life.

Reinforcing the identification of woman as nourishment, he imagines works of art as "beautiful fruits" that a serving girl might set before him at the end of a dinner. While the tables of the gods "provide no spiritual food and drink," as no one worships them any longer, the works of art from this period exist for the phenomenologist like so many luscious fruits presented for his consideration and pleasure. The "spirit of the fate" that presents the phenomenologist with these works of art exceeds "the ethical life and the actual world of that nation" by producing "*inwardizing* in us," just as the serving girl is "more than the nature" that provides the fruit "because she sums them up in a higher mode, in the gleam of her self-conscious eye and in the gesture with which she offers them" (¶753). Her "gleam" may be no more than the reflection of his leer, as he exercises his right of assessment and objectification. At least he accords her some self-consciousness, so that she is more than fruit, if still only a principle of nourishment, to be assessed through her effect on men.[7]

Hegel appropriates female generativity by repeatedly describing absolute knowing as "giving birth to itself." It is "to give birth to itself from its own concept" (¶702). The array of shapes "stands impatiently expectant round the birthplace of spirit as it becomes self-consciousness. The grief and longing of the unhappy self-consciousness which permeates them all is their center and the common birth-pang of its emergence—the simplicity of the

---

6. In the Eleusinian mysteries, this is Ceres's longing for her daughter Persephone. In the Christian Eucharist, it is Mary's grief for her crucified son.

7. On the Aristotelian roots of Hegel's treatment of woman as nourishment, see Caroline Whitbeck, "Theories of Sex Difference," in *Women and Philosophy: Toward a Theory of Liberation*, ed. C. C. Gould and M. W. Wartofsky (New York: Putnam, 1976), 54–80.

pure concept, which contains those forms as its moments" (§754). Woman is to be silent, to nourish masculine activity, and to find her own generativity supplanted by the generativity of the concept. On the one hand, she is absolutely necessary to the unfolding of the concept; on the other, she is left behind and effaced in it. Only thus can absolute knowing—in violation of everything phenomenology teaches about the indelible dependence of identity on a relation to the other, on difference—"give birth to itself." Only thus can the "immortal" concept be said to be "living."

---

Hegel means to install an absolute knowing that has freed itself from determinateness, that has detached from life and from his own mortality, that knows the other as like himself, and that knows himself as a moment in the life of the concept. The master narrative of the *Phenomenology* will have mastered difference by locating each one in its own proper place in a totalized system of differences. Yet, there remains the irreducible two of sexual difference, the ineffaceable difference of the singleton in his mortality, and the multiplicity of signatures in art, each one not an instance of a type or kind but a way of generating a world.

Hegel's own method seems to undermine his desire to install a master narrative of the one, of absolute knowing. Under his analysis, every unity immediately sunders itself into its constitutive moments. He repeatedly recognizes that spirit is (at least) two, even as he leaves the sister behind. He erases the difference through the sequestration of women in domestic space and the exclusion of the feminine voice from the 'I' of philosophy. The idea of absolute knowing "giving birth to itself" seems to contradict the fundamental Hegelian principle that any identity is itself only in relation to an other. The logic of forgiveness captures the *inequality* of the mutual recognition of community: the forgiving is not the forgiven, though each self plays both roles. Man's intellectual activity exists only in relation to the feminine work of nourishment. The slave begins to discover his freedom in the "formed thing." At every moment, self-consciousness finds itself mediated by the radically other, not "giving birth to itself."

Hegel has constantly reminded us that the concept is only realized as an infrastructure of life. Yet, he has assiduously tried to tear the concept away from its adherence to the sensuous. The thinking of absolute knowing positions the self in a purely conceptual realm, where any possible experience has been anticipated, and history is no longer philosophically interesting. In his most powerful metaphorical move, Hegel recruits the reader to the *life of the concept*. But, the concept on its own, as Hegel told us in the preface, is a "lifeless husk." The concept lives only when it is thought by the singleton and functions as an infrastructure of life. It too is infinitely mediated by its sensuous other.

Hegel's desire to install absolute knowing—the master narrative, the complete and totalized system of concepts of experience—also undermines his own phenomenological demonstration that the truth of organic being is "incommensurability" (¶706). In absolute knowing, Hegel would render the singleton a purely conceptual being, in whom all the constitutive differences and distinctions would be resolved.[8] But the pure 'I' of self-consciousness remains distinct from the concrete, substantial 'I' of consciousness or determinate being, just as the form of the 'now' remains distinct from every determinate 'now.' The one will never be commensurate with the other.[9]

In a decisive conceptual coup of the phenomenological analysis, Hegel terminates the endless dissemblances of morality and the regression to the spiritual animal kingdom, where all vie for wealth, power, and the authority over truth, in the suspension of the law and unequal reciprocity of forgiveness. This revolutionary moment contrasts sharply with the conventional political philosophy of contract, property, and sovereignty that Hegel

---

8. Indeed, this gesture of resolution was visible at least as early as his discussion of the man of culture. See section 4.b.

9. Comay designates absolute knowing as "trauma," the "measure" of a hierarchy of traumas, and what treats or redeems the traumas: "the illness for which it presents the cure" or "interminable analysis." But Hegel means to terminate the phenomenological interrogation in absolute knowing, so that he can erect the vast edifice of the encyclopedic project. In place of "interminable analysis," there will be the mastery of the diffusion of life in classes and laws, the erasure of novelty in history and art through a taxonomy of epochs and forms, the (mis)representation, over and over again, of the incommensurabilities of language and forgiveness, of experience itself. Experience will have been made commensurate with itself in absolute knowing, and philosophical practice will never be the same again. Absolute knowing is the Bacchanalian revel of complete repose: the appearing and vanishing *that does not vanish*, in which the loss of the singleton leaves no trace, in which each one is replaced as soon as he drops out. In the asymmetrical reciprocities of forgiveness, it may be that Hegel "reins back, if only for a moment, the chronic temptation to slide from a phenomenology of embodied freedom to a noumenology of the pure will," and that, with this philosophical gesture, Hegel "returns thought to the order of experience." (Comay, *Mourning Sickness*, 153.) But the philosophical perspective of the logic is only possible if the path of the phenomenological interrogation has been completed and *left behind*. I note that Comay ends her book not with Hegel but, at least indirectly through Benjamin, with Proust.

develops later in *The Philosophy of Right*. Later on, it seems that politics could not arise from a suspension of the law, because politics is by definition the domain of law, and above all the law of property and of what is proper, which prescribes who has a right to what. Hegel's analysis of the dependency of community on forgiveness suggests a politics that begins not from the articulation of rights and laws, but from an assessment of structural inequities and injustices and systemic precarities. It suggests a politics based not on the power of judgment and punishment, but on generating the community that will sustain each and all. Later on, the incommensurabilities of a politics of forgiveness are replaced by the fictive equalities of the logic of property.

The speculative rhetoric of an absolute knowing, a self-consciousness that is detached from determinateness, from life, from mortality, from sexual difference, from the signatures of art, turns away from phenomenology toward a logic of concepts and takes up philosophy as an *encyclopedic* project, a complete and systematic conceptual mapping of nature, history, and human experience. To the extent that Hegel leaves the phenomenological project behind, he cuts his tether to the impression and to the immediate certainty of the self-interrogating, incommensurate singleton in his sensuous existence, the seed or germ that guaranteed and nourished the entire project.

Given its magisterial prose and the grandeur of its conceptual project, its satirical wit and indelible images, few other texts can be read alongside Hegel's *Phenomenology*. Proust's *À la recherche du temps perdu* can and should be, not only because its prose and project are equally magnificent, but, more importantly, because Proust achieves Hegel's aim of thinking the whole of experience without losing the guarantee of the impression or the specificity of the singleton and the work of art.[10] Like Hegel, Proust begins with the germ of an impression and unfolds the whole of a life from it in such a way as to implicate all life in the narrative. Instead of the voluntary and contrived method of the *Phenomenology*, Proust's phenomenological narrative unfolds via the involuntary and articulates only what the narrator is forced to think by life itself. "Ideas are substitutes for sorrows" (6:315). Proust, like Hegel, aligns philosophical truth with the traversal of time and

---

10. Marcel Proust, *In Search of Lost Time*, trans. C. K. Scott Moncrieff, Andreas Mayor, and Terence Kilmartin, 6 vols. (1913–27; New York: Modern Library, 1982–83). References in the text are to volume and page number.

the "creation of inwardness," but he produces these in the reader not as abstract ideas, but as actual experiences of grief and loss. Hegel's analysis of the ritualized disappointment and contrived suffering of the unhappy consciousness, who projects his truth into the beyond, seems shallow compared to Proust's account of the absolute loss of the mortal other. What Hegel would erase Proust makes the wellspring of his philosophy.

Whereas Hegel reduces the work of art to an instance of a general kind or type, as if the work could not speak on its own but only as an example, Proust locates the truth of the work of art in the signature:

> [Style] is the revelation, which by direct and conscious methods would be impossible, of the qualitative difference, the uniqueness of the fashion in which the world appears to each one of us, a difference which, if there were no art, would remain forever the secret of every individual. Through art alone are we able to emerge from ourselves, to know what another person sees of a universe which is not the same as our own and which, without art, the landscapes would remain as unknown to us as those that may exist on the moon. (6:299)

The thought of the whole would consist not in the fiction of a master narrative but in thinking this expanding universe of individual worlds.

What creates inwardness and gives joy in art lies precisely in the differences between Vermeer and Rembrandt, Mozart and Beethoven. Whatever categories or general concepts might be applied to them, the signatures would always exceed them. Each name presents not only an easily recognizable style, but also a *specific universal*. Style exhibits the unity that Hegel accorded to absolute knowing, as a universe of universalizable styles of experience. Each name embodies a power to unfold the whole of a world in a distinct way that proves its universality by creating for itself a community of adherents. "The idea of the edifice that I had to construct did not leave me for an instant. Whether it would be a church where little by little a group of faithful would succeed in apprehending verities and discovering harmonies or perhaps even a grand general plan, or whether it would remain, like a druidic monument on a rocky isle, something forever unfrequented, I could not tell" (6:521). Hegel thought he would articulate *the truth*. Proust, less grandiose and more bound to the specificity of sensuous life, knows he creates only a "monument" to truth, which may or may not create a community of "faithful." Truth occurs—or the concept is realized—only when others come to revivify the work.

In a few short passages, Hegel reduces maternal love to a formal principle, and this proved to be an essential gesture in his mastery of sexual difference. Proust, in contrast, devotes thousands of pages to the dynamics of maternal love, to its subtle and disciplined character, its unbounded generosity, its intergenerational generativity. Rather than approach the "creation of inwardness" as a purely conceptual unfolding, Proust sets the reader up for the revelation of inwardness through the scene of an involuntary memory of the experience of profound grief at the absolute loss of his grandmother. The conventions of grief have dulled his sense of her: "I'm so sorry for your loss. Thank you for your condolences." The rituals of grief seem shallow and fail to yield an experience of the depth of his loss. But, in the involuntary kinesthetic memory that floods him as he bends over to tie his shoe on his second visit to Balbec—just as she had done on his first—he experiences her absolute loss. On the one hand, it is an experience of the greatest possible despair because he feels the depth of the loss, how she was lodged within him as the horizon of his experience. On the other, it is an experience of profound joy, because *he has found her again* in remembering the self that he was in her presence. This very specific experience of grief in the loss of the mortal other provides one of the "constitutive moments" of Proust's philosophical account of experience. His analysis makes philosophically significant an experience that is irreducibly singular and at the same time universal—a *specific universal*.

When Hegel turns from phenomenology to logic, he leaves behind the phenomenon of incommensurability that on his own account defines organic life. Absolute knowing effaces the difference between saying and meaning, between certainty and truth, that drives the phenomenological interrogation. Philosophical science concerns itself only with conceptual relations among the "pure essentialities" that undergird "the development of all natural and spiritual life."[11] Proust eschews this move to abstraction that is required by the aim of the master narrative and the hegemony of the one: "The ideas formed by the pure intelligence have no more than a logical, a possible truth, they are arbitrarily chosen.... Only the impression ... is a guarantor of truth" (6:273). The real exhibits the incommensurable

---

11. G. W. F. Hegel, *Science of Logic*, trans. A. V. Miller (1816; New York: Humanities, 1969), 28.

difference between the determinate self of consciousness and the pure movement of self-consciousness, the irreducibilities of sexual difference,[12] the mortality of the singleton for which there is no compensation, and the multiplicity of signatures in art and literature against the abstract fiction of the master narrative or the logic of the one. Hegel cannot write with both hands, maintaining the concept as an infrastructure of life, while erasing mortality, sexual difference, and the difference of style in art and literature. The difference of the singleton always remains the element of philosophical thought and of the concept. The purified 'I' of the master narrative of the one or absolute knowing will always have been an abstraction from the truth.

Hegel admonishes the reader over and over again to be taught by experience, not to import any of her own bright ideas, and to think of the concept not as an abstraction but as an infrastructure of life. Over and over again he reminds us that any identity exists only in difference, in relation to its other, that any unity was always already two. Perhaps, Hegel's own style always forestalls the closing of the circle in absolute knowing and undoes the erasure of time.

---

12. Proust's analysis complicates the two-ness of sexual difference, so that sexual difference becomes a portal for thinking not only the complexities of sexual difference but also other differences of gender, race, and class.

# BIBLIOGRAPHY

Benhabib, Seyla. *Situating the Self.* New York: Routledge, 1992.
Butler, Judith. *Antigone's Claim: Kinship Between Life and Death.* New York: Columbia University Press, 2000.
Comay, Rebecca. *Mourning Sickness: Hegel and the French Revolution.* Stanford, CA: Stanford University Press, 2011.
de Condillac, Étienne Bonnot. *An Essay on the Origin of Human Knowledge.* Translated by Thomas Nugent. 1746; New York: AMS, 1974.
Danto, Arthur. *The Philosophical Disenfranchisement of Art.* New York: Columbia University Press, 1986.
Derrida, Jacques. *Dissemination.* Translated by Barbara Johnson. 1972; Chicago: University of Chicago Press, 1981.
———. *Paper Machine.* Translated by Rachel Bowlby. Stanford, CA: Stanford University Press, 2005.
———. *Speech and Phenomena.* Translated by David B. Allison. 1967; Evanston, IL: Northwestern University Press, 1973.
Forster, Michael N. *Hegel's Idea of a Phenomenology of Spirit.* Chicago: University of Chicago Press, 1989.
Foucault, Michel. *Abnormal: Lectures at the Collège de France, 1974–1975.* Translated by Graham Burchell. 1999; London: Verso, 2003.
———. *The Care of the Self.* Vol. 3, *The History of Sexuality.* Translated by Robert Hurley. 1984; New York: Random House, 1986.
———. *An Introduction.* Vol. 1, *The History of Sexuality.* Translated by Robert Hurley. 1976; New York: Pantheon, 1978.
———. *Les Mot et les choses.* Paris: Gallimard, 1966.

———. *"Society Must Be Defended": Lectures at the Collège de France, 1975–76*. Translated by David Macey. 1997; London: Penguin, 2003.

———. *The Use of Pleasure*. Vol. 2, *The History of Sexuality*. Translated by Robert Hurley. 1984; New York: Random House, 1985.

Freud, Sigmund. "Femininity." In *New Introductory Lectures on Psychoanalysis*. Vol. 22, *The Complete Psychological Works of Sigmund Freud*, 112–35. 1933; London: Hogarth Press, 1964.

Gadamer, Hans-Georg. *Hegel's Dialectic: Five Hermeneutical Studies*. Translated by P. Christopher Smith. 1971; New Haven, CT: Yale University Press, 1976.

Gilligan, Carol. *In a Different Voice: Psychological Theory and Women's Development*. Cambridge, MA: Harvard University Press, 1982.

Grosz, Elizabeth. "Irigaray and Darwin on Sexual Difference: Some Reflections." In *Engaging the World: Thinking After Irigaray*, edited by Mary C. Rawlinson, 157–72. Albany: State University of New York Press, 2016.

———. *Time Travels: Feminism, Nature, Power*. Durham, NC: Duke University Press, 2005.

Hegel, G. W. F. *Encyclopedia of the Philosophical Sciences in Basic Outline*. Part 1, *The Science of Logic*. Translated by Klaus Brinkmann and Daniel O. Dahlstrom. 1827; Cambridge: Cambridge University Press, 2010.

———. *Phenomenology of Spirit*. Translated by A. V. Miller. 1807; New York: Oxford University Press, 1977.

———. *The Phenomenology of Spirit*. Translated by Terry Pinkard. 1807; Cambridge: Cambridge University Press, 2018.

———. *The Philosophy of History*. Translated by J. Sibree. 1837; New York: Dover, 1956.

———. *Science of Logic*. Translated by A. V. Miller. 1816; New York: Humanities, 1969.

Hobbes, Thomas. *Leviathan*. 1651; Oxford: Oxford University Press, 1996.

Holtzman, Jeffrey S. "Normative Moral Neuroscience: The Third Tradition of Neuroscience." *Journal of the American Philosophical Association* 4, no. 3 (2018): 411–31.

Honig, Bonnie. *Antigone Interrupted*. New York: Cambridge University Press, 2013.

Hyppolite, Jean. *Genesis and Structure of Hegel's* Phenomenology of Spirit. Translated by Samuel Cherniak and John Heckman. 1946; Evanston, IL: Northwestern University Press, 1974.

———. *Studies on Marx and Hegel*. Translated by John O'Neil. 1955; New York: Harper Torchbooks, 1969.

Irigaray, Luce. *Democracy Begins Between Two*. Translated by Kirsteen Anderson. 1994; London: Athlone, 2000.

———. *Speculum of the Other Woman*. Translated by Gillian C. Gill. 1974; Ithaca, NY: Cornell University Press, 1985.

Johnston, Adrian. *Prolegomena to Any Future Materialism*. Vol. 2, *A Weak Nature Alone*. Evanston, IL: Northwestern University Press, 2019.

Kant, Immanuel. *Critique of Practical Reason*. Translated by Mary Gregor. 1788; Cambridge: Cambridge University Press, 2015.

———. *Critique of Pure Reason*. Rev. 2nd ed. Translated by Norman Kemp Smith. 1787; New York: St. Martin's, 1964.

———. *Groundwork of the Metaphysic of Morals*. Translated by H. J. Paton. 1785; New York: Harper Torchbooks, 1964.

## BIBLIOGRAPHY

——. *Idea for a Universal History with Cosmopolitan Intent*. Translated by Carl J. Friedrich. In *Basic Writings of Kant*, edited by Allen W. Wood, 117–32. 1784; New York: Modern Library, 2001.
——. *The Metaphysics of Morals*. Translated by Mary Gregor. 1797; Cambridge: Cambridge University Press, 1991.
Kojève, Alexandre. *Introduction to the Reading of Hegel: Lectures on the Phenomenology of Spirit*. Translated by James H. Nichols, Jr. 1947; Ithaca, NY: Cornell University Press, 1969.
MacIntyre, Alasdair. "Hegel on Faces and Skulls." In *Hegel: A Collection of Critical Essays*, edited by Alasdair MacIntyre, 219–36. Notre Dame, IN: University of Notre Dame Press, 1976.
Maurois, André. *A History of France*. Translated by Henry L. Binsse. 1949; London: Methuen, 1960.
Merleau-Ponty, Maurice. *Phenomenology of Perception*. Translated by Colin Smith. 1945; New York: Humanities, 1962.
Miller, Elaine. *The Vegetative Soul: From Philosophy of Nature to Subjectivity in the Feminine*. Albany: State University of New York Press, 2002.
Mills, Patricia Jagentowicz. "Hegel's Antigone." In *Feminist Interpretations of G. W. F. Hegel*, edited by P. J. Mills, 59–88. University Park: Pennsylvania State University Press, 1994.
Naas, Michael. *Turning: From Persuasion to Philosophy: A Reading of Homer's Iliad*. Atlantic Highlands, NJ: Humanities, 1995.
Nares, Robert. *A Glossary: Or, Collection of Words, Phrases, Names, and Allusions to Customs, Proverbs, etc., Which Have Been Thought to Require Illustration in the Works of English Authors, Particularly Shakespeare and His Contemporaries*. Stralsund: Charles Loeffler, 1825.
Nietzsche, Friedrich. *Beyond Good and Evil*. Translated by Walter Kaufmann. 1886; New York: Vintage, 1966.
——. *Ecce Homo*. Translated by Walter Kaufmann. 1908; New York: Vintage, 1996.
——. *The Gay Science*. Translated by Walter Kaufmann. 1887; New York: Vintage, 1974.
Pinkard, Terry. *Hegel's Phenomenology: The Sociality of Reason*. Cambridge: Cambridge University Press, 1994.
Pippin, Robert B. "Hegel's Social Theory of Agency." In *Hegel on Action*, edited by Arto Laitinen and Constantine Sandis, 59–78. Basingstoke, UK: Palgrave Macmillan, 2010.
——. "You Can't Get There From Here: Transition Problems in Hegel's *Phenomenology of Spirit*." In *The Cambridge Companion to Hegel*, edited by Frederick C. Beiser, 52–85. Cambridge: Cambridge University Press, 1993.
Plato. *Complete Works*. Edited by John M. Cooper. Indianapolis, IN: Hackett, 1997.
Proust, Marcel. *In Search of Lost Time*. 6 vols. Translated by C. K. Scott Moncrieff, Andreas Mayor, and Terence Kilmartin. New York: Modern Library, 1982–83.
Rawlinson, Mary C. "Beyond Antigone: Ismene, Gender, and the Right to Life." In *The Returns of Antigone*, edited by Tina Chanter and Sean Kirkland, 101–24. Albany: State University of New York Press, 2014.
——. *Just Life: Bioethics and the Future of Sexual Difference*. New York: Columbia University Press, 2016.

———. "Liminal Agencies: Literature as Moral Philosophy." In *Literature and Philosophy: A Guide to Contemporary Debates*, edited by David Rudrum, 129–41. London: Palgrave Macmillan, 2006.

———. "Women's Work: Ethics, Home Cooking, and the Sexual Politics of Food." In *The Routledge Handbook of Food Ethics*, edited by Mary C. Rawlinson and Caleb Ward, 61–71. London: Routledge, 2017.

Robinson, G. G., and J. Robinson. *The Sportsman's Dictionary, or the Gentleman's Companion for Town and Country*. 4th ed. London: R. Noble, 1800.

Roland de la Platière, Marie-Jeanne. *Mémoires*. 1793; London: Barrie and Jenkins, 1989.

Rousseau, Jean-Jacques. *Emile: Or, On Education*. Translated by Allan Bloom. 1762; New York: Basic, 1979.

Ruddick, Sara. *Maternal Thinking: Toward a Politics of Peace*. Boston: Beacon, 1989.

Sartre, Jean-Paul. *Being and Nothingness: An Essay on Phenomenological Ontology*. Translated by Hazel Barnes. 1943; New York: Washington Square, 1969.

Soboul, Albert. *A Short History of the French Revolution*. Translated by Geoffrey Symcox. 1965; Berkeley: University of California Press, 1977.

Sophocles. *Antigone*. Translated by F. Storr. Cambridge, MA: Harvard University Press, 1912.

Spinoza, Baruch. *Ethics*. Translated by Samuel Shirley. 1677; Indianapolis, IN: Hackett, 1992.

Starobinski, Jean. *1789: The Emblems of Reason*. Translated by Barbara Bray. Charlottesville: University of Virginia Press, 1982.

Taylor, Charles. "Hegel and the Philosophy of Action." In *Hegel on Action*, edited by Arto Laitinen and Constantine Sandis, 22–41. Basingstoke, UK: Palgrave Macmillan, 2010.

Tolstoy, Leo. *The Death of Ivan Ilych*. Translated by Rosemary Edmonds. 1886; New York: Signet Classics, 1960.

Whitbeck, Caroline. "Theories of Sex Difference." In *Women and Philosophy: Toward a Theory of Liberation*, edited by Carol C. Gould and M. W. Wartofsky, 54–80. New York: Putnam, 1976.

Wolf, Maryanne. *Proust and the Squid: The Story and Science of the Reading Brain*. New York: Harper Perennial, 2007.

# INDEX

Abraham (biblical), 58–59
Absolute difference, 17–20
Absolute fear, 44
Absolute freedom, 31, 76–77; alienation and, 152–53; death and, 157; morality and, 170; reason and, 149; terror and, 150–58; as universal, 154
Absolute knowing, xiv–xv, 10; art and, xviii–xx; birth of, 194–95; Comay on, 196$n$9; consciousness and, 187–91, 194–200; freedom and, 195–96; religion and, 185, 186–91; spirit and, 194–200; women and, xvi–xvii
Absolute truth, xxxix, 8, 31
Abstraction, 12–14, 18, 23, 94, 129–30, 154, 163
Acknowledgment, 39, 41–43
Action, 71, 78–79; Antigone, law, and, 95–110; body and, 97$n$24, 100$n$28; community of, 96–105; consciousness and, 99, 102–4; defining, 99$n$26; doing, 100–1, 162, 166, 170–71; immediacy and, 98, 102; morality and, 159–60, 159$n$52, 162–63, 166, 170–71, 175–76; movement of, 100–5; as self-realization, 100$n$28; sexual difference in, 117–31; of singleton, 66–68, 96–105; from singleton to individual, 96–105; speech and, 132, 132$n$16, 176; time and, 98–99; work and, 100–1
Agency, 77$n$7; custom and, 84–88; etymology of, 134$n$20; world of culture and, 134–35
Alienation: absolute freedom and, 152–53; culture or, 131–58; freedom and, 170; law and, 133–34; man of culture and, 133–38; world of culture and, 133–38
American Revolution, 153$n$37
Animals, 53; animal "functions," xxv, 8–9, 63–64; difference between humans and, 39–40, 76–77; self-consciousness of, 39–40
Annihilation of the world, 49–51
Antigone, 122$n$5, 190–91; action, law, and, 95–110; sexual difference and, xvi, 120–22; story of, 109
Appearance, xxxi; experience and, 23–33; Kant on, 23; law and, 28–29; logic of, xvii, 140; reason and, 27–28; sensuous things and, 27, 28

## INDEX

Art: absolute knowing and, xviii–xx; freedom and, xix; hierarchy of, xix; literature and, xviii–xxi, 192–95; religion and, 189–90; spirit and, 189–90, 192–95; style and, xx–xxi, 189–90, 198; truth in, xviii–xix, xx
Aspect, 12, 15–16, 18–19, 102
Attitude: first, of double relation, 58–59; second, of double relation, 59–63; third, of double relation, 63–69
*Aufheben* (Unfold), xxv–xxvi, xxvn4, xxxv, 12, 148, 177–78, 184

Bacchanalian revel, xxx–xxxi, 12n4, 91n21, 184, 193; first critique of law, 28–30; life and, 38–40; organic metaphor in, xxxi–xxxii; self-consciousness and, 36; spirit and, 116; unhappy consciousness and, 55–57; violence of, 72–73, 75
Bacchus, 3–4
Beautiful soul, 174–77, 187
Becoming, xv, xxiii, 38, 140, 187–89
Beginning: last, 186–91; truth in, xxiv–xxv
*Begriff*. *See* Concept
Being: conscience and, 146; consciousness and, xli–xlii; doing and, 100–1; immediacy and, 4–5; language and, 172; as "two-ing," xxi, 142; unconditioned, xli
*Being and Nothingness* (Sartre), 40
Being-for-Others, 17–20, 32–33
Being-for-self, 113
Being-in-Itself, 17–20, 17n6, 30, 32–33, 43, 47
Belonging-together (*Zusammenhang*), 46–47, 96n92, 97n25, 139, 149n31, 160, 172, 188
Benhabib, Seyla, 122n5
The Beyond, 27; unhappy consciousness and, 51–69
Bird and lime-twig analogy, xxxvii–xxxviii, xxxviiin3
"Birdlime" (Robinson, J., and Robinson, G. G.), xxxviiin3
Birth, 194–95

Body: action and, 97n24, 100n28; bodily functions, 63–65; as enemy, 63–64; gender division of labor and, 120–21; history and, 87; purity and, 64–66; reason and, 72; religion and, 64–65; as sensuous things, 64–66; unhappy consciousness and, 64–65, 64n22; women and, xvi, 120–21, 159n54
Body politic, xxxi, 32, 35, 66
Brain, 81, 82, 83
British Museum, 130n15
Butler, Judith, 122n5

*Care of the Self, The* (Foucault), 64, 64n22
Censorship, 87n20
Ceres, 3, 8–9
Certainty: immediacy and, 8–11; interrogation between truth and, 3–11; knowledge and, 9–11; self-certainty, 173, 175; sense-certainty, 3, 4–11
Chiasmatic effects, 14–17
Church, 63–69
Citizenship, 120, 122–25
Cloak: of morality, 168; of virtue, 94
Cognition, xxxviii; Kant on, 15–16, 158; self-consciousness and, 81; truth and, 15–16, 72, 107
Comay, Rebecca, 157n50, 158n51, 177n69, 193n5; on absolute knowing, 196n9
Common sense, xxxv, xl–xlii, 18
Community: of action, 96–105; death and, 124; eternal irony of, 117; faith and, 185; freedom and, 153–54; mutual recognition of, 195; nation and, 121–22; of others, 36, 56–57, 94, 104, 147; political, 13n5; of properties, 12–16, 13n5, 18, 24–25; singleton in, xxxii, 31, 177–78; spirit and, 117–18; thinghood and, 13n5; wealth and, 135–36; women and, 125–26
Concept (*Begriff*), xli, xlii, 39–40; life of, 187, 196; movement of, 188–89; singleton as, xvii; time and, 188–89
Condillac, Étienne Bonnot de, 5, 183
Confession, 115, 143, 176–79, 187

# INDEX

Conscience: being and, 146; man of, 169–74; morality and, 160, 169–79
Conscious freedom, 153
Consciousness: absolute knowing and, 187–91, 194–200; action and, 99, 102–4; being and, xli–xlii; common sense and, xl–xlii; death of, xliv; experience of, xliii; forgiveness and, 115; happiness and, 86–87, 86*n*19; heart and, 90–91; knowledge and, xlii–xliii, 114; law and, 30; movement of, 25–26, 71, 187–88; plurality of, 120; reason and, 70–73, 77–81, 95–96; religion and, 185, 186–91; reversal of, xliii; spirit and, 82, 133–34, 187–91; truth and, xl–xliii; understanding and, 25–28; as universal, 16–17; virtue in, 93–94. *See also specific types of consciousness*
Contradiction, 138; judgment or, 58–59; in Sophistry of perception, 11–20
Corpse, 150, 152
Critical philosophy, xxxvi*n*1, xxxvii–xxxix, xxxvii*n*2
*Critique of Pure Reason* (Kant), xxxv–xxxvi, 19, 19*n*7, 23
Culture, 134*n*19; alienation or, 131–58; man of, 133–38, 159–60; of possibilities, 25*n*12, 85, 106; world of, 131–38
Custom, 84–88

Danto, Arthur, xviii, xix
Death: absolute freedom and, 157; community and, 124; of consciousness, xliv; embracing, xxvii–xxviii; the encounter and, 40; family and, 124–25; fear of, 44–45, 61*n*20, 124, 157–58; inversion and the thing, 42–45; knowledge of, 53–54, 53*n*12; life and "Trial by Death," 38–40; mortality of the singleton and, xv, xvii–xviii, xxxiii, 31, 53–54, 193; mutual recognition of life and, 41–42; nation and, 124; self-consciousness and, 34–45; sexual difference and, 120–21; slavery and, 41–45; struggle unto, 34–45, 136–37; terror of, 154–56; as universal, 141*n*27; violence and, 151, 154–55
*Death of Ivan Ilych, The* (Tolstoy), xviii*n*14, 141*n*27, 193
Deception: experience as, 11–12; movement, assignment of truth, and, 14–17; self-deception, 32
Derrida, Jacques, xxxiii, 56, 132*n*16
Desire: for life, 35–38, 86, 87; self-consciousness and, 36–38, 55–56; sexual, 64–65, 127–28, 128*n*10; unhappy consciousness and, 54; women and, 125–28
Detachment from life, 45–51, 61*n*20
Determinate duty, 168
Determinate negation, xl, 3–11, 191
Devotion, 61
Difference: absolute, 17–20; abstraction and, 12–14; between human and animal, 39–40, 76–77; identity and, xv; between inner and outer, 73–82, 75*n*4; of I/Others, 82–95; between one and many, 12–14; in perception, 17–23; sensuous things and, 17–23; truth and, xiii–xiv. *See also* Sexual difference
Dionysus, xxx–xxxi
Disease, 79
Dishonesty, 103–4, 108
Dissemblance: forgiveness and, 158–79; morality and, 164–69
"Distinction which is no distinction," xiii–xiv, xiii*n*7, xxxix
Doing, 100–1, 162, 166, 170–71
Double reading and writing, xv, xlii
Double relation: first attitude of, 58–59; religion and, 58–69; second attitude of, 59–63; of singleton, 57–69; third attitude of, 63–69; in unhappy consciousness, 57–69, 58*n*18
*Durchdringen* (Intercalate), 13, 95, 96, 99, 101–2
Duty, 162–69, 163*n*59, 171; determinate, 168; pure, 165–69

Earth, xxxi, xxxi*n*10, 31, 38, 76, 88, 120, 140, 194
Eating, xxv, 8–9
*Ecce Homo* (Nietzsche), xxx*n*9
Educating consciousness, xxvi–xxvii
Education, 25
*Einzelne, das. See* Singleton
Element, 23–27, 36–37, 94, 96, 118, 125, 171
Eleusinian mysteries, 3, 194*n*6
The Encounter, 40
Enlightenment, 142–50
*Entzweiten. See* "Two-ing"
Envy, 159
Essential/inessential distinction, 12, 18, 30, 42, 42*n*4, 184
Ethical life, 85–86, 108
Ethics: family and, 123; of family and nation, 117–31; law and, 106–8
*Être suprême*, 145–46, 152
European civilization, xxviii
Experience: appearance, or Hegel's concept of, 23–33; of consciousness, xliii; as deception, 11–12; defining, xxviii–xxix, xliii; history and, 80–81, 115–16; inversion and, 23–33; language and, 23; law and, 29; learning by, 3–4; now and, 26; perspective and, xxxvi, 3–4; reason and, 80–81; self-consciousness and, 67; sense-certainty and, 3, 4–11; suffering and, 4; unhappy consciousness and, 57, 66–67; will and, 66–67. *See also* Life
Explanation, law and, 28–30

Faith, 142–50, 185; terrestrial, 120, 140
False beliefs, xxxvi–xxxvii, 3–4
Family: death and, 124–25; ethics and, 123; ethics of nation and, 117–31; home and, 118–19; law and, 123–25; nature and, 119; sexual difference and, 113, 117–31; singleton and, 118–20
Faust, 88
Fear, 44–45, 61*n*20, 124, 157–58
Feminism, 122, 122*n*7
Fixed thought, xxx–xxxi, xxxiii
Forgiveness, 114, 177, 184*n*1, 197; consciousness and, 115; dissemblance and, 158–79; nation and, 177*n*69, 178–79; punishment and, 178–79
Forster, Michael, 149*n*32
Fortune, 101, 102
Foucault, Michel, xix*n*17, 21–22; *The Care of the Self* by, 64, 64*n*22
Freedom: absolute, 31, 76–77, 149, 150–58, 170; absolute knowing and, 195–96; alienation and, 170; art and, xix; community and, 153–54; conscious, 153; in detachment from life, 45–51, 61*n*20; life and, 76–77, 77*n*8; nation and, 86–87, 130; reason and, 76–77; slavery and, 44–51; will and, 151–52, 152*n*35, 155–56
Free market, 135, 135*n*21
Free reality, 90
French Revolution, 108*n*32, 151, 154–57, 156*n*45, 156*n*49
French *salons*, 143
Freud, Sigmund, 64–65, 84*n*17, 128*n*10
Frick, Henry Clay, 93

Gender division of labor, 54*n*14, 194; body and, 120–21; law and, 126–27; women and home relating to, xii*n*2, xvi, xvi*n*10
General will, 151
Goethe, 88
Good, 92–95, 162*n*57
Governance, 130, 130*n*15
Greeks, 20–21, 119*n*2
Greeks v. modernity, 27
Grief, 199
Grosz, Elizabeth, 127*n*9, 128*n*11
Guilt, 156

Happiness: consciousness and, 86–87, 86*n*19; morality and, 163, 167–68; nation and, 86–87, 86*n*19
Hardheadedness, xxxi, 44–45, 48, 75, 122, 184, 187, 190
Hard-heartedness, xxxi, 75, 122, 160, 176–78, 184, 187
Head of household, 122*n*4
Healthy reason, 105–8

INDEX

Heart: consciousness and, 90–91; hard, 176–78; law of, 89–91; pure, 60–61; violence and, 89
Hegel, Georg Wilhelm Friedrich. *See specific topics*
Here, xxix, 6, 7–9
Hermeneutical circle, 99, 99n27
History: body and, 87; experience and, 80–81, 115–16; as left behind, 189; life and, xxiii–xxiv, xxv, xxxi, xliv, 21, 115–16; modern politics and, 21–22; movement and, 8; reason and, 80–81; self-consciousness and, 132–33; time and, 189; truth and, xxiii–xxiv, xxv–xxviii, xxxi; world of culture and, 132–33
*History of France* (Maurois), 154–55
Hobbes, Thomas, 38, 53–54, 67–68, 67n25, 130, 133n17; on mastery, 34; on women, xvin11
Home: family and, 118–19; women and, xiin2, xvi, xvin10
Honest consciousness, 102–4
Honesty, 108
Human exceptionalism, 73–82
Humiliation, xvii, xxi, 132
Hypocrisy, 159
Hyppolite, Jean, 51, 58, 145n28

Identity: difference and, xv; as fluid, xxxi; language and, 139; narratives of, xxviii; natural consciousness and, 21–23; self-consciousness and, 35–38; of singleton, xii–xv, 30–31, 54–55, 109; spirit and, xxviii
Immediacy, xxiii, xxxivn1, xli, 88, 114–15; action and, 98, 102; being and, 4–5; certainty and, 8–11; here and, 6–8; knowledge and, 9–11; movement and, 7–8; natural consciousness and, 8–11; now and, 6–7; return to, xxxii, 10, 56; of sense-certainty, 4–7; sensuous things and, 27; truth and, 4–8, 132
Immortality, 119n2
Impurity, 167; women as impure, 68
Incarnation, 59–63

Incommensurability, xii–xiv, xiiin5, 66, 199–200
Independence, 88, 124, 152
Individual (*das Individuum*), xxviin7, 134; action, from singleton to, 96–105; singleton compared to, xiin4
Inessential/essential distinction, 12, 18, 30, 42, 42n4, 184
Inner/outer distinction, 73–82, 75n4
"Insofar as," xxxv, 12, 14–19, 25
"Insolence" of reason, 95–105; law and, 105–10
Inspiration, xxxv
Intercalate (*Durchdringen*), 13, 95, 96, 99, 101–2
Interrogation, xii, xxxiv, xlii, 3–11
Intuition, xxxv–xxxvi
Inversion, 52; critique of law and, 28–30; experience and, 23–33; sensuous things and, 30–33; the thing and, 42–45; truth and, 32; of understanding, 32
Inverted world, 27, 31
Irigaray, Luce, 127n9, 128n11

Johnston, Adrian, 70
Judging, 173, 176–77, 197
Judging consciousness, 175–76
Judgment, contradiction or, 58–59

Kant, Immanuel, 20n9, 164nn61–62; on appearance, 23; on cognition, 15–16, 158; critique of, 158–79; *Critique of Pure Reason* by, xxxv–xxxvi, 19, 19n7, 23; on knowing, 19; on mastery, 34; on morality, 108n34, 158–59; on reason, 72n2, 83
Knowing, 19–20. *See also* Absolute knowing
Knowledge: absolute knowing and, xiv–xv, 10; certainty and, 9–11; consciousness and, xlii–xliii, 114; of death, 53–54, 53n12; as "distinction which is no distinction," xxxix; immediacy and, 9–11; logic and, xiv–xv, 114; as medium, xxxvii; perception and, xxxvi–xxxvii, 11–12;

Knowledge (*continued*)
as ruse, xxxvii–xxxviii; sense, 12–14; sense-certainty and, 3, 4–11; thought and, xxxvi–xxxvii, xxxvi*n*1; truth and, xxxvi–xliv

Kojève, Alexandre, 61*n*20

Labor, 85–87. *See also* Gender division of labor

Language: being and, 172; experience and, 23; identity and, 139; meaning and, 10; nation and, 137; power of, 9; reason and, 142–43; self-consciousness and, 139–40, 192–93; singleton and, xvii, 131–33, 138–42; spirit as, 140

Last beginning, 186–91

Law: action, Antigone, and, 95–110; alienation and, 133–34; appearance and, 28–29; consciousness and, 30; critique of, 28–30; ethics and, 106–8; experience and, 29; explanation and, 28–30; family and, 123–25; gender division of labor and, 126–27; of heart, 89–91; "insolence" of reason and, 105–10; morality and, 108, 164–67, 170; of motion, 29–30, 75–76; of nation, 85, 122–25; now and, 29–30; physics and, 28–30; politics and, 196–97; punishment and, 178–79; reason and, 74–81, 76*n*5, 105–10; of refraction and representation, xxxvii; sexual difference and, 126–27; singleton and, 84–85; supplementary practices to, 29; testing of, 107, 166*n*63; truth and, 107

Learning by experience, 3–4

"Legal person," 129–31; v. "absolute person, 133

Life: Bacchanalian revel and, 38–40; of concept, 187, 196; desire for, 35–38, 87; ethical, 85–86, 108; freedom and, 76–77, 77*n*8; freedom in detachment from, 45–51, 61*n*20; history and, xxiii–xxiv, xxv, xxxi, xliv, 21, 115–16; logic of, 38–40; mastering, 51–69; mutual recognition of death and, 41–42; natural science and, xxviii–xxix, xxxi; reason and, 74–79, 83–84; skepticism on, 49–51, 54, 56–57, 65–66; of spirit, xxvii–xxviii, xxxii; Stoicism on, 47–48, 56–57; "Trial by Death" and, 38–40; truth and, xliv, 198–200; women as, 21–22, 194–95

Life world, 114

Literature: art and, xviii–xxi, 192–95; as exception, xxxiii–xxxiv; logic and, xxxiii–xxxiv; style and, 191

Logic, xi; of appearance, xvii, 140; knowledge and, xiv–xv, 114; of life, 38–40; literature and, xxxiii–xxxiv; in organic metaphor, xxxii; perception and, 26; pure, xiv–xv; truth and, 4

MacIntyre, Alasdair, 52–53, 80–81
Mandela, Nelson, 177*n*69, 178–79
Man of conscience, 169–74
Man of culture, 133–38, 159–60
Man of reason, 145–51
Man of the world, xii, 82–95
Man of virtue, xii, 94–95
Master morality, 51
Mastery, 34, 133, 133*n*17; of nature, 73–82; slavery and, 41, 42–45, 54–55, 61, 61*n*20
Maternal love, 128–29, 199
Maurois, André, 154–56
Meaning, 3–4, 10
Mediated simplicity, 5–6, 8, 12
Medicine, 79
Merleau-Ponty, Maurice, xxxvi*n*1, xxxvii*n*2, 25*n*12
Miller, A. V., xi*n*1, xii*n*4, xxvii
Miller, Elaine, 53
Mills, Patricia Jagentowicz, 122*n*5
Modern politics, 21–22
Moral insolence, 52
Morality: absolute freedom and, 170; action and, 159–60, 159*n*52, 162–63, 166, 170–71, 175–76; beautiful soul and, 174–77; conscience and, 160, 169–79; critique of, 158–79; dissemblance and, 164–69; duty and,

162–69, 163*n*59, 171; happiness and, 163, 167–68; judging consciousness and, 175–76; Kant on, 108*n*34, 158–59; law and, 108, 164–67, 170; master, 51; moral "insolence" of reason and, 95–110; nature and, 161–63, 161*n*56; religion and, 163*n*60, 164–65; representation of, 163–64; self-consciousness and, 167, 167*n*64, 172; sensuous things and, 161; slave, 51; spirit and, 160; thought and, 168–70; unity and, 161–62; will and, 161, 164–65; as worldview, 160–64
Moral purity, xii, 98
Mortality of the singleton, xv, xvii–xviii, xxxiii, 31, 53–54, 193
Movement: of action, 100–5; of concept, 188–89; of consciousness, 25–26, 71, 187–88; deception, assignment of truth, and, 14–17; history and, 8; immediacy and, 7–8; law of motion and, 29–30, 75–76; in perception, 15–17; revolutionary, 148–49; of self-consciousness, 187; of singleton, 30–31, 57; of spirit, 188–89; of time, 188–89; of truth, xliii, 14–17; of unchangeable, 57, 57*n*17
Mutual recognition, 41–42, 195

Naas, Michael, xxiv*n*1
Name, power of, 137
Narrative, 22, 31–32, 184; master, 196, 198
Narrator, xxxi–xxxii, 57, 63–64, 77*n*7, 82, 191, 197; philosophical consciousness and, xl, xli, xliii–xliv, 10
Nation, 153*n*37; community and, 121–22; death and, 124; ethics of family and, 117–31; forgiveness and, 177*n*69, 178–79; freedom and, 86–87, 130; governance and, 130, 130*n*15; happiness and, 86–87, 86*n*19; labor and, 85–86; language and, 137; law of, 85, 122–25; "legal person" and, 129–31; man of culture and, 136–37; politics and, 87; singleton and, 114; sovereignty of, 35; "state of right"

and, 130–31; violence and, 87*n*20; war and, 124; women and, 121–22, 126
Natural consciousness, xi–xii, 42*n*4; Greeks and, 20–21; identity and, 21–23; immediacy and, 8–11; now and, 8; perception and, 14–20; philosophical consciousness and, xl–xli; reader as, xxiv–xxvi, xxv, xxv*n*2, xxvi*n*5, xxix–xliv, xxxv; spirit and, xxix; time and, xxv; truth and, xxix, xliii
Natural science: life and, xxviii–xxix, xxxi; reason and, 74–81; thought and, xxxix–xli; truth and, xliv
Nature, xv, 35, 76*n*6; family and, 119; mastery of, 73–82; morality and, 161–63, 161*n*56; reason in, 73–82, 96–99; sexual difference and, 126–27
Nazi regime, 156*n*46
Needs, 85
Negative, "tarrying with," 184
Neurology, 81, 82
Nietzsche, Friedrich, xxiii, xxx, xxx*n*9, 45, 48, 51
Nothingness, xl, 8–9
Now, xxix, 6–9, 54*n*15, 139; experience and, 26; law and, 29–30; plurality of "nows," 11*n*2, 12–13

Oedipus, 84*n*17, 120
Organic metaphor, xiii*n*5, xxvii–xxviii, xxxi–xxxii
Originary violence myth, 34–35, 52
Otherness, xv, xl–xli, 77
Our time, xxiv, xxix, xxx, 21, 27, 32, 94, 120, 192

Patriarchy, 122
Penis, 82–84
Perceiver, xxxvi, 23–25
Perception: difference in, 17–23; knowledge and, xxxvi–xxxvii, 11–12; logic and, 26; movement in, 15–17; natural consciousness and, 14–20; in perceiving of things, 12–14; reason and, 27–28; representation and, 27–28; sensuous things and, 23–24;

Perception (*continued*)
  Sophistry of, 11–20; thought and, 24–25; truth and, 3–4, 11–12, 23–33; unity and, 12–13
Personhood, 133*n*17
Perspective: experience and, xxxvi, 3–4; thought and, xxxvi, xxxvi*n*1; truth and, xxxvi–xxxvii, 19
Perversion, 91–92, 94
Phenomenology (method), xli–xlii, 5, 114, 139, 197–98
*Phenomenology of Perception* (Merleau-Ponty), xxxvi*n*1, xxxvii*n*2
Philosophical consciousness, xl, xli, xliii–xliv, 10
Physics, xiii, 28–30
Piety, 61–62
Pinkard, Terry, 64*n*22, 79, 133*n*17; on free market, 135, 135*n*21; on pure insight, 146*n*29
Pippin, Robert, 99*n*26, 100*n*28, 109*n*35, 149*n*32
Plants, 76*n*6
Plato, xviii
Plurality, 11*n*2, 12–13, 120
Political community, 13*n*5
Politics, 21–22, 177*n*69, 196–97
Polyneices, 109
Practical consciousness, 86
Proceduralism, 123
Properties, 12–16, 13*n*5, 18, 24–25
Property, 54*n*14, 197
Proust, Marcel, 192, 197–99, 200*n*12
Psychoanalysis, 84*n*17
Punishment, 178–79
Pure duty, 165–69
Pure heart, 60–61
Pure insight, 143–48, 146*n*29, 149, 157
Pure logic, xiv–xv
Purified "I," xxi, 53, 139–42, 199–200
Purifying, xxi
Purity: moral, 98; reason and, 67–68

Reader, xi–xii, xv, 63–64; contradicting, xxvi; going beyond himself, xli; as natural consciousness, xxiv–xxvi, xxv, xxv*n*2, xxvi*n*5, xxix–xliv, xxxv

Reading philosophy, xxxii–xxxiii
Real issue (*Die Sache selbst*), xxvi, xxix, 31–33, 42, 46, 51–52, 114, 178; in action, law, and Antigone, 95–110; as intercalation, 101–2; in reason, 76, 95–96, 110
Reason, 49*n*9, 91*n*21; absolute freedom and, 149; appearance and, 27–28; body and, 72; consciousness and, 70–73, 77–81, 95–96; Enlightenment, faith, truth, and, 142–50; experience and, 80–81; freedom and, 76–77; healthy, 105–8; history and, 80–81; in human exceptionalism, 73–82; "insolence" of, 95–110; Kant on, 72*n*2, 83; labor and, 85–87; language and, 142–43; law and, 74–81, 76*n*5, 105–10; life and, 74–79, 83–84; man of, 145–51; natural science and, 74–81; in nature, 73–82, 96–99; penis and, 82–84; perception and, 27–28; as pure insight, 143–48, 146*n*29, 149, 157; purity and, 67–68; real issue in, 76, 95–96, 110; representation of, 71–72; self-consciousness and, 67–68; self-realization and, 74–75; sensuous things and, 74; sexual difference and, 82–83, 85–86; time and, xxiv–xxv; in virtue and man of the world, 82–95; women and, 73*n*3
Reciprocity, 59–63
Recognition: mutual, 41–42, 195; recognizing and, 127; of self-consciousness, 39–40
Relationships, 109, 109*n*37, 190
Religion: absolute knowing and, 185, 186–91; art and, 189–90; body and, 64–65; consciousness and, 185, 186–91; double relation and, 58–69; faith and, 142–50; incarnation in, 59–63; morality and, 163*n*60, 164–65; piety and, 61–62; resolution and Church, 63–69; sexual desire in, 64–65; spirit and, 183–86; unhappy consciousness and, 145, 145*n*28, 185–86
Representation, 185; law of refraction and, xxxvii; of morality, 163–64;

# INDEX

perception and, 27–28; of reason, 71–72; of thinghood, 15–16
Resolution and the Church, 63–69
Return from otherness, xl–xli
Return to immediacy, xxxii, 10, 56. *See also* Immediacy
Revolutionary movement, 38, 148–49, 196
Robespierre, 154–56
Robinson, G. G., xxxviii$n$3
Robinson, J., xxxviii$n$3
Rousseau, Jean Jacques, xvi$n$12

*Sache selbst, Die. See* Real issue
Sameness, 85–86
Sartre, Jean-Paul, 40
Science of consciousness, xxviii–xxix
Self-certainty, 173, 175
Self-consciousness, xvii, 30, 32–33; of animals, 39–40; Bacchanalian revel and, 36; cognition and, 81; death and, 34–45; desire and, 36–38, 55–56; experience and, 67; history and, 132–33; identity and, 35–38; language and, 139–40, 192–93; mastering life and, 51–69; morality and, 167, 167$n$64, 172; movement of, 187; reason and, 67–68; recognition of, 39–40; skepticism and, 49–51, 54; slavery and, 41–51; violence and, 61; will and, 66–67
Self-deception, 32
Self-interrogation, xlii–xliv, 32–33, 87
Self-realization, 74–75, 100$n$28
Sense-certainty, 3, 4–11
Sense knowledge, 12–14
Sensibility, 167, 167$n$64, 168–70
Sensuous things, 3, 22; appearance and, 27, 28; body as, 64–66; difference and, 17–23; immediacy and, 27; inversion and fate of, 30–33; meaning and, 10; morality and, 161; nothingness of, 8–9; perception and, 23–24; reason and, 74; thought and, 24–25; understanding and, 24–28
Sexual desire, 64–65, 127–28, 128$n$10

Sexual difference, xii$n$2, xv, 200$n$12; in action, 117–31; Antigone and, xvi, 120–22; death and, 120–21; family and, 113, 117–31; head of household and, 122$n$4; law and, 126–27; nature and, 126–27; overview of, xvi–xvii; reason and, 82–83, 85–86; spirit and, 117–31, 193–95, 197
Sexuality, of women, 127–28, 128$nn$10–11
Shakespeare, William, xxxviii$n$3
Signature, 195, 197, 198
Singleton (*das Einzelne*), 136; action of, 66–68, 96–105; agency and custom for, 84–88; in community, xxxii, 31, 177–78; as concept, xvii; double relation of, 57–69; family and, 118–20; identity of, xii–xiii, xii–xv, 30–31, 54–55, 109; individual compared to, xii$n$4; language and, xvii, 131–33, 138–42; law and, 84–85; as "left behind," xvii–xviii, 131–33, 138–42, 141$n$26; mortality of, xv, xvii–xviii, xxxiii, 31, 53–54, 193; movement of, 30–31, 57; nation and, 114; as organic, xiii$n$5; power of thought and, xxviii–xxix; from singleton to individual, 96–105; spirit and, 184; "Trial by Death" and, 38–40; truth and, xii–xiii; unchangeable and, 57–63, 66, 67–68; will of, 151–52
Skepticism, 49–51, 54, 56–57, 65–66, 143
Slave morality, 51
Slavery: absolute fear and, 44; death and, 41–45; freedom and, 44–51; inversion and the thing, 42–45; mastery and, 41, 42–45, 54–55, 61, 61$n$20; self-consciousness and, 41–51; slave narratives and detachment from life, 45–51, 61$n$20; Stoicism and, 47–48; thought and, 47–48; unhappy consciousness and, 54–55
Social norms, 109$n$37
Sophistry, 11–20
Sophocles's Theban plays, xix, 109. *See also* Antigone
Sovereignty, 35
Speech, 65, 131–32, 132$n$16, 176

# INDEX

Spinoza, Baruch, 46
Spirit: absolute knowing and, 194–200; art and, 189–90, 192–95; Bacchanalian revel and, 116; common sense and, xl–xli; community and, 117–18; consciousness and, 82, 133–34, 187–91; of Earth, 88; fluidity of, xxxiii; forms of, 116–18; identity and, xxviii; as language, 140; life of, xxvii–xxviii, xxxii; morality and, 160; movement of, 188–89; natural consciousness and, xxix; religion and, 183–86; sexual difference and, 117–31, 193–95; singleton and, 184; thought and, 190–91; time and, 184
Starobinski, Jean, xix*n*17
"State of right," 130–31
Stoicism, 45–48, 56–57, 65–66, 129
Struggle unto death, 34–45, 136–37
Style, xx–xxi, 189–90, 191, 193, 198
Substance, xxi, xxx, 94, 141, 188, 192, 193
Suffering, 4, 198, 199
Supersensible world, 27

Taylor, Charles, 100*n*28
Terrestrial faith, 120, 140
Terror: absolute freedom and, 150–58; of death, 154–56; French Revolution and, 108*n*32, 151, 154–57, 156*n*45, 156*n*49
Thinghood, 12–14; community and, 13*n*5; inversion and the thing, 42–45; representation of, 15–16
This, 5, 9
This, here, now, 6–9
Thought: fixed, xxx–xxxi, xxxiii; knowledge and, xxxvi–xxxvii, xxxvi*n*1; metamorphoses of, xxx–xxxi; morality and, 168–70; natural science and, xxxix–xli; negative power of, xxviii–xxix, 188; perception and, 24–25; perspective and, xxxvi, xxxvi*n*1; sensuous things and, 24–25; slavery and, 47–48; spirit and, 190–91; truth and, 48
Time: action and, 98–99; concept and, 188–89; erasure of, 188–89; history and, 189; movement of, 188–89; natural consciousness and, xxv; in our time, xxiv, xxix, xxx, 21, 27, 32, 94, 120, 192; reason and, xxiv–xxv; spirit and, 184; truth and, xxiv–xxvi, xliv, 6–8
Tolstoy, Leo, xviii*n*14, 141*n*27, 193
Tragic philosopher, xxx, xxx*n*9
"Trial by Death," 38–40
Tribalism, 122
Truth, xi–xii; absolute, xxxix, 8, 31; in art, xviii–xix, xx; in becoming, xv; in beginning, xxiv–xxv; cognition and, 15–16, 72, 107; consciousness and, xl–xliii; difference and, xiii–xiv, xiii*n*7; Enlightenment, reason, faith, and, 142–50; history and, xxiii–xxiv, xxv–xxviii, xxxi; immediacy and, 4–8, 132; interrogation between certainty and, 3–11; inversion and, 32; knowledge and, xxxvi–xliv; law and, 107; life and, xliv, 198–200; logic and, 4; movement, deception, and assignment of, 14–17; movement of, xliii, 14–17; natural consciousness and, xxix, xliii; natural science and, xliv; perception and, 3–4, 11–12, 23–33; perspective and, xxxvi–xxxvii; philosophical consciousness and, xliii; self-interrogation of, xlii–xliv, 32–33; sense-certainty and, 3, 4–11; singleton and, xii–xiii; in this, here, now, 7–9; thought and, 48; time and, xxiv–xxvi, xliv, 6–8
"Two-ing" (*Entzweiten*), xii*n*3, xxi, 114–15, 142

Ultimacy of concreteness, 52–53
Unchangeable, 57–63, 57*n*17, 66, 67–68
Unconditioned being, xli
Understanding: consciousness and, 25–28; by Greeks, 20–21; inversion of, 32; knowing and, 19–20; object of, 25–28; as play of forces, 25–28; sensuous things and, 24–28
Unfold (*Aufheben*), xxv–xxvi, xxv*n*4, xxxv, 12, 148, 177–78, 184

## INDEX

Unhappy consciousness, 83–84, 174; Bacchanalian revel and, 55–57; the beyond and, 51–69; body and, 64–65, 64$n$22; desire and, 54; double relation in, 57–69, 58$n$18; experience and, 57, 66–67; first attitude of double relation and, 58–59; religion and, 145, 145$n$28, 185–86; second attitude of double relation and, 59–63; slavery and, 54–55; third attitude of double relation and, 63–69

Unity: morality and, 161–62; perception and, 12–13

Universal, 9, 53, 198–99; absolute freedom as, 154; consciousness as, 16–17; death as, 141$n$27; driving forth of, 27; order, 91$n$21; specific, 189–99; unchangeable as, 59–63; will, 13$n$5, 155–56

Utility, 146–47, 149

*Vegetative Soul, The* (Miller, E.), 53$n$12

Violence, xxiv, xxx, xl, 4, 76, 133$n$17; of Bacchanalian revel, 72–73; censorship and, 87$n$20; death and, 151, 154–55; heart and, 89; myth of originary, 34–35, 52; nation and, 87$n$20; self-consciousness and, 61

Virtue, 55; in consciousness, 93–94; critique of, 92–95, 97$n$24; good and, 92–95; man of, xii, 94–95; man of the world and, 92–93; reason in, 82–95; world and, 92–95

War, xxiii, xxiv; American Revolution, 153$n$37; French Revolution and, 108$n$32, 151, 154–57, 156$n$45, 156$n$49; nation and, 124

Wealth, 101–2, 101$n$29, 135–36, 135$n$21

Will: experience and, 66–67; freedom and, 151–52, 152$n$35, 155–56; good and, 162$n$57; morality and, 161, 164–65; self-consciousness and, 66–67; of singleton, 151–52; universal, 13$n$5, 155–56

Women: absolute knowing and, xvi–xvii; body and, xvi, 120–21, 159$n$54; community and, 125–26; desire and, 125–28; Freud on, 128$n$10; Hobbes on, xvi$n$11; home and, xii$n$2, xvi, xvi$n$10; as impure, 68; as "left behind," xvi–xvii, 117–31, 128; as life, 21–22, 194–95; maternal love and, 128–29, 199; nation and, 121–22, 126; reason and, 73$n$3; Rousseau on, xvi$n$12; sexuality of, 127–28, 128$nn$10–11. *See also* Gender division of labor; Sexual difference

World: inverted, 27, 31; life, 114; man of, xii, 82–95; skepticism and annihilation of, 49–51; supersensible, 27; virtue and, 92–95

World of culture, 131–38

Worldview, 160–64

*Zusammenhang. See* Belonging-together

GPSR Authorized Representative: Easy Access System Europe, Mustamäe tee 50, 10621 Tallinn, Estonia, gpsr.requests@easproject.com

www.ingramcontent.com/pod-product-compliance
Lightning Source LLC
Chambersburg PA
CBHW021358290426
44108CB00010B/300